For Peter,

With very Best Wishes,

Mike

Stock Markets, Investments
and Corporate Behavior
A Conceptual Framework of Understanding

Stock Markets, Investments and Corporate Behavior

A Conceptual Framework of Understanding

Michael Dempsey

RMIT University, Melbourne, Australia

Imperial College Press

Published by

Imperial College Press
57 Shelton Street
Covent Garden
London WC2H 9HE

Distributed by

World Scientific Publishing Co. Pte. Ltd.

5 Toh Tuck Link, Singapore 596224

USA office: 27 Warren Street, Suite 401-402, Hackensack, NJ 07601

UK office: 57 Shelton Street, Covent Garden, London WC2H 9HE

Library of Congress Cataloging-in-Publication Data
Dempsey, Michael (Michael J.)
    Stock markets, investments and corporate behavior : a conceptual framework of understanding /
by Michael Dempsey.
      pages cm
    Includes bibliographical references and index.
    ISBN 978-1-78326-699-9 (alk. paper)
    1. Corporations--Finance--Mathematical models. 2. Capital assets pricing model. 3. Stocks--
Prices. 4. Corporations--Valuation. 5. Capital market. I. Title.
    HG4012.D46 2016
    332.64'2--dc23
                                                        2015011284

British Library Cataloguing-in-Publication Data
A catalogue record for this book is available from the British Library.

In-house Editors: Catharina Weijman/Dipasri Sardar

Typeset by Stallion Press
Email: enquiries@stallionpress.com

Printed by FuIsland Offset Printing (S) Pte Ltd Singapore

The text is dedicated to Mary, Frank and children and their loved ones, the great Hugh Williams, who dictated the destiny of more than one of us, Tony Naughton, whom I remember with great affection, and the girls in Bangkok. All of them have been good to me.

By three methods we may learn wisdom: First, by reflection, which is noblest; Second, by imitation, which is easiest; and third by experience, which is the bitterest.

Confucius

All I ask is the chance to prove that money can't make me happy.

Spike Milligan

Mathematical finance can take us only so far.

The rest is economics and management

There are many patterns in finance, but few immutable rules.

And the Sun comes up tomorrow
It just doesn't know she's gone

Gram Parsons
–for Yokie–

A Short Bio for the Author (Official Version)

RMIT official photo: Spot the rather forced smile aimed at showing how enthusiastic I am at my work, how happy I am to be at RMIT, and how I will say almost anything if it might give me a salary increase at my next performance meeting.

Michael Dempsey joined RMIT University as Professor and Head of the Finance Discipline in early 2013. Prior to this, he was an Associate Professor at Monash University, before which he was an Associate Professor with Griffith University, having previously been at Leeds University, UK. He also has many years' experience working for the petroleum exploration industry, in the Middle East, Egypt, Aberdeen and London. His teaching expertise includes corporate and investment finance, international finance, derivatives and financial engineering. He is an active researcher and research supervisor across financial markets, in which he has published over fifty articles that have appeared in leading international journals, including *Journal of Banking and Finance* (2), *Financial Analysts Journal* (2), *European Financial Management* (1), *Abacus* (3), *Journal of Investment Management* (2), *Australian Journal of Management* (2), *Journal of Business Finance and Accounting* (3), *Accounting and Business Research* (3), *Critical Perspectives on Accounting* (3), *Journal of Asset Management* (1), and *Accounting and Finance* (1). He has a first degree in Mathematics and a PhD in Astrophysics, as well as an MBA and Masters degrees in Theoretical physics and Petroleum engineering.

Unofficial Bio

Mike Dempsey has failed in many aspects of life. He has failed to learn a second language despite (numerous) attempts, to ski with anything approaching style, or to hang-glide a significant distance cross-country. He is also been mostly unsuccessful in his stock trading strategies (the reader of the text should bear this in mind*). Nevertheless, his poker-playing skills are improving significantly. He is currently working at RMIT University in Melbourne, Australia under the delusion that the royalties from the present text along with movie rights will make him immensely rich and famous.

Unofficial photo: of myself (third from left) at one of our academic soirées in my Melbourne flat. Where were you Riley and Larry? Yes, that's Jimi Hendrix almost falling over in the background. I tell my nieces that they must listen to Jimi at least once a month in their formative years. And lots of Van Morrison. (And early Bob Dylan.)

Comment or suggestions on the text are welcomed at:
Michael.Dempsey@rmit.edu.au

Cover design concept: Michael Dempsey; above photo by John Vaz.

The bull and bear on the front cover are in front of the Frankfurt Stock Exchange.

---

*Or, place it back on the shelf if you are one of those people who reads books at bookstores (go on, buy it!).

Prologue

First there was barter
Then we had money
Then we had financial markets
These changed everything . . .

It is an interesting story.

It is not just the story of financial markets and large firms, but also the story of how finance academics have developed their understanding of financial markets and such firms over time.

Financial markets function to gather from millions upon millions of individuals, their financial savings — each insignificant individually — that are in excess of their immediate needs, so that investments of billions of dollars can be invested in large firms — which attain such finance by either borrowing (debt finance) or issuing stocks or shares as certificates of ownership of the firm (equity finance). Without access to such financing arrangements, large firms would not exist. And without such firms, we would be without the capacity to develop modern civilization; from the technologies of electronics and airplanes, urban infrastructure and highways, to the mass, and therefore affordable, production of our housing, pharmaceuticals, cars, agriculture, and so on. In addition to this, we would be without services such as banking and financing arrangements for smaller firms, and our insurance and pension arrangements.

In short, the history of the landscape of modern civilization is inseparable from the history of financial markets and their provisions for large firms. The human brain that developed the aerodynamics of the boomerang many thousands of years ago would one day develop the capacity to send a spacecraft around the moon and have it return. But ingenuity without the means of production afforded by large firms financed by capital markets, can take us only so far. The aboriginals of Australia did not see the need to develop large firms with capital markets. Whereas other societies did. That was the difference.

Finance academics have attempted to understand financial markets and large firms as they might understand the laws that govern physics. In their models, financial capital, like rainwater seeking the steepest downhill path as it flows, is forever looking for the highest return. In the models, the market's *required* rate of return on the investment of financial capital identifies the firm's *cost of financial capital*. It follows that the activities of large firms and financial markets must be understood in terms of each other. The criterion for the firm's activities is that they provide a rate of financial return that at least meets shareholders' required rate of return.

Unfortunately, there is a problem with these models. Stated simply, it is that *finance is not physics*. Markets and firms do *not* operate as the outcome of mathematical models applied mechanically. Rather, they must be understood as the outcome of real people in organizations, who are called on to make decisions against an uncertain future. For this reason, the present text begins by deconstructing the traditional foundations of financial theory, before reshaping a quantitative model of markets in the context of the mathematics of growth combined with market psychology, which leads us to an assessment of the decision-making processes of firms in response.

The present text represents an invitation to share an intellectual journey that, hopefully, will appeal to anyone with an interest in the interplay between stock markets, investments and corporate activity — and who is not altogether allergic to mathematics, provided it remains intuitive, not overly demanding, and, most definitely, elegant — as well as to academics with openness to new ideas. And it should be of interest to anyone who has been subject to the models and theories of standard finance theory, and who is prepared to have those models and theories dismantled and ultimately contradicted.

Contents

Chapter 1

Introduction:
Stock Markets, Investments and Corporate
Financial Decision Making

Market fundamentalism...contributed directly to the financial crisis and the associated erosion of social capital.

Mark Carney, the governor of the Bank of England

Companies are not charitable enterprises: They hire workers to make profits. In the United States, this logic still works. In Europe, it hardly does.

Paul Samuelson

Markets are designed to allow individuals to look after their private needs and to pursue profit. It's really a great invention, and I wouldn't underestimate the value of that. But they're not designed to take care of social needs.

George Soros

It is a kind of spiritual snobbery that makes people think they can be happy without money.

Albert Camus

The text is aimed at examining the interplay between stock markets, investments, and corporate financial decision making.

A large firm[1] is typically financed by a combination of *equity* finance, which is raised by issuing shares or stocks as certificates of ownership in the company,[2] and *debt* finance, or borrowing, which is created by issuing bonds

---

[1]The terms "company" and "firm" are close to interchangeable. "Firm" may carry with it the connotation of professional services (we speak of a law firm) and that the firm is registered and acts under a trade name ("firm" derives from the Italian word *firma*, a signature). The term "company" indicates a firm that is registered under the Corporation Law of the state (the Companies Act in the US and UK). The present text has a tendency to move between the two terms without implying any great distinction.

[2]The terms "stocks" and "shares" are also pretty much interchangeable. The term "stocks" is more US-inclined; the term "shares" more UK-inclined.

(an "I Owe You") that obliges the company to return the borrowed amount (the principle) at some designated date together with interest payments over the loan. Such a large firm is likely incorporated as a *legal entity* under the Corporation Law of the state. One implication of incorporation is that the firm's shareholders as owners of the company have *limited liability* (responsibility) for the firm's behaviour. By submitting itself to the rules of a *stock exchange*,[3] the firm's shares and bonds can be listed for trading on the exchange. This means that a firm can raise funds by issuing equity and debt (which we refer to as a *primary* market) and thereafter have its stocks and bonds traded second-hand between sellers and new buyers (in what we refer to as a *secondary* market, but which more generally is referred to as the stock market, whose prices are reported daily in the news). The holders of bonds and stocks in a firm are naturally seeking the highest returns on their investments for a given level of risk. Such investors' *expectation of return*, reciprocally, may be viewed as identifying the firm's *cost of financial capital*. So firms must seek to invest in projects and ventures that satisfy the risk–return expectations of their sources of finance — as both equity and debt. From such a perspective, we can say that (i) the investment activities of large firms and (ii) the investment activities in their bonds and stocks that take place in stock and other financial markets, are different sides of the same investment coin, connected by the cost of financial capital.

The stock market, in its pricing of the firm's equity shares or stocks in the marketplace, is making a judgment about the firm's ability to meet investor expectations. When such expectations are downgraded, investors continue to purchase the firm's stocks — but at a *lower* price: thus, the stock price declines. At this point, the firm's current shareholders take a financial loss. Another implication of stock market declines, which became a reality during the global financial crisis (GFC), is that the company is held in law to be viable as an ongoing concern provided that its capitalized value — as determined by the stock market — exceeds its financial liabilities. When the firm's market value drops below the value of the firm's financial

---

[3]The words stock exchange and stock market are often interchangeable. The three largest in the world are the New York Stock Exchange (NYSE), the London Stock Exchange (LSE) and the Tokyo Stock Exchange (TSE).

obligations, the firm can be declared bankrupt, and allowed to die. From such perspectives, the motive of the firm is the profit motive.

When I was an engineer, I viewed large companies as existing to produce and deliver the goods and services that are associated with their brand names. At my induction as a new petroleum engineer at British Petroleum (BP), a person from human resources (HR) introduced the organizational setup of the company by placing a transparency on the light projector (in the days before PowerPoint presentations). The transparency highlighted the various departments of the company spreading out like spokes on a wheel from a central hub. And there at the center in the hub was the department of HR. For the HR presenter, a firm represented first and foremost a number of people in some cooperative activity. As for the significance of the department of petroleum engineering, the presenter was at first actually unable to locate it on his transparency. Only when he moved the transparency to the right a little did it show up at the very outer edge — literally falling off the end of his perception of the firm.

In this text — in contrast to the concept of the firm as exiting primarily as either a provider of goods and services or as a social construct — we are, in effect, adopting a third perspective of the firm; namely, the firm as that which is sustained by financial markets, provided that the firm continues to meet the market's demands for financial performance.

This perspective leads to a rather impersonal view of firms and financial markets. Indeed, we typically refer not to the individual *people* who manage or are responsible for large firms, or those who are active in the financial markets that provide services for these firms, but to the firms and markets *of themselves* — to the extent, in fact, that we speak of the actions of the organization as of the organization itself — and not of the individuals who are engaged in the organization. In law, the company typically stands as an individual legal entity in its own right.

Motivated by profit, large firms provide us with the enhanced benefits of the material world as we know them: Our cars, highways, hospitals, homes, affordable technologies, etc., as well as financial services such as banking and provision for pensions and insurance services. In return, we are beholden to large firms. In the workplace, we may even feel that we are dwarfed by them. Large firms regularly lobby politicians for policies that accord with their profit motive. We might say that we have created a self-reliant entity — for better or for worse — that is powerfully motivated to satisfy its pay-masters, which are the financial markets that sustain the firm with finance on conditions that the firm continues to demonstrate its ability to perform financially satisfactorily.

It is an intriguing concept, that the colossal funds made available to financial markets are ultimately derived from the investment savings of "mere" households. The function of financial markets is to gather and transfer these savings to the productive enterprises of firms. Commercial (otherwise known as retail or high street) banks perform this function by gathering our individually not-very-significant savings deposits and making them available as more substantial financial investments. Investment banks[4] perform the function by liaising with those institutions that manage our additional savings — our savings, for example, in firms that manage our regular contributions such as for retirement and life and property insurance, as well as additional savings we might make in professionally managed funds — and connecting those savings with opportunities to invest in commercial firms that are seeking such funds (through new issues of their stocks or bonds) to finance their investments.

In seeking to enrich ourselves, from time to time, we are perhaps given to invest our valuable savings in opportunities with highly uncertain outcomes (a flutter on a horse race, the lottery, etc.). In these cases, we are "risk-seeking". We need some excitement in our lives from time to time! Nevertheless, when it comes to making more substantial investments, such as an investment of one's total wealth, provisions for loved ones, or for retirement plans, the same person is likely to be much more "risk-averse". The stock market has traditionally rewarded long-term investment. But the markets are "risky" in that they are prone to quite large-scale fluctuations as the economy moves through cycles of prosperity and decline,

---

[4]An investment bank is an institution that provides financial services for other firms, for example, by providing advice and underwriting the raising of capital for firms (new issues of their equity or bonds). Unlike commercial banks, investment banks do not take deposits. Some names are associated with both commercial and investment banking activity (Citigroup, Barclays, The Royal Bank of Scotland Group), while other names are associated with specific investment banking activities (Goldman Sachs, Morgan Stanley, JP Morgan Chase). In a sense, in the services it offers, an investment bank is to the large firm as the commercial bank is to the individual or small company.

optimism and pessimism — in addition to being prone to self-induced gyrations as market sentiment swings between greed and fear. We may be fearful that the market will encounter a "global financial crisis" from which we cannot recover before we have withdrawn from the market. The interplay between risk (to which we are averse) and high returns (which we are seeking) identifies the essential dynamic at the heart of market behavior.

Thus, in the models, it is assumed that risky investments demand an expected rate of return over and above a *risk-free* rate as offered, say, by a bank deposit rate, or by the government's short-term treasury bills. The difference between the expected return offered by the market and a risk-free rate is termed the *market risk premium* (*MRP*). The expected rate of return on any individual asset j should, therefore, in principle, be determined as the risk-free rate (r_f) plus the *MRP* multiplied by the asset's sensitivity to the market (which is termed the asset's beta; β_j[5]), so that we have the expected return on asset j, $E(R_j)$, as

$$E(R_j) = r_f + \beta_j(MRP). \tag{1.1}$$

Notwithstanding its simplicity, the above equation is referred to somewhat grandly as the "capital asset pricing model", or the CAPM (pronounced "cap-em").[6] Prior to the GFC, a stock MRP in the range of 6–8% was commonly referenced. Following the GFC, the concept has become more nebulous. A premium of at most 6% is now regarded

---

[5]If the asset's performance has an exposure to the market that equates with the market itself, its beta is equal to 1.0. If the asset's performance represents only a partial exposure to the market's performance, the asset's beta is less than 1.0, whereas if the asset's performance tends to exaggerate the market's (positive or negative) performance, the asset's beta is greater than 1.0. A more formal definition of beta is presented in Chapter 6.10.6.

[6]The idea underlying the CAPM was developed by various US academics at roughly the same time. The idea was first introduced by Jack Treynor (1961, 1962), followed by developments of the idea by William Sharpe (1964), John Lintner (1965), and Jan Mossin (1966), each more or less independently building on the earlier work of Harry Markowitz (1952) on diversification and modern portfolio theory. Sharpe, Markowitz, and Merton Miller (of the Modigliani and Miller propositions fame, see footnote 9 of this chapter) jointly received the 1990 Nobel Prize in Economics for their contributions to the field of financial economics.

as realistic.[7] The CAPM nevertheless represents the foundation for how academics understand the formation of asset prices in a market.

In reciprocation, it is assumed that the firm's obligation is to obtain a return on its financial capital from shareholders that exceeds or is at least equal to that determined by the CAPM. Thus, consider the three essential sequential decisions of corporate financial investment (the three pillars of corporate finance):

(i) The "investment" decision: Where should the firm be allocating limited resources of plant, employees, as well as finance?

(ii) The "financing" (capital structure) decision: Having identified its investment decisions, how should the firm be financing those investments as between debt and equity finance? and

(iii) The "repatriation" decision: At what point in the firm's life-cycle should the firm be returning the profitable outcomes of its investments to shareholders (as dividends or buy backs of shares)?[8]

For the investment decision, we have the clear guideline: invest in projects that provide shareholders with an expectation of return that exceeds or at least matches the rate implied by the CAPM.

The sequential "financing" and "repatriation" decisions of corporate financial investment identify the circulation of funds (as equity or debt finance) into the company before funds are returned, on a profitable basis, hopefully, to the firm's investors who hold the firm's equity and debt. Franco Modigliani and Merton Miller argued that, fundamentally, the firm's investments determine the firm's value, and declared that the "financing" and "repatriation" decisions of the firm are actually "irrelevant" to the firm's value. They articulated their arguments as the Modigliani and Miller (MM) propositions of the late 1950s and early 1960s, where they argue that the firm's value is the value of its future cash flows in relation to

---

[7]Reflecting the more downbeat sentiment of that time, *The Economist* newspaper (March 17th, 2012) reported research that indicated a market risk premium closer to 3.5% as more realistically attainable.

[8]In regards to the firm's debt holders, the decision to honour interest repayments and the repayment of the borrowed principal at maturity is typically not regarded as a "decision" as the firm is committed to such obligations by the contractual arrangements of the bond.

risk, and that this value is independent of how the cash flow is ultimately distributed between shareholders and bond holders. Thus, the firm's value is, in principle, independent of its capital structure (its level of debt or leverage). Similarly, the firm's current value should be independent of the future timing of how shareholders choose to return the firm's profitability to themselves. And, thus, the firm's value is, in principle, independent of its dividend policy (or policy of buy backs of its shares).[9]

On the foundations of the CAPM and the MM propositions, traditional finance has attempted to understand financial markets and commercial companies as a mechanistic construct, rather as physicists approach their subject matter. It is on this point that this book takes issue with traditional theory. Stated simply, finance is not physics. The academic's approach falsely assumes that financial markets can be understood as systems within which self-interested maximizers behave in logical ways, which are coordinated by the invisible hand of the price mechanism. This book recognises that finance is more appropriately understood as a field in which investors and finance managers may or may not use rational calculations as the basis of their decision making.

The book opens with an effective dismantling of the traditional mathematical approach used to understand and describe markets and corporate financial behaviour. Thus, Part A critiques how academics have chosen to understand stock price formation founded on the CAPM (Chapters 2–4), while Part B critiques the adequacy of the MM propositions as principles of corporate finance (Chapter 5). Notwithstanding that the CAPM and MM propositions are of themselves perfectly reasonable, we shall argue that adherence to the mathematical development of the principles has created an edifice of finance theory that fundamentally misses the human reality of

---

[9]The story goes that Merton Miller and Franco Modigliani were set to teach corporate finance for business students despite the fact that they had no prior experience in corporate finance. When they read the material that existed they found it inconsistent so they sat down together to try to figure it out. The result of this was a theorem on capital structure, arguably forming the basis for modern thinking on capital structure. Their Modigliani–Miller theorem is also often called the capital structure irrelevance principle. Modigliani was awarded the 1985 Nobel Prize in Economics for this and other contributions. Miller was awarded the 1990 Nobel Prize in Economics, along with Harry Markowitz and William Sharpe with Miller specifically cited for "fundamental contributions to the theory of corporate finance".

how markets react and over-react to economic cycles, as investors respond in bouts of psychological greed and fear that are capable of sending markets into self-fuelling upturn "bull" and downturn "bear" markets; and the models miss the reality of how people in organizations actually behave and make important decisions that determine and guide the firm's direction. Why academic finance has chosen to remain oblivious to these realities is in itself an interesting story.

In the second part of the book (Parts C and D), the mathematics of growth and decline is developed anew, while holding to the realisation that the decisions of organisations rely on the choices of real people with limited information available to them. Thus, in Part C, we refine our understanding of the nature of stock markets and financial growth, the dynamics of risk and return in financial markets, optimal portfolio allocation, stock mispricing, and option pricing (Chapters 6–12). Deviations from the core mathematical models are understood in terms of the mispricing of stocks, induced market cycles of booms and slumps within economic cycles, and the psychology of markets. We conclude that (investment) finance can take us only so far. The rest is economics and the psychology of markets. Part D advances a framework for corporate financial decision making that complements the mathematics of cash flow valuation (Chapter 13) with a framework that captures the distinctly human dimension of corporate financial activity, and what it means to be ethical in our financial institutions (Chapters 14 and 15). Again, we conclude that (corporate) finance can take us only so far. The rest is principles of management and an understanding of organizations.

The final chapter (Chapter 16) concludes with a review of the text.

The text is "academic" in allowing for a fair deal of abstraction and mathematical application. Nevertheless, the hope is that the reader will find the text *enjoyable*: Enjoyable because the shared intellectual journey is found to be worthwhile — as we share observations of how academic thinking in finance has taken shape over 60 years, discover a mathematical behavior of stock price formation, and consider how we might understand corporate financial decision making in the context of such stock price formation.

Let us commence our intellectual journey.

PART A

**Foundations of Stock Pricing:
A Critical Assessment**

Chapter 2

The Capital Asset Pricing Model

It is the first responsibility of every citizen to question authority.

Benjamin Franklin

Capitalism loses its sense of moderation when the belief in the power of the market enters the realm of faith.

Mark Carney, the governor of the Bank of England

Not to be absolutely certain is, I think, one of the essential things in rationality. Some things are believed because people feel as if they must be true, and in such cases an immense weight of evidence is necessary to dispel the belief.

Bertrand Russell

Castles made of sand, fall into the sea, eventually.

Jimi Hendrix

2.1. Introduction[1]

The Capital Asset Pricing Model (CAPM) was introduced in Chapter 1 as a foundation of financial models. Since its inception in the early 1960s, it has served as the bedrock of capital asset pricing theory and its application to practitioner activity.[2]

The CAPM commences with the concept that when we invest in a broad portfolio of stocks, a good deal of the risk exposures to individual stocks can be relied on to simply cancel with one another — a case of not having all one's eggs in one basket, as one stock in our portfolio prospers beyond expectations while another stock in our portfolio underperforms against expectations. Thus, we say that *idiosyncratic* risk, which is to say, risk that

---

[1]This chapter develops ideas that were presented in the journal *Abacus* (Dempsey 2013a, 2013b). I am indeed grateful and indebted to the editors and reviewers of this journal for supporting and publishing this work notwithstanding its unorthodoxy. The above journal issue offers a spirited debate on the CAPM (*Abacus*, 49(S1), 2013).

[2]The model has dominated financial economics to the extent of being labeled "the paradigm" (Ross, 1978; Ryan, 1982).

11

is peculiar to the firm, can be *diversified* away by holding many stocks. However, the risk that the larger economy and hence the stock market *in total* might suffer cannot so easily be diversified away. This risk we refer to as *market* risk (or non-diversifiable risk, or non-idiosyncratic risk), which an investor remains exposed to no matter how many stocks are held in a well-diversified portfolio. If investors are *risk averse*, they will be unwilling to invest in the market unless the market offers a *risk premium* — in the form of an expectation of return over and above the risk-free rate — to compensate for holding risk. Logically, the risk premium for a particular asset should be in proportion to that asset's sensitivity to the market. This is the tenet of the CAPM. The tenet appears to represent a perfectly acceptable principle of rational behavior, and following its inception, a good deal of empirical work was performed aimed at supporting the prediction of the CAPM that an asset's excess return over the risk-free rate should be proportional to its exposure to overall market risk. The asset's exposure (sensitivity) to the market, we call beta (β).

The CAPM is a model of investor *ex ante* expectations or requirements. In designing a test of the model that can be referenced to market data, the challenge is to somehow relate *past* stock price movements (which is what we have available) to a model that predicts *expectations* of stock price movements. The approach of Fischer Black, Michael Jensen and Myron Scholes (BJS hereafter), who published their findings in 1972, represents what is generally recognized as the first methodologically satisfactory test of the CAPM.[3] In its essentials, it remains the method by which academics continue to test asset pricing models.

In this chapter, we first present the historical background in relation to the CAPM (Section 2.2). We proceed to present the experimental setup of BJS (Section 2.3). Their findings do not actually support the CAPM as Eq. (1.1), but have been interpreted as supporting a weakened form of the CAPM, which is Black's CAPM (Section 2.4). In Section 2.5, we argue that the findings of BJS fail to provide substantial support even for Black's version of the CAPM. Section 2.6 concludes with a discussion of these viewpoints.

---

[3]The same Myron Scholes and Fischer Black of the Black–Scholes option pricing formula fame (Chapter 12).

2.2. Background to the CAPM

The CAPM holds out a conception of US stock markets as having matured from a freewheeling casino in the past, generally held in disdain, to a market of information that allows prices to efficiently clear the market and which inspires an efficient allocation of capital. Such a market represents an important component of a capitalist system. The founders of modern finance theory were anxious (perhaps too anxious as we shall see) to confirm such a reality. In such a world, financial capital circulates to achieve those rates of return that are most attractive to investors, so that when they choose among the securities that represent ownership of firms' activities, they can do so under the assumption that they are paying fair prices given what is known about the firm (Fama, 1976).

With such perceptions, in the late 1960s, academics in the US had begun to demonstrate how financial markets might be made susceptible to quantitative scrutiny.[4] Already, from the late 1950s, institutional investors had begun to apply the analysis of data, as well as the judgments of management teams, to the selection and allocation of stocks in their investment portfolios.

In *Fisher Black and the Revolutionary Idea of Finance*, Perry Mehrling (2007) considers the CAPM as the "revolutionary idea" that runs through finance theory. Mehrling recounts that the first major step in the development of modern finance theory was the *efficient markets hypothesis*, followed by the second step, which is the CAPM.

The efficient market hypothesis — the notion that market prices react rapidly to new information (weak, semi-strong, or strong form) — is claimed to be the most extensively tested hypothesis in all the social sciences. Michael Jensen (1978) went as far as to claim that "there is no other proposition in economics which has more solid empirical evidence supporting it than the efficient market hypothesis".

In accordance with this principle, prices of securities observed at any time "fully reflect all information available at that time", so that it is impossible to make consistent economic profits by trading on such available

---

[4]Some academics, such as Fischer Black, were engaged directly with the funds management industry.

information (e.g., Modigliani and Miller, 1958; Fama, 1976). Consistent with the hypothesis, detailed empirical studies of stock prices at the time indicated it is difficult to earn above-normal profits by trading on publicly available data because such data has already been incorporated into security prices. Fama (1976) reviews much of this evidence, though the evidence is not completely one-sided (e.g., Jensen, 1978).

Yet even allowing that empirical research has succeeded in broadly establishing that successive stock price movements are systematically uncorrelated, thus establishing that we are unable to reject the efficient market hypothesis, this does not describe *how* markets respond to information and how *how* information is impounded to determine stock prices. That is to say, the much-vaunted efficient market hypothesis does not in itself actually enable us to conclude that capital markets allocate financial resources "efficiently". If we wish to claim efficiency for capital markets, we must show that markets not only rapidly impound new information, but also "meaningfully" impound that information.

Thus, while the efficient market hypothesis states that at any time, all available information is imputed into the price of an asset, the CAPM gives content to how such information should be imputed. As observed in Chapter 1, the CAPM states that investors can expect to attain a risk-free rate plus a "market risk premium" multiplied by their exposure to the market (Eq. (1.1)). The model may be presented formally as

$$E(R_j) = r_f + \beta_j[E(R_M) - r_f], \tag{2.1}$$

where $E(R_j)$ is the expected return on asset j over a single time period, r_f is the riskless rate of interest over the period, $E(R_M)$ is the expected return on the market over the period, and β_j identifies the exposure of asset j to the market return.[5]

Mehrling's (2007) text captures the sense of excitement of the early researchers who believed that they were at the forefront of understanding

---

[5]Formally, the market beta of an asset is defined as the asset's proportional contribution to the *variance* of the market's returns, which is to say, the *co-variance* of the asset's returns with the market returns divided by the market's variance of returns. This formal definition follows naturally in Chapter 6.10.6.

markets, and, ultimately, being able to control them. Mehrling recounts how Black recognized that a rational market effectively *requires* the CAPM. As Black saw it, if the market of all assets offers investors a "risk premium" — $[E(R_M) - r_f]$ — in compensation for bearing risk exposure to the market, then, all else being equal, each individual stock, j, must rationally offer a risk premium equal to $\beta_j[E(R_M) - r_f]$, since β_j measures the asset's individual risk exposure to the market. Market frictions (limited access to borrowing at the risk-free rate, for example) might imply adjustments, but, at the core, the CAPM must be maintained (Black, 1973).

Nevertheless, the question remains: Does the CAPM capture how investors set prices in the marketplace? Can it claim to be what its name proclaims? The answer requires that we are able to *test* the proposition.

One response might be simply to ask anyone who holds stocks, either as individuals or as a portfolio or fund manager: What are your estimates of beta and expected return on each of the stocks you have chosen to hold? Then, test their responses against the model. Such an exercise would bring us to recognize that the concept of an investor's *expectation of return* is actually quite a *nebulous* concept. Even sophisticated fund managers typically do not think explicitly in terms of expected returns on the stocks they hold, but, rather, of their *portfolio* of stocks in broad *strategic* terms, which is typically in accord with the mandate of the fund as entrusted to the fund trustees (e.g., that the fund invest in the firms of a given index in proportion to each firm's market value).

Nevertheless, the rationale of the CAPM allowed BJS (1972) to believe that investors implicitly — if not explicitly — should determine stock prices in accordance with the underlying concept of the model. The challenge however remained: How to test the model?

As we shall see, the approach of BJS was innovative, clear and concise, and I intend to share it with you; not as a labor of algebraic equations, but as an intellectual joy. Their clarity and purposefulness of thought as portrayed in their contribution represents a high point of academic finance. It represents what is generally recognized as the first methodologically satisfactory test of the CAPM, and in its essentials, it remains the method by which academics continue to conduct their tests of whatever asset pricing model they have in mind.

2.3. A Test for the CAPM

In the absence of reliable investor expectations of stock returns, researchers had already realized that they must somehow turn to *past* returns as a proxy for investor *expectations*. The idea became that each recorded monthly return for a stock is a random selection from the possible outcomes that were anticipated by investors on a probability-weighted basis for that stock at the outset of each month. We might imagine a sack with balls representing all possible outcomes in proportion to their probability of outcome (that is, outcome returns with a higher probability of outcome have proportionally more balls in the sack) and interpret each monthly return as a random selection from the sack. The assumption is perhaps reasonable. Nevertheless, we should perhaps give some consideration to the following.

1. The outcome return in each month is affected by information and unpredicted outcomes that occur *during* the month itself, which are capable of influencing the returns of assets for that month uniformly in the *opposite* direction of investors' required expectations. For example, suppose that information is forthcoming that has negative implications for market price stability, and that, consistent with the CAPM, investors perceiving themselves as being exposed to an increased risk, increase their required expectation of return. But increased returns can only be operationalized in the market by stocks becoming *cheaper to buy*; which is to say, current shareholders (in response to *higher* expectations) encounter a stock price loss and a *lower* return.[6] When it hits home, risk is not something that rewards investors; it is something that *punishes* them.[7]

---

[6]This is readily appreciated by bonds. An investor holds $100 of bonds with an annual coupon rate of 3% in perpetuity, which is the current market rate on bonds of that risk. Now, suppose inflation increases to the extent that the holders of such bonds now "demand" a rate of 6% in perpetuity to compensate for inflation. This is achieved by the market value of the $100 bond dropping to $50. By demanding *more*, investors receive *less*! In reverse, a drop in inflation will lead to investors being satisfied with a *lower* return and thereby benefitting with a windfall *gain* in the market value of the bonds.

[7]Justin Fox (2009) quotes Alan Greenspan in his valedictory speech as chairman of the Federal Reserve Board, "The vast increase in the market value of asset claims is in part the indirect result of investors accepting lower compensation for risk... Any onset of increased investor caution elevates risk premiums and, as a consequence, lowers asset values..."

2. Beta is actually a rather nebulous concept. We might think of a high-beta firm as one that is sensitive to the cycles of the economy with attendant major movements in markets (high-rise construction companies, purveyors of luxury goods, or marketing enterprises) and low-beta stocks as those that are less exposed (food and drinks, beverages). But beta is not assessed by such considerations. A stock's beta is measured in relation to the covariance (sensitivity) of the stock price to the market over a series of prior (typically 60) monthly periods. It is simply assumed that the monthly fluctuating movements of a stock in relation to the market capture long-term exposure. This, however, is not necessarily the case. It may be, for example, that a high-risk firm considers day-to-day news of, say, economic consumption patterns, that does not affect the bigger picture of economic cycles as more or less irrelevant, but that such information is relevant to, say, the food and beverage industry, leading to firms of the food and beverage industry being accorded a high beta, whereas high-rise construction companies, whose price remains stationary to such news, are accorded a low beta. In this case, measurements of beta are failing systematically to capture risk exposure as perceived by investors.

3. Some market sectors are so large that their movements of themselves are capable of leading the market either up or down. For example, if the economy and thereby the market benefit from low energy prices, we might expect that energy firms have a somewhat negative relation to the economy (and hence a negative beta). However, the oil and gas sector is sufficiently large as to be capable of leading the market up or down. For this reason, its beta is typically positive.

4. When a stock outperforms against a generally rising market (a generally rising market has generally been the background of historical research), a firm's outperformance *of itself* generates an outperformance association between the stock's return and the market return, and, thereby, a beta greater than one. In this case, the direction of causality is from stock

---

(p. 317); and observes that the precursor to the steep falls in the prices of dot-com internet companies in 2000 was a tilt from optimism surrounding such stocks to a concern with their *risk* (p. 265).

price performance to beta, and *not* from beta to stock price performance (as the CAPM assumes).

5. Allowing that the observed price at the end of the month is a random selection from the sack of probability-weighted price outcomes, we must allow that each such price outcome is, in turn, logically determined in accordance with how investors at the end of each month anticipate how investors one month later must predict returns for the following month, and so on. Thus, the only way that an investor can attach probability-weighted outcomes to a stock price at the end of the month is by attaching probability-weighted outcomes to the stock price at the end of each subsequent month to infinity.

6. Roll's (1977) critique has pointed out that if the market is return-risk efficient, meaning that no sub-section of the market offers a superior relation of expected return to risk, then all of the market's contributing component assets must necessarily relate to the expected return on the market in accordance with the CAPM. In other words, the CAPM is a logical necessity if the market can be assumed to be return-risk efficient. However, the other side of Roll's critique is that because the equity market fails to represent the full total of investment assets (equities, bonds, property, one's foreseeable income as an individual, antiques, etc.), we cannot be certain that it is return-risk efficient in relation to the complete market of investors' opportunities.[8] Roll argues that if the equity market imposed on the CAPM is not return-risk efficient in the context of all investors' opportunities, the CAPM is invalidated. For Roll, it follows that, conventional tests of the CAPM are not a test of the CAPM, but, rather, a test of whether the equity market is return-risk efficient in the context of the (unknown) total set of available investments assets.

The above considerations were not explicitly considered by BJS. Perhaps, they considered that these effects should "wash through" on the aggregate. Or, perhaps, they considered that at some point they had, somehow, to make a stand on how an acceptable econometric test of the

---

[8]We note that in tests of the CAPM, the "market" portfolio typically ignores even the bond component of markets.

CAPM might be conducted. The financial academic world was after all becoming anxious for a proclamation of the model's applicability, which would give the go-ahead to continued advancement of an understanding of market behavior using econometric analyses of stock price data. As we have observed, in the late 1960s and early 1970s, researchers believed that they were at the forefront of significant discovery as they moved to understand financial markets in relation to rational models that would advance how such markets might be manipulated and improved.

Although they appear to have allowed themselves not to be overly concerned with the characteristics of monthly return data as discussed above, BJS did, however, identify a subtle effect in the data that they realized should not be ignored. They realized that, even it were the case that beta is actually *ignored* by investors, beta would still be captured in the data of stock returns, as $\beta_j[R_M - E(R_M)]$, where β_j is the beta for a stock j and $[R_M - E(R_M)]$ represents the actual market return (R_M) over what it was expected to be $(E(R_M))$.

To see where the $\beta_j[R_M - E(R_M)]$ term comes from, consider that a researcher wishes to test the "non-model" hypothesis that investors actually *ignore* a stock's sensitivity to the market as beta when setting prices and simply seek those stocks offering the highest returns, with the outcome that all stocks are priced to deliver the same expected return, say 10%, in a given year. Now, suppose that the actual market return for this year turns out to be 18%. In accordance with the "non-model" hypothesis (all stocks are priced to deliver the same return), should the researcher now expect to find that outcome returns for this year are distributed around 18% and that beta has no explanatory role?

Surprisingly, the answer is "no". Consider, for example, that Stock A has a sensitivity to the market described by its beta of 1.5, and Stock B has a sensitivity to the market described by its beta of 0.5. BJS recognized that the researcher should expect to find that each stock has achieved a return equal to the initial expectation (10%) plus the "surprise" additional market return (8% $=$ 18% $-$ 10%) *multiplied* by that stock's sensitivity to this market return (the stock's beta). In other words, the researcher expects to find that the outcome return for Stock A is 10% $+$ 1.5 $\times$ 8% $=$ 22%, and for Stock B is 10% $+$ 0.5 $\times$ 8% $=$ 14%, even though both stocks were priced to give the same expected outcome of 10%.

Thus, for BJS, the relation between actual outcome returns, R_j, for an asset j in relation to the expectation of return, $E(R_j)$, for the asset, becomes

$$R_j = E(R_j) + \beta_j[R_M - E(R_M)] + \varepsilon_j, \qquad (2.2)$$

where $E(R_j)$ formulates the model to be tested (for example, the right-hand side of the CAPM expression in Eq. (2.1)) and $[R_M - E(R_M)]$ is the "unexpected" excess market return multiplied by the asset beta (β_j), while ε_j allows an error term.[9] The clarity and conciseness of thought of BJS at this point is exemplary. I take my hat off to it. Note again that the explicit β_j term in Eq. (2.2) does not depend on any assumptions regarding investor expectations.

In seeking to test the CAPM, BJS therefore formed their hypothesized relation by substituting the CAPM equation for $E(R_j)$ as Eq. (2.1) into Eq. (2.2) to give

$$R_j = r_f + \beta_j[E(R_M) - r_f)] + \beta_j[R_M - E(R_M)] + \varepsilon_j. \qquad (2.3)$$

The $E(R_M)$ terms cancel out and the implied relation between the excess asset return ($R_j - r_f$) and the excess market return ($R_M - r_f$) in relation to the CAPM becomes

$$R_j - r_f = \beta_j(R_M - r_f) + \varepsilon_j. \qquad (2.4)$$

At this point, BJS had struck gold, so to speak, on account of that the non-directly measureable expectation terms, $E(R_j)$ and $E(R_M)$, have dropped out of the hypothesized relation to be tested. So now, BJS had to work out how to apply Eq. (2.4) to the data of monthly returns.

BJS proceeded to apply Eq. (2.4) to the data following a double-pass regression method, so as to achieve a number of testable predictions. In this way, they founded the elements of the methodology that underpins all subsequent tests of asset pricing models. The method can be explained briefly. In a first-pass, Eq. (2.4) is run as a time-series regression of each stock j's monthly excess return ($R_{j,t} - r_f$) at time t on the monthly excess market return ($R_{M,t} - r_f$) for that month so as to determine each stock's

---

[9] Equation (2.2) is BJS's Eq. (3).

beta (β_j) as the "slope" of the regression:

$$R_{j,t} - r_f = \alpha_j + \beta_j(R_{M,t} - r_f) + \varepsilon_{j,t}, \tag{2.5}$$

where α_j denotes the "intercept" of the regression and $\varepsilon_{j,t}$ are the regression error terms, which are expected to be symmetrically distributed about zero.[10] The parameters α_j and β_j for each firm j are now determined as those values that provide the "best overall fit" of Eq. (2.5) with the empirically observed data combinations of the stock j's performance, $R_{j,t}$, in any month, t, and the market's performance, $R_{M,t}$, in that month (with empirically observed risk-free rates, r_f), which is achieved by computerized algorithms that minimize the "error" terms ($\varepsilon_{j,t}$) in the alignment of Eq. (2.5) with the historical combinations of $R_{j,t}$ and $R_{M,t}$.

The stocks are then ranked by their beta and ten decile portfolios are partitioned from lowest beta to highest beta stocks. In this way, an average intercept (α_P) and average slope (beta, β_P) of the stocks in the portfolio may be assigned to each portfolio ($P = 1 \rightarrow 10$). We can see that if the CAPM of Eq. (2.1) is well specified in describing expectations, the intercepts α_j averaged as α_P for each portfolio should be close to zero. In the second-pass, Eq. (2.4) can now be run as a single cross-section regression[11] of the excess portfolio returns ($R_P - r_f$) on their portfolio betas (β_P) (as determined in the prior time-series regression)[12]:

$$R_P - r_f = \gamma_0 + \gamma_1 \beta_P + \varepsilon_P. \tag{2.6}$$

Again, if the CAPM of Eq. (2.1) is well specified, the intercept, γ_0, term should be statistically indistinguishable from zero, and the coefficient, γ_1, on the β_P's should identify the average excess market return, ($R_M - r_f$).

In the first-pass time-series regressions, the BJS studies determine that the average of the intercepts (α_j) for the portfolios α_P ($P = 1 \rightarrow 10$) is consistently negative for the high-risk portfolios ($\beta > 1$) and consistently

---

[10]Equation (2.5) is BJS's Eq. (6).

[11]The term "cross-sectional" regression captures the idea of a static relation between variables *at* a given point or points in time, in contrast to a time-series analysis, which traces a relation between variables *through* time.

[12]Equation (2.6) is BJS's Eq. (10).

positive for the low-risk portfolios ($\beta < 1$). In the second-pass cross-sectional regression, they find that the intercept (γ_0) is positive and the slope (γ_1) is too low to be identified with an average excess market return, $(R_M - r_f)$.

Both pass regressions, therefore, contradict the CAPM.

2.4. The Black Model

As highlighted in Mehrling's biography, Black realized that without some meaningful version of the CAPM, markets cannot be held to be rational. As Black (1993) explained, if the market does not appropriately reward beta, no investor should invest in high-beta stocks. Rather, the investor should form a portfolio with the lowest possible beta stocks and use leverage (purchasing additional stocks with debt financing) to achieve the same market exposure, but with a superior return performance as compared with a high-beta stock portfolio.

The simplest way to make the CAPM fit the data is to replace the risk-free rate, r_f (typically the return on short-term US Treasury bonds), with some larger value, R_z, since, as we shall see, that would justify a higher intercept term in both the first and second pass regressions, and explain the lower slope of the second-pass cross-sectional regressions. In fact, BJS use the data to calculate the required substitute rate, R_z, that offers the best fit. As Mehrling's biography recalls, "the R_z term was a statistical fix in search of a theoretical explanation" (p. 114). Accordingly, Black proposed his version of the CAPM as

$$E(R_j) = E(R_z) + \beta_j[E(R_M) - E(R_z)], \qquad (2.7)$$

where R_z is postulated as representing the return on a portfolio that has zero covariance with the return on the market portfolio. Black argued that the model is consistent with relaxing the assumption of the existence of risk-free borrowing and lending opportunities.

The test of whether the data are being generated by the process of Eq. (2.7) is then that of whether the actual returns are explained by the relation Eq. (2.4) with the standard risk-free rate r_f replaced by R_z:

$$R_j = R_z + \beta_j(R_M - R_z) + \varepsilon_j, \qquad (2.8)$$

which (because we wish to maintain the regression format of a dependence of $R_j - r_f$ on $R_M - r_f$ as the independent variable) can be rewritten as

$$R_j - r_f = (R_z - r_f)(1 - \beta_j) + \beta_j(R_M - r_f) + \varepsilon_j, \qquad (2.9)$$

That is, the first-pass time-series regressions of the excess return ($R_j - r_f$) for each stock, j, on the excess market return ($R_M - r_f$) should now produce an average intercept, α_P, for the stocks in each portfolio (formed on low to high measured betas, $P = 1 \rightarrow 10$) as

$$\alpha_P = (R_z - r_f)(1 - \beta_P), \qquad (2.10)$$

where β_P is the average sensitivity to the market of the stocks in each portfolio. Equation (2.10) (and therefore, Eq. (2.7)) could, therefore, be declared consistent with the JBS findings that the intercept α_P is increasingly negative (positive) with increasing (decreasing) beta from the base $\beta_P = 1$. In addition, the second-pass cross-section regressions of the excess portfolio returns ($R_P - r_f$) on their portfolio betas (β_P) as Eq. (2.6) above:

$$R_P - r_f = \gamma_0 + \gamma_1 \beta_P + \varepsilon_P,$$

now predicts (with Eq. (2.8))

$$\gamma_0 = R_z - r_f \quad \text{and} \quad \gamma_1 = R_M - R_z, \qquad (2.11)$$

which is consistent with the empirical determination by BJS in the cross-section regressions for the portfolios of a positive intercept ($R_z - r_f$) and a slope ($R_M - R_z$) that understates the excess market return over the risk-free rate.

Subjecting the data to sub-periods, Table 2.1 presents results taken from BJS (1972) (Table 4, p. 98) for 1939–1965, and from Black (1993) for 1966–1991. The outcomes are from their cross-sectional regression of portfolio excess returns ($R_P - r_f$) on portfolio betas (β_P) as Eq. (2.6) above:

$$R_P - r_f = \gamma_0 + \gamma_1 \beta_P + \varepsilon_P.$$

In the table, Row 1 reports the average excess market return $R_M - r_f$ for each period of the study. Rows 2 and 3 are the regression intercepts (γ_0) and slopes (γ_1) for the periods. The CAPM predicts $\gamma_0 = $ zero and $\gamma_1 = R_M - r_f$, whereas Black's version of the CAPM model implies $\gamma_0 = R_z - r_f$ and $\gamma_1 = R_M - R_z$.

Table 2.1. Summary of cross-sectional intercepts and slopes: The BJS and Black studies.

	1939–1948 (%)	1948–1957 (%)	1957–1965 (%)	1966–1991 (%)
1. Excess market return $R_M - r_f$:	18	13	10.5	8
2. Intercept γ_0	5	9	12	6
3. Slope γ_1	13	4	−1.5	2

The results above are taken from Black, Jensen, and Scholes (1972) (Table 4, p. 98) for 1939–1965, and from Black (1993) for 1966–1991. The outcomes are from their cross-sectional regression of portfolio excess returns $(R_P - r_f)$ on portfolio betas (β_P), as Eq. (2.6):

$$R_P - r_f = \gamma_0 + \gamma_1 \beta_P + \varepsilon_P.$$

In the Table, Row 1 reports the average excess market return $(R_M - r_f)$ for each period of the study. Rows 2 and 3 are the regression intercepts (γ_0) and slopes (γ_1) for the periods. BJS interpret the regression γ_0 and γ_1, either as zero and $R_M - r_f$, respectively, allowing the CAPM, or as $R_z - r_f$ and $R_M - R_z$, respectively, allowing Black's version of the CAPM. Following the null-hypothesis model in relation to beta (Eq. (2.12) below) γ_0 and γ_1, are interpreted, respectively, as $E(R_M) - r_f$ and $R_M - E(R_M)$.

The table highlights the contortions that must be attributed to $R_z - r_f$ and $R_M - R_z$ through time so that Black's CAPM can be made to fit the data. For the period 1957–1965, γ_1 is negative, implying that through this period, and notwithstanding a market excess return over the risk-free rate, $R_M - r_f = 10.5\%$, the market return (R_M) was, on average, less than Black's proposed "risk-free" rate (R_z).

On the face of it, the data does little to inspire confidence in either the conventional or Black's CAPM. The implications of rejecting market rationality as encapsulated by the CAPM would, however, have been considerable. In capturing the idea that markets are inherently rational, the CAPM had made finance an appropriate subject for econometric studies. The fact that the test showed that higher stock returns are generally associated with higher betas was taken as evidence in support of the CAPM, while the fact that the findings contradicted the CAPM as an adequate model of asset pricing did not discourage enthusiasm for the model.[13]

---

[13]For example, empirical work as far back as Douglas (1969) confirms that the average realized stock return is significantly related to the variance of the returns over time, but not to their covariance with the market index of returns, thereby contradicting the CAPM.

Miller and Scholes (1972) and Fama and McBeth (1973) also subsequently demonstrated positive relationships between beta and asset return outcomes that were interpreted as confirming the CAPM.

2.5. A Test of the Irrelevancy of Beta

Suppose, that we wish to test the possibility that investors are *not* in accord with Black's CAPM and can be modeled as adhering to a "non-model" hypothesis, whereby all assets j have the *same* expected rate of return, $E(R_j)$, which is then necessarily that of the market, $E(R_M)$:

$$E(R_j) = E(R_M). \tag{2.12}$$

How do the regressions separate the hypotheses as preferable explanations of the data? To test the Eq. (2.12) hypothesis, we form the implied relation between the observed returns for asset j, R_j, and the expected return for the asset, $E(R_j)$, as Eq. (2.2), which with Eq. (2.12) gives

$$R_j = E(R_M) + \beta_j[R_M - E(R_M)] + \varepsilon_j. \tag{2.13}$$

Note again how β_j above identifies the "pull" of the excess market return on the return on asset j. Equation (2.13) (again for the purpose of expressing a preferred regression dependence of $R_j - r_f$ on $R_M - r_f$ as the independent variable) can be rewritten as

$$R_j - r_f = (1 - \beta_j)[E(R_M) - r_f] + \beta_j(R_M - r_f) + \varepsilon_j. \tag{2.14}$$

The first-pass time-series regressions (of $(R_j - r_f)$ on $(R_M - r_f)$) should now produce an average intercept for the stocks in each portfolio (formed, as above, on low to high measured betas), α_P, as

$$\alpha_P = (1 - \beta_P)[E(R_M) - r_f], \tag{2.15}$$

where β_P is the average beta of the stocks in each portfolio, and the second-pass cross-section regressions as Eq. (2.6):

$$R_P - r_f = \gamma_0 + \gamma_1\beta_P + \varepsilon_P,$$

Douglas also summarizes some of Lintner's unpublished results that also appear to be inconsistent with the CAPM (reported by Jensen, 1972). This work finds that asset returns appear to be related to the idiosyncratic (non-market) volatility that is diversifiable.

should now reveal the parameters γ_0 and γ_1 as

$$\gamma_0 = E(R_M) - r_f \quad \text{and} \quad \gamma_1 = R_M - E(R_M). \qquad (2.16)$$

Thus, we find that the differences in predictions between the traditional CAPM (Eq. (2.1)), Black's CAPM (Eq. (2.7)) and the "non-model" of Eq. (2.12) are as follows. For the traditional CAPM hypothesis, the predictions (as above) are:

$$\alpha_P = 0,$$

$$\gamma_0 = 0, \quad \text{and} \quad \gamma_1 = R_M - r_f.$$

For Black's CAPM hypothesis (as above), we have Eqs. (2.10) and (2.11):

$$\alpha_P = (1 - \beta_P)(R_z - r_f),$$

$$\gamma_0 = (R_z - r_f), \quad \text{and} \quad \gamma_1 = R_M - R_z.$$

And for the "non-model" hypothesis, we have Eqs. (2.15) and (2.16):

$$\alpha_P = (1 - \beta_P)[E(R_M) - r_f],$$

$$\gamma_0 = E(R_M) - r_f, \quad \text{and} \quad \gamma_1 = R_M - E(R_M).$$

Thus, the original CAPM hypothesis predicts $R_z = r_f$, and Black's CAPM hypothesis predicts $R_z = $ a value greater than r_f, but less than $E(R_M)$. The non-model hypothesis predicts $R_z = E(R_M)$. So what do the data say? BJS actually observe:

> "This (the beta factor, R_z) seems to have been significantly different from the risk-free rate and indeed is *roughly the same size as the average market return* (R_M) of 1.3 and 1.2% per month over the two sample intervals (1948–1957 and 1957–1965) in this period" (our italics) (p. 82).

In other words, the BJS results would appear to validate the "non-model" hypothesis of Eq. (2.12), in favor of either the CAPM of Eq. (2.1) or Black's CAPM of Eq. (2.7)!

Recall also that in Table 2.1, the null-hypothesis model interprets $\gamma_0 = [E(R_M) - r_f]$ and $\gamma_1 = [R_M - E(R_M)]$. In contrast to the *ad hoc* variations that must be attributed to $R_z - r_f$ and $R_M - R_z$ through time so that Black's CAPM can be made to fit the data, the null-hypothesis model offers a coherent story; namely, that from inauspicious times in the later 1930s, market expectations as to the market's ability to deliver wealth as $E(R_M) - r_f$ have increased consistently (5%, 9%, 12% over the risk-free rate) up to the mid-1960s, from which time, expectations have been moderated (to a risk-premium of 6%). Consistently, the outcome market performance as $R_M - E(R_M)$ has progressed from very much outperforming expectations (13%) in the 1940s to a more modest surpassing of expectations (4%) until actually underperforming against expectations by 1.5% (although still surpassing the risk-free rate by 10.5%), until in the period 1966–1991, the market again exceeded expectations (by 2%).

The traditional approach to an assessment of the forward-looking equity risk premium $[E(R_M) - r_f]$ has been to take the average of historical equity performances over and above the risk-free rate, $R_M - r_f$. Following such an approach, textbooks in the late 1990s regularly quoted an equity risk premium as approximately 8% (which is consistent with Black's historical estimate for the period 1966–1991 for $R_M - r_f$ in Table 2.1). However, the assumption that the historical $R_M - r_f$ can be identified with $E(R_M) - r_f$ requires that the CAPM is fully embedded in the data. If the CAPM is without influence in the data (the "non-model" hypothesis), the historical observation for $R_M - r_f$ in Table 2.1 is decomposed as constituting an $E(R_M) - r_f$ component (row 2) in combination with an unexpected market outcome $R_M - E(R_M)$ component (row 3). Thus, for the period 1966–1991 in Table 2.1, the intercept γ_0 provides an estimate of the forward looking equity risk premium $E(R_M) - r_f$ as 6%, and the slope γ_1 provides an *ex post* estimate of the market's divergence from expectations, $R_M - E(R_M)$, as 2%.

2.6. Time for Reflection: What Have We Learned?

The success of US (and other) stock markets has led academics to observe that markets offer a premium in compensation for investing in a risky market. The CAPM states that investors expect to avail of the market risk premium in proportion to their exposure to market risk. Otherwise, one set of investors is gaining at the expense of some other set. So why is the CAPM not evident in the data?

Generically, two sets of reasons might be offered. Firstly, there are arguments that the *tests* of the CAPM are invalid, as outlined earlier in the chapter. Notably, Roll's statement of the non-testability of the CAPM provides empiricists with a get-out clause when their findings do not accord with CAPM predictions. As such, Roll's critique has been evoked many times.

Secondly, it is possible that investors are sufficiently insensitive to beta as to actually disqualify the CAPM. We note that the CAPM is a model of markets *in equilibrium*, whereas actual markets are always in flux, which is to say, in *dis*equilibrium. In a world of disequilibrium, it may be that beta really is more or less irrelevant as institutional investors and professional portfolio managers compete in the business of picking winners in competition with other portfolio managers. A rational investor (investing h/h own money) might be aware of the commensurate downside to high beta stocks if the market should turn. But for institutional investors, as they compete for accolades of higher than average performance, the race is to the short run, over which they are assessed. For institutional investment, the risk is not the risk of losing (other people's) money, but of underperforming against the competition. Thus, when markets appear to be in the ascension, exposure to the market with higher beta stocks appears as a sensible strategy — with the longer-term *downside* potential of high beta stocks suppressed as a concern for risk. Justin Fox (2009) in *The Myth of the Rational Market* (p. 260) quotes a survey whereby professional investors, while agreeing pretty much unanimously that the Standard and Poor's (S&P's) price-to-earnings ratios in the high 20s in 1999 would likely fall in the near future, nevertheless regarded that betting against such a drop could be a career killing move so long as the markets continued to grow. A case of the market can stay irrational longer than the rational institutional investor can keep his job. In which case, an understanding of capital markets requires an understanding of the *institutional imperatives* encountered by fund managers rather than an understanding of individual stock sensitivities to beta.

However, at a time when researchers were convinced that markets could and should be made subject to something like scientific inquiry, evidence against the CAPM was not what researchers were wishing to hear. Such a revelation would have fundamentally undermined the determination of finance to be accepted as a domain of economics with its study of "efficient markets" in terms of econometric techniques. Thus, notwithstanding that the evidence from the beginning has always been squarely against the notion that investors set stock prices rationally in relation to stock betas, the industry of writing papers in support of the CAPM grew vibrantly over the decades following its inception. A blind eye was purposefully turned to the evidence. Lo and Mueller (2010) — themselves proficient exponents of empirical research — observe that up to the early 1990s, any challenge to the notion of market efficiency was anathema, and that papers claiming to have discovered departures in the data from what was predicted by CAPM were "routinely rejected from the top economics and finance journals, in some cases, without even being sent out to referees for review" (p. 18). In the introduction to their paper, they explain: "The quantitative aspirations of economists and financial analysts have for years been based on the belief that it should be possible to build models of economic systems — and financial markets in particular — that are as predictive as those in physics" (p. 13).

Ultimately, however, the issue is not whether the CAPM should be accorded "true" or "false". The CAPM presents a rather straight-forward principle of additive rationality. Following the scientific philosopher Hilary Putnam (1979), theories/models are never ultimately "true" or "false", but, rather, are ultimately "useful" or "not useful".[14] Similarly, the scientific philosopher Thomas Kuhn (1962) considers that the theory is not a hypothesis in need of confirmation, but a "view of the world", on the basis of which we set out to explore and explain.[15] In this manner, the

---

[14]The *usefulness* of a model is that it allows us to organize our perceptions, insights and experiences. The model facilitates relationships, which is to say, *patterns* of recognition that are *repeatable*. The model breaks down (to a greater or lesser extent) when observations fail to fit the pattern. We then progress to models that are more "useful". On such a basis, Putnam (1979) refuses to accept the separation of science and behavioral science, arguing that what previous scientific philosophers — Popper in particular — fail to recognize is that "practice is primary", meaning that our ideas are not just an end in themselves; rather, they exist to "guide practice", to structure whole forms of life:

> "We judge the correctness of our ideas by applying them and seeing if they succeed; in general, and in the long run, correct ideas lead to success, and ideas lead to failures where and insofar as they are incorrect. Failure to see the importance of practice leads directly to failure to see the importance of success. Practice is primary" (pp. 374–375).

[15]Kuhn developed the idea that at any time, researchers are expected to "buy into" the prevailing paradigm of the day. A refutation does not actually threaten the central paradigm, but rather, is deemed to be an "anomaly", stimulating only the need to relax or refigure the simplifying assumptions surrounding the central paradigm. Kuhn stresses that theories are by their nature highly immune to falsification. It is difficult, if not impossible, to refute theories completely since any empirical test always involves the target hypothesis in conjunction

usefulness of a model is that it allows us to organize our perceptions, insights and experiences of the observed data. The manifestation of such patterns creates a conceptual framework — a way of seeing the world. Ultimately, the CAPM fails as a worthy paradigm for understanding markets because, as an *empirical* fact, its core prediction succeeds in advancing only a succession of "anomalies" that contradict its core premise.

As an outcome of continued academic championing of the CAPM, however, the model has achieved broad acceptance in industry as a model with which to estimate a firm's cost of equity capital. And this is not irrational. If the *principle* of the CAPM is accepted, Eq. (2.1) represents the *logical* determination of a rational shareholder's long-term expectation of return for the firm (and its investments). We might say that the CAPM fails as a "capital asset pricing model" of markets, but remains as an entirely valid "cost of equity formula" for the firm. This is an important observation. In developing rational models of portfolio allocation (Section C) we shall find that the CAPM appears naturally in the analysis. The principle of the CAPM is not denied. Our point in this chapter is that (for whatever reasons) the CAPM fails abjectly as an explanation of the observed formation of stock returns.

Finally, we note that our "non-model" representation of the data has allowed for an interpretation of *ex post* market premium data, $R_M - r_f$, as the component (1) $E(R_M) - r_f$ — which is to say, investors' actual anticipated equity premium — in conjunction with the component (2) $R_M - E(R_M)$ — which provides an estimate of the market's over/underperformance against actual expectations. Thus, for example, the historical market premium of 8% in Table 2.1 is interpreted as the outcome of investors' expected risk premium of 6% combined with an outperformance of the market above investor expectations of 2%.

---

with a whole set of auxiliary hypotheses — which are often of the form of simplifying assumptions that are *known* to be *un*true. It follows that any refutation is a refutation of only a particular conjunction of hypotheses, not of the target hypothesis. For Kuhn, complexity around the core paradigm thereby accumulates until a new paradigm arrives with a Gestalt explanation of facts that had previously defied a satisfactory explanation, so that the old edifice collapses in the face of the alternative paradigm that simultaneously simplifies the conceptual framework and stimulates new enquiry that actually goes beyond the domain of the original paradigm.

Chapter 3

The Fama and French Three-Factor Model

*If past history was all there was to
the game, the richest people would be
librarians.*

Warren Buffett

*To understand the actual world as it is, not
as we should wish it to be, is the beginning
of wisdom.*

*The fact that an opinion has been
widely held is no evidence whatever that
it is not utterly absurd.*

Bertrand Russell

*The financial markets generally are unpre-
dictable. So that one has to have different
scenarios. . . The idea that you can actually
predict what's going to happen contradicts
my way of looking at the market.*

George Soros

Reality leaves a lot to the imagination

John Lennon

3.1. Introduction[1]

As we observed in Chapter 2, for academics into the 1990s, the capital asset
pricing model (CAPM) — as a model for understanding the pricing of assets
in a market — was pretty much the only game in town. Additionally, the
CAPM had achieved broad industry acceptance.

Nevertheless, as was also observed, the CAPM entirely fails as a model
of historical asset pricing, which prompted our belief in a non-beta model
as providing a more coherent explanation of the data. In 1992, the CAPM's
inability to function as a model of asset pricing was recognized by Eugene
Fama and Kenneth French. Rather than dismiss the CAPM, however, they

---

[1]This chapter develops ideas that were presented in the journal *Abacus* (Dempsey 2013).
I am indeed grateful and indebted to the editors and reviewers of this journal for supporting
and publishing this work notwithstanding its unorthodoxy.

31

chose to present their three-factor model, which is the CAPM with two additional variables. Their model is now generally accepted as having superseded the CAPM.

In this chapter, we introduce what is now referred to as the Fama and French three-factor (FF-3F) model (Section 3.2). In Section 3.3, we question the Fama and French interpretation of their model as a risk-return model refinement of the CAPM. Section 3.4 concludes with a discussion.

3.2.   The Fama and French Three-Factor Model

Altogether not actually the first to do so,[2] in the early 1990s, Fama and French were particularly aggressive in pronouncing the ineffectiveness of the relation between historical average returns and beta (β). In 1992 — while holding to the principle of market efficiency — they introduced their paper in the prestigious *Journal of Finance* with the pronouncement that beta had effectively no explanatory power in regard to asset pricing:

> "When the tests allow for variation in β that is unrelated to size, the relation between β and average return is flat, even when β is the only explanatory variable" (Fama and French, 1992, p. 427).

Fama and French introduced two variables in addition to beta, which, they claimed, administered most of the "heavy work" in explaining historical stock price movements. These variables were the market equity (ME) value or size of the underlying firm, and the ratio of the book value of the firm's common equity to its market equity value (BE/ME), which together "provide a simple and powerful characterization of the cross-section of average stock returns for the 1963–1990 period" (FF, 1992, p. 429). The authors concluded that "if stocks are priced rationally, the results suggest that stock risks are multidimensional" (p. 428).

As Black, Jensen, and Scholes (1972) before them, Fama and French wished to retain the notion of a risk-based model of asset pricing. In the absence of such a model, the rational integrity of markets is undermined. Thus, in their 1996 paper, they place their model squarely in the tradition

---

[2]For example, Reinganum (1981) and Lakonishok and Shapiro (1986).

of the CAPM, stating that

> "this paper argues that many of the CAPM average-return anomalies are related, and that they are captured by the three-factor model in Fama and French (1993)".

The FF-3F model states that the expected return on an equity portfolio, j, in excess of the risk-free rate, $E(R_j) - r_f$, is explained by the sensitivity of its return to three factors:

(i) $E(R_M) - r_f$, the excess market return: the expected difference between the risky equity market return and the risk-free rate (as in the CAPM),

(ii) $E(R_{SMB})$, Small minus Big: the expected difference between the return on a portfolio of small firm stocks and the return on a portfolio of large firm stocks, and

(iii) $E(R_{HML})$, High minus Low: the expected difference between the return on a portfolio of the stocks of high-book-to-market firms (which tends to represent the stocks of more mature "non-growth" — termed "value" — firms) and the return on a portfolio of the stocks of low-book-to-market firms (which tends to represent the stocks of "growth" firms).

Specifically, the FF-3F model states that the expected return $E(R_j)$ on portfolio j is determined as (Fama and French, 1996):

$$E(R_j) - r_f = b_j[E(R_M) - r_f] + s_j E(R_{SMB}) + h_j E(R_{HML}) \quad FF - 1,$$

(3.1)

where $E(R_M) - r_f$, $E(R_{SMB})$, and $E(R_{HML})$ are expected premiums, and the factor sensitivities or loadings, b_j, s_j, and h_j, are the slopes in the time-series regression:

$$R_j - r_f = \alpha_j + b_j(R_M - r_f) + s_j R_{SMB} + h_j R_{HML} + \varepsilon_j \quad FF - 2,$$

(3.2)

where α_j and ε_j represent, respectively, the intercept and error terms of the regression.

Fama and French interpreted their model as preserving the structure of the CAPM, while extending it with two additional risk premiums. Thus,

$[E(R_M) - r_f]$ is the CAPM risk premium — the expected return on the market portfolio of all risky stocks, $E(R_M)$, minus the return on non-risky treasury bonds, r_f. In analogy, $E(R_{SMB})$ is the risk premium for stocks of small firms, which is identified as the expected return on a portfolio of stocks of the smallest firms (Fama and French choose the 30% of stocks with the smallest firm size) minus the return on a portfolio of stocks of the largest firms (Fama and French choose the 30% of stocks with the largest firm size), and, similarly, $E(R_{HML})$ is the risk premium for a portfolio of stocks of the highest book-to-market value minus the return on a portfolio of stocks of the lowest book-to-market value.

In seeking to establish their model as a strictly risk-based model, Fama and French argued that the size of the underlying firm (ME) and the ratio of the book value of equity to market value (BE/ME) are "risk-based" explanatory variables, with the former being a proxy for the required return for bearing exposure to small firm stocks, and the latter being a proxy for investors' required return for bearing "financial distress", neither of which are captured in the market return (FF, 1995). They also claimed that their model provided both a resolution of the CAPM (FF, 1996) and a resolution of prior attempts to generalize a risk-based model of stock prices:

> "At a minimum, the available evidence suggests that the three-factor model in *FF 1* and *FF 2* [Eqns. (3.1) and (3.2), above], with intercepts in *FF 2* equal to 0, is a parsimonious description of returns and average returns. The model captures much of the variation in the cross-section of average returns, and it absorbs most of the anomalies that have plagued the CAPM. More aggressively, we argue in FF (1993, 1994, 1995) that the empirical successes of *FF 1* suggest that it is an equilibrium pricing model, a three-factor version of Merton's (1973) inter-temporal CAPM (ICAPM) or Ross's (1976) arbitrage pricing theory (APT). In this view, R_{SMB} and R_{HML} mimic combinations of two underlying risk factors or state variables of special hedging concern to investors" (FF 1996, p. 56).

3.3. Critique of the Fama and French Three-Factor Model

There is an obvious inherent contradiction between, on the one hand, Fama and French's repeated denouncement of β, and, on the other hand, their inclusion of β as an explanatory variable in their model.

In fact, in their formal test of their model, Fama and French do not trouble to allow for a beta effect. Thus, in FF (1996) they form 25 (5×5) portfolios on "book-to-market value" and "firm size", but not on β, with the outcome that the b_j coefficients of the 25 portfolios are all very close to 1.0 (none diverge by more than 10% as shown in Table 1 of FF (1996)). The FF-3F model has simultaneously included β and made it redundant as an explanatory variable.

We thereby have a disconnect between the FF-3F model and the CAPM. Whereas the CAPM states that all assets have a return equal to *the risk-free rate* "as a base" plus a market risk premium multiplied by the asset's exposure to the market, the FF-3F model states that all stocks have *the market return* "as a base" plus or minus an element that depends on the stock's sensitivity to the differential performances of high and low book-value-to-market-equity (BE/ME) stocks and big and small firm size (ME) stocks. The FF-3F model is more truthfully (and parsimoniously) expressed as a "two"- rather than a "three"-factor model:

$$E(R_j) = E(R_M) + s_j E(R_{SMB}) + h_j E(R_{HML}). \qquad (3.3)$$

But to express it thusly would be to concede that investor rationality, as captured by the CAPM, is now abandoned, whereas by allowing the loading b_j coefficients on the excess market return $[E(R_M) - r_f]$ to remain in the model, a formal continuity with the CAPM and the illusion that the three-factor model can be viewed as a refinement of the CAPM is maintained. Nevertheless, it can be noted that even on its own terms, the FF-3F model does not work entirely satisfactorily. As Fama and French (1996) concede, there are large negative unexplained returns for the stocks in their smallest size and lowest BE/ME quintile portfolios, and large positive unexplained returns for the stocks in the largest size and lowest BE/ME quintile portfolios.

There is a correspondence here with the arguments developed by the scientific philosopher Thomas Kuhn (1962) introduced in Chapter 2 (p. 29). In Kuhn's view, "normal science" generally consists of a protracted period of adjustments to the surrounding framework of a central paradigm with "add-on" hypotheses aimed at defending the central hypothesis against various "anomalies". Facts always serve to justify more activity without ever seriously being allowed to threaten the paradigm core. The continued defense of the CAPM — adding more factors to the CAPM to explain more anomalies — has led the single-factor CAPM model to become the three-factor model of Fama and French. And, subsequent to the FF-3F model, additional factors have been added for idiosyncratic volatility, liquidity, momentum, and so forth (we shall encounter them in Chapter 4), all of which typify Kuhn's understanding of "normal science".

Lakonishok, Shleifer, and Vishny (1994) have argued that the Fama and French risk premiums are not risk premiums at all, but rather are the outcome of mispricing. They argue that investors consistently underestimate future growth rates for "value" stocks (captured as high BE/ME value) and therefore, underprice them. This results in value stocks outperforming growth stocks.[3] From another perspective, Daniel and Titman (1997) provide evidence against the premiums as risk premiums by finding that the return performances of the Fama and French portfolios do not relate to covariances with the risk premiums as the Fama and French model dictates, but, rather, relate directly to the book-to-market and size of the firm as attributable "characteristics" of the stock.

3.4.   Time for Reflection: What Have We Learned?

The FF-3F model derives from a fitting of data rather than from theoretical principles. Black (1993), for example, attributed the then fledgling FF-3F model to "data mining". Conceptually, the model leaves much to be desired. The model states that US institutional and retail investors (a) care about market risk, but (b) do not appear to care about how such risk might be magnified or diminished in particular assets as captured by their beta (thereby contradicting the CAPM), while (c) simultaneously appearing to care about the BE/ME ratio and the firm size of their stocks. But, if sensitivity to market risk as captured by beta does not motivate investors, it is, on the face of it, difficult to envisage how the BE/ME and firm size variables can be expected to motivate them.

---

[3]Other authors provide evidence against the Fama and French premiums as proxies for risk premiums by arguing that the risk of bankruptcy is negatively rather than positively related to expected returns; for example, Dichev (1998) and Campbell, Hilscher, and Szilagyi (2008), although Griffin and Lemmon (2002) report that distressed firms often do have high book-to-market ratios.

On the one hand, Fama and French have rejected an explanatory capacity for beta, while, on the other hand, they insist that their two factors are *additional* — designed to capture "certain anomalies with the CAPM". There is an evident self-contradiction in rejecting beta and simultaneously retaining the CAPM as the conceptual foundation of the FF-3F model.

If the blind eye purposefully turned to the evidence confirming that the CAPM does not even approximately fit with the data represents a pretense of the previous chapter, the pretense of the present chapter is that the FF-3F model represents some kind of upgrading or refinement of the CAPM.

Notwithstanding, the FF-3F model is now academically mainstream in having effectively replaced the CAPM.

Chapter 4

Beyond the Fama and French Three-Factor Model

If investing is entertaining, if you're hav- ing fun, you're probably not making any money. Good investing is boring. Markets are constantly in a state of uncertainty and flux and money is made by discounting the obvious and betting on the unexpected.

The trouble with institutional investors is that their performance is usu- ally measured relative to their peer group and not by an absolute yardstick. This makes them trend followers by definition.

George Soros

There is nothing so useless as doing effi- ciently that which should not be done at all.

Peter Drucker

Successful investing is anticipating the anticipations of others.

John Maynard Keynes

First get your facts, then you can distort them anyway you want.

Mark Twain

4.1. Introduction[1]

The capital asset pricing model (CAPM) and Fama and French three-factor (FF-3F) models continue to stimulate substantial contributions in the academic asset pricing literature. This work typically aims to test the model and record an "anomaly" when a new variable adds to the description of the cross-section of *ex post* stock returns. The new variable may then be incorporated in an extended factor model.

Thus, the "value" and "size" effects in the FF-3F model have been augmented by a stock return momentum effect, which is now viewed as a standard variable in asset pricing models (the Carhart 1997 model). The model captures the observation that stocks that have recently performed well

---

[1]This chapter develops ideas that were presented in the journal *Abacus* (Dempsey 2013a). I am indeed grateful and indebted to the editors and reviewers of this journal for supporting and publishing this work notwithstanding its unorthodoxy.

are likely to continue such a performance over a period of many months. It is also common to include a premium for stock illiquidity.

The trend of adding explanatory variables continues. Academia, it appears, is not yet prepared to abandon the belief that stock prices are determined rationally on the basis of inputs to its factor models.

This chapter is arranged as follows. Section 4.2 summarizes the elaboration of the FF-3F model with additional variables. In Section 4.3, we question the worth of this work and discuss why it is that academics devote such effort (whole careers) to data mining for each and every market anomaly. In Section 4.4, we consider the implications of abandoning the CAPM. Section 4.5 concludes with a discussion.

4.2. Asset Pricing Research

Since Jegadeesh and Titman (1993) demonstrated a momentum effect based on three to 12 months of past returns, the effect and its relation to other variables has spurred considerable research effort.[2]

Although it is possible to conjecture how momentum may come about as an outcome of a stock's attractiveness continuing to build on its recent performance, it is difficult to justify stock return momentum (which, in principle, offers a level of predictability for a stock's price movement) as an inherent *risk* factor. The challenge has been recognized more recently by Fama and French (2008) who indicate that momentum as such may need to be incorporated in asset pricing explanations (with the momentum effect allowed to differentiate across firm size).

As well as momentum, Fama and French (2008) have reported accruals and stock issues as robustly associated with the cross-section of returns, while, Cooper, Gulen, and Schill (2008) argue that growth in assets predicts

---

[2]For example, Chordia and Shivakumar (2002) argue that momentum profits in the US can be explained by business cycles, the findings of which are elaborated by Grinblatt and Moskowitz (2004), Griffin, Ji and Martin (2003) and Rouwenhorst (1998), who report evidence of momentum internationally. Heston and Sadka (2008) also report how winner stocks continue to outperform the same loser stocks in subsequent months; while Hong, Lim, and Stein (2000) relate the momentum effect negatively to firm size and analyst coverage. Allied with momentum over six- to 12-month horizons, researchers such as DeBondt and Thaler (1985, 1987) have also reported evidence of long-term *reversal* in stock under- and over-performance over three- to five-year periods. This finding, although challenged by Conrad and Kaul (1993), finds essential support from Loughran and Ritter (1996) and Chopra, Lakonishok, and Ritter (1992).

returns. Haugen and Baker (1996) consider past returns, trading volume, and accounting ratios such as return on equity and price/earnings, as the strongest determinants of expected returns, and go so far as to report that they find no evidence that risk measures (such as systematic or total volatility) are influential in the cross-section distribution of equity returns.

A good deal of research has followed aimed at replacing the Fama and French "high book-to-equity value" and "small firm size" explanatory variables with economic variables that appear to relate more naturally to investors' concerns.[3] It should, of course, come as no surprise that aspects of the economy relate to stock price formation. Neither is it a surprise that the relations are evident as covariances in the data of stock price returns. This is, in fact, what we expect. We should be clear that the purpose of an asset pricing model is to show how the essential dynamic of markets — *the playoff between risk and return* — is monitored and priced in the market — not to merely confirm expected pricing effects. As John Cochrane (2005) — himself a highly regarded contributor to asset pricing research — observes in a classic text, *Asset Pricing*, such observations need "not cause a ripple" (p. 453).

Indeed, it is now the convention for models not to make the claim to be "asset pricing" models in the risk-return sense, but rather to be "factor" models. The identification of the correlation of a variable with asset returns is then presented as either an "anomaly" or as the demonstration that the variable is "priced" by the markets. This is what Fischer Black meant by saying that the exercise amounts to data mining.

---

[3]As examples of the work in this area, Petkova (2006) shows that a factor model that incorporates the term and credit spreads of bonds makes redundant the Fama and French (1993) risk proxies for the Fama and French 25 portfolios sorted by size and book-to-market. Also working with the Fama and French 25 portfolios, Brennan, Wang, and Xia (2004) report that the real interest rate and the Sharpe ratio (the ratio of market excess return to market standard deviation) together describe the expected returns of assets in equilibrium. Again with reference to the Fama and French portfolios, Da (2009) reports that the expected return of an asset is the outcome of the asset's covariance with aggregate consumption and the time pattern of market cash flows; while Campbell and Vuolteenaho (2004) argue for focussing on an asset's covariance with market cash flows as the important risk factor. Jagannathan and Wang (1996) argue that a conditional CAPM, where betas are allowed to vary with the business cycle, works well when returns to labor income are included in the total return on the market portfolio (which is supported by Santos and Veronesi (2006) who show that the labor income to consumption ratio is a useful descriptor of expected returns).

Observed stock returns can also be related to "micro-finance" — the institutional mechanics of trading equities. Thus, Amihud and Mendelson (1986) relate asset returns to stock liquidity, measured, for example, by the quoted bid-ask spread.[4] More recently, studies have begun to identify cross-sectional predictability with frictions due to the cognitive limitations of investors.[5] But, again, it is difficult to see how such variables might be interpreted as proxies for non-divesifiable "risk" factors.

4.3. Asset Pricing and Data Mining

A good deal of finance is now an econometric exercise in mining data, either for confirmation of a particular factor model or for the confirmation of deviations from a model's predictions as anomalies. The accumulation of explanatory variables advanced to explain the cross-section of asset returns has been accelerating, albeit with little overall understanding of the structure between them. Subrahmanyam (2010) documents more than 50 variables used to predict stock returns. We might venture that these papers exist on the "periphery of asset pricing" — they show very little attempt to model a robust risk-return relationship that differentiates across assets.

Although we have failed to identify an essential risk-return relationship for the markets, it might be suggested that analyses of covariances of market returns with economic or psychological considerations, or with market institutional (liquidity attributes) considerations, have at least provided us with a fairly detailed *description* of correlations in asset pricing over a sustained period of stock market history. Interesting as the findings might be, however, we should be clear that the findings fail to satisfactorily generalize the functioning of markets. With regard to value stocks — which constitute the dominant factor in the Fama and French model — Burton Malkiel (2004) observes,

> "While there appears to be long periods when one style seems to outperform the other, the actual investment results over a more than 65-year period are little different for value and growth mutual funds.

---

[4]Liquidity is also promoted as an explanatory variable in understanding asset returns by Chordia, Roll, and Subrahmanyam (2002, 2008) and Chordia, Sarkar, and Subrahmanyam (2005).

[5]For example, Cohen and Frazzini (2008) and Chordia, Huh, and Subrahmanyam (2009).

Interestingly, the late 1960s through the early 1990s, the period Fama and French use to document their empirical findings may have been one of the unique long periods when value stocks outperformed growth stocks" (p. 132).

With reference to the funds of small firm capitalization, Malkiel (2004) also observes that periods of small firm outperformance are followed by periods of underperformance. On the whole, he finds no consistency of performance that points to a dependable strategy of earning excess returns above the market, quite independent of any risk consideration. Reflecting the above, Cochrane (2005) advocates caution in making definite conclusions due to the difficulty of measuring average returns with statistical meaningfulness, even over a period of many years.

If the question is asked as to why academics are not pursuing more interesting lines of enquiry in their publications, such as the relation between the propensity of banks to offer credit and the cycle of the real economy, and the extent to which each is the cause of the other, the answer is that the job of writing papers and achieving citations for papers is most efficiently achieved not by thinking long and hard about financial economic issues, but by mining data until some arguably (statistically) significant relation is found and around which a narrative can be spun so as to have the finding published (and subsequently cited by other academics).[6] Academics do not prosper by experiencing reality and thereby attaining a firsthand understanding of reality. Academics prosper by *writing papers* on perceptions of reality as advanced by other academics.

In a review of the US Center for Research in Security Prices (CRSP) database, *The Economist* magazine (November 20–26, 2010) observes that the high level of "data mining" is the outcome of the opportunity that the CRSP database offers financial economists (it estimates that more than one third of published papers in finance represent econometric studies of the database). Robert Shiller in the same article in *The Economist* is quoted as saying that with the creation of the CRSP database, economists

---

[6]There is a corrupting influence here when university members vie for prestige and personal reward on the basis of attaining "production targets" for their output. Universities might lecture on the merits of free market enterprise, but many of them are governed by centrally planned (Soviet-style in Australia) systems.

have been led to believe that finance has become scientific, and that conventional ideas about investing and financial markets — and about their vulnerabilities — are out of date. He states that to have seen the global financial crisis coming, it would have been better "to go back to old-fashioned readings of history, studying institutions and laws. We should have talked to grandpa". For many years, Shiller had been a rare voice advocating the possibility of price movements and bubbles unrelated to information.[7]

4.4. Implications of Abandoning the CAPM

The early researchers in asset pricing theory recognized that the integrity and rationality of markets must be based on their ability to monitor and price risk. The CAPM captures the idea that markets are rational in this manner and hence are an appropriate subject for scientific inquiry. Unfortunately, the facts do not support the CAPM. Furthermore, the additional variables brought in to describe the distribution of asset returns generally resist interpretation as contributing to a risk-return relation. For this reason, we cannot interpret more recent models as refinements of a fundamentally robust risk-return relation. Nevertheless, the impression is often given that the CAPM model of rational markets has simply paved the way for more sophisticated models. This is not the case and the perception is unfortunate.

The implications of abandoning the idea of a risk-return relation at the heart of asset pricing are considerable. Without such a model, we are left with a market where stock prices generally respond positively to good news and negatively to bad news, and where as John Maynard Keynes put it, market players are not independently assessing fundamental values, but are "anticipating what average opinion expects the average opinion to be", with the outcome that market sentiment and crowd psychology play a role that

---

[7]But he came in from the cold when his work earned him the Nobel Prize for Economics in 2013 (shared with Lars Peter Hansen and Eugene Fama). Shiller (1981) argues that stock market fluctuations show far too much variability to be explained by an efficient market theory of pricing, and that one must look to behavioral considerations and to crowd psychology to explain the actual process of price determination.

is never easy to determine, but which at times appears to produce tipping points, sending the market to booms and busts. In a non-CAPM world, the practitioner needs to understand how markets function in disequilibrium, as well as in equilibrium. As a market trend consolidates, we are naturally seduced into considering that such consolidation represents "the way the market works". But a market trend can prove to be a fickle friend. There are many patterns in finance, but few immutable rules. We venture that it is in this sense that markets are ultimately risky.

There are additional implications of not having a reliable model that relates market exposure to potential returns. A derivation of the appropriate discount factor for valuation of cash flows requires such a model. Without a rationalized discount factor, attempts to value a firm or its projects, to impose fair prices for regulated industries, or to set realistic benchmarks for fund managers and for managers seeking bonuses, will have even more the appearance of "guesstimating". For academics, an inexact science becomes even more inexact. For professionals, the image of professional expertise in the management of risk is compromised.

4.5. Time for Reflection: What Have We Learned?

The usefulness of an asset pricing model — and hence the motivation in constructing such a model — lies in the degree to which it succeeds in encapsulating the market's interplay between risk and return. On this basis, we might question the usefulness of data mining research dedicated to demonstrating that certain economic, finance institutional and psychological factors (which are unrelated to market risk) are apparently "priced" by investors.

If the "pretenses" of the previous two chapters are (i) the CAPM is applicable to the historical data of stock prices (Chapter 2), and (ii) the FF-3F model represents a refinement of the CAPM (Chapter 3), the pretense in this chapter is the upholding of data mining as a significant contribution to an understanding of the risk-return dynamic of markets.

Unless it can be demonstrated that the markets are actually capable of balancing risk and return in a meaningful manner, the revelation of each additional "priced" attribute across sufficiently large aggregates of stocks has little purport. Academics, however, continue to adhere to the illusion that their models are meaningfully illuminating the dynamic of market behavior.

In the absence of a working model that purports to capture the risk-return dynamic at the heart of asset pricing in markets, the status and authority of the discipline is undermined. Ultimately, however, we must seek to understand markets on their own terms and not on our own.

PART B

**Foundations of Corporate Financial Activity:
A Critical Assessment**

Chapter 5

The Modigliani and Miller Propositions and the Foundations of Corporate Finance

Imaginary' universes are so much more beautiful than this stupidly constructed 'real' one; and most of the finest products of an applied mathematician's fancy must be rejected, as soon as they have been created, for the brutal but sufficient reason that they do not fit the facts.

G. H. Hardy[1]

Beware of false knowledge; it is more dangerous than ignorance.

George Bernard Shaw

When you combine ignorance and leverage, you get some pretty interesting results.

Warren Buffett

I have so much debt, I might start a government.   Michael Dempsey

5.1. Introduction[2]

By the late 1950s, the prestige of the natural sciences had encouraged the belief that decision making and resource allocation problems could

---

[1] Godfrey Hardy was an extremely gifted Professor of mathematics at Oxford in the early 1900s — days of sherry before dinner, silver waiter service at one's hall, and an almost complete absence of females. At an interview, Hardy stated that his collaboration with Ramanujan — the self-taught mathematical genius whom Hardy brought to prominence — was "the one romantic incident in my life". Hardy later became depressed and attempted suicide. Poor man, I can console myself that I am at least normal (actually, my friends think I am rather odd. Goodness knows why).

[2] This chapter encapsulates ideas that have appeared in *Abacus* (Dempsey, 2014), *Critical Perspectives on Accounting* (Dempsey, 1996, 1999 (with Hudson, Keasey, and Littler)) and *Accounting, Accountability and Performance* (Dempsey, 2003). I am grateful and indebted to the editors and reviewers of these journals for supporting and publishing this work notwithstanding its unorthodoxy. More journals such as these would be welcomed.

be identified with the elaboration of models and the general extension of techniques from applied mathematics. The writings of Karl Popper had also contributed to exalt the philosophical basis of science as *the* rational process, progressing towards objective truth on the basis of the falsification method of theory selection.

In a scientific world, the logical structure of decision making implied that practising managers were likely to make more optimal decisions when supplied with a richer set of positive theories that provided a better understanding of the consequences of their choices. It was natural, therefore, that finance theory (along with other social science disciplines) should seek to identify with the scientific method. It was into this environment in the late 1950s that Merton Miller and Franco Modigliani ushered in their agenda for the modern theory of corporate finance.

The Modigliani and Miller (MM) propositions are regarded as the bedrock of corporate financial decision making. Nevertheless, this chapter will argue that the focus on the MM propositions as the foundation of corporate management has led to a stylized representation of corporate financial decision making that is far removed from reality. Specifically, it has brought about a disengagement from the institutional, behavioral, and corporate strategic contexts within which corporate financial decision making actually functions.

In developing our arguments, the chapter is structured as follows. In Section 5.2, we highlight how, prior to MM, corporate strategy and corporate finance were unified, allowing for a behavioral context, but that subsequent to MM, the two disciplines of corporate strategy and finance came to be developed almost entirely independently, with behavioral considerations in the finance models suppressed. In Section 5.3, we highlight the development of corporate financial decision making from the foundation of the MM propositions. Section 5.4 provides a critique of the MM propositions as a foundation for understanding corporate finance. Such perspectives have traditionally been muted, but, following the global financial crisis, have been gaining support. The following section, Section 5.5, argues that although the corporate finance literature now allows for "behavioral finance", this occurs in a narrow, restricted sense. It has worked to popularize an awareness of certain psychological idiosyncrasies, but not a recognition of the socialization of decision making. The final section, Section 5.6, concludes with a discussion.[3]

5.2. Corporate Financial Management prior to MM

Prior to the MM propositions, textbook writers' recommendations and prescriptions on corporate finance were formulated as a distillation of experience interpreted by the writer. The major corporate finance textbook prior to the late 1950s was published by Arthur Dewing (1919), who advanced principles of *judgment* for a firm's investment, financing, and dividend policies on the basis of his observations and experiences over a career covering a variety of firms.

Dewing's argument was that a firm's most fundamental investment decision was that of determining whether economic circumstances call for either the firm's *expansion* or *contraction*. At any one time, for example, should the firm be looking to expand or contract its workforce? As simple as the concept may appear, Dewing regarded the enactment of the principle as the essential determinant of a firm's success or failure — as well as being the decision that most called on management acumen and entrepreneurial skill. For Dewing, the firm is in equilibrium when its investment strategy is at the point of decreasing returns with expansion. Dewing considered that the production of a firm was a direct result of a relatively constant factor in the form of fixed capital investment and a variable factor in the form of human labour, the whole administered by an intangible economic value called entrepreneurial ability.

Dewing's text progresses to discuss the financial problems incident to obtaining financing for extensions, with special reference to sources of new capital. Nevertheless, his understanding of entrepreneurial activity is never divorced from an understanding of what he terms the humanity of business. His text emphasizes repeatedly that motives other than economic are at play: "The impelling springs of human action are difficult to fathom". For Dewing, business managers retain their human attributes and their solutions

---

[3]Equations that are referenced in subsequent chapters are bordered.

of the difficult problems of business expansion often cannot be reconciled readily with economic tenets.[4]

Although these managers generally would not have used discounting methods in their investment decision making, the concept of, and the mathematical apparatus for net present value (NPV) calculations were nevertheless familiar to textbook writers by this time. For example, Irving Fisher's (1930) economic text considers the choice between alternative investments on the basis of discounted earning streams, with examples of choosing between the allocation of land between farming, forestry, and mining (p. 133). It is even pointed out that the undesirable time shape of an earnings stream can be remedied by borrowing in early years against future income and paying back with interest in later years. Nevertheless, Fisher is at pains to emphasize that the choice is being analyzed under *unrealistic* assumptions of certainty. With regard to the appropriate discount rate under conditions of general *uncertainty*, he considers:

> "To attempt to formulate mathematically in any useful, complete manner the laws determining the rate of interest (return) under the sway of chance would be like attempting to express completely the laws which determine the path of a projectile when affected by random gusts of wind. Such

---

[4]Dewing (1919) established the tone of his study of corporate investment decision making with the opening passage to his text:

> "Four main motives have led men to expand business enterprises. On the whole they are not economic, but rather psychological; they are the motives incident to the struggle for conquest and achievement — the precious legacy of man's 'predatory barbarism'. Primarily a man measures the success of a business by increased size, and secondarily by increased profits.... The race-old instinct of conquest becomes translated in our twentieth century economic world into the prosaic terms of corporate growth. Business expansion is the spirit of a modern Tamerlane seeking new markets to conquer. It is a pawn for human ambition. The second motive, less significant, one is led to believe, is the creative impulse.... It is a common place of psychology that somewhere in the mental structure of all of us lies the impulse to build, to see our ideas take form in material results.... The third motive is the economic. My own observation is that the vast majority of businessmen who plan enlargements, consolidations, and extensions of their business are not actuated primarily by the impulse to make more money, although they unquestionably place this motive uppermost when they need to present plans for enlargement to directors and stockholders.... And it appears foremost in every business manager's mind when he attempts to justify a business policy which may have been in the first instance subconsciously prompted by less obvious and more basal motives.... The fourth motive is the satisfaction in taking speculative chances.... All men enjoy the game they think they can play." (Vol. 4, p. 4).

formulas would need to be either too general or too empirical to be of much value. . . We must, therefore, give up as a bad job any attempt to formulate completely the influences which really determine the rate of interest." (p. 316)

In the absence of a formal model of risk, Fisher recognizes that risk and return are closely correlated, and states:

"But evidence that in general risk tends to raise the commercial rate of return (interest) is abundant. The proposition is a matter of such common observation that no special collection of facts is necessary. Every lender or borrower knows that the rate of interest varies directly with risk. A bird in the hand is worth two in the bush. The principle applies not only to the explicit interest rate in loan contracts, but also to the implicit interest which goes with the possession of all capital. Where there is uncertainty whether income saved for the future will ever be of service, but the certainty that it can be of service if used immediately, the possessor needs the possibility of a very high future return in order to induce him to save." (p. 382)

Application of probability theory to an assessment of risky outcomes was also quite familiar at this time. Unlike modern finance academics, however, decision makers at the time distinguished naturally between the problem of predicting outcomes under *risk* — when the probabilities might be difficult to estimate — and the problem of predicting outcomes under *uncertainty* — when the possibilities themselves, let alone their probabilities, are difficult to estimate. "Our knowledge of the factors that will govern the yield of an investment in some years hence is usually very slight and often negligible" (Keynes, 1936, p. 149). Among theoreticians at the time, the notion of reducing uncertainty to probability distributions was in fact well recognized, but regarded as impractical, to the extent that enthusiasm for the potential applications of probability to economic issues had been more or less extinguished as economists acknowledged the insurmountable problems. Put simply, the modeling of uncertain future cash flows in terms of probability density functions did not at this time answer a need among managers in their bid to face uncertainty (McGoun, 1995).

In the time of Dewing's writing, managers believed that their *experience* must recognize the well-run *processes* combined with satisfied customers that would make their companies competitive and profitable. The firm's value resides in the complexity of managing and motivating divisional performance and of identifying synergies between them. The implementation of such perspective, in turn, requires a sustained commitment to managing the multiple challenges of product improvement, production management, costing, budgeting, human resources, marketing, and strategy.

For such reasons, a sound basis for investment decision making was identified not with mathematical proofs, but with the application of proven principles based on experience. Accordingly, textbook writers' recommendations and prescriptions at this time were substantiated by the evidence of experience. Theory at this time *was* the distillation of experience as interpreted by the writer.

In the MM world, however, the intuitive, normative approach of such authors would be ignored. Insights prior to the MM propositions have been effectively airbrushed from our collective memory. Brennan (1995, p. 11), for example, dimisses Dewing's contribution as, "detailed institutional fussiness"; and Smith's (1990, p. 3) *The Theory of Corporate Finance: an Historical Overview* singles out Dewing for dismissal while requiring only a single paragraph to account for corporate finance theory prior to the late 1950s:

> "The finance literature through the early 1950s consisted in large part of *ad hoc* theories and institutional detail, but little systematic analysis. For example, Dewing (Financial Policy of Corporations, 1919; 1953), the major corporate finance textbook for generations, describes the birth of a corporation and follows it through various policy decisions to its death (bankruptcy). Corporate financial theory prior to the 1950s was riddled with logical inconsistencies and was almost totally prescriptive, that is, normatively orientated. The major concerns of the field were optimal investment, financing, and dividend policies, but little consideration was given to the effects of individual incentives, or to the nature of equilibrium in financial markets" (p. 5).

The rejoinder, of course, might be that markets *are not in equilibrium*, and that the pre-MM texts were accordingly — *by choice* — concerned with communicating overall observations (which, yes, were sometimes contradictory) of the functioning of actual companies as opposed to theoretical outcomes of individual incentives in equilibrium markets.

5.3. Corporate Finance and the Paradigm of the MM Propositions

MM proclaimed that the objective of the firm must be to maximize the wealth of its shareholders as owners of the firm. Thus, the "value" of the firm was no more or less than its price in the marketplace. The discipline of "corporate financial management" was transformed thereby from an institutional normative literature — motivated by and concerned with topics of direct practitioner relevance, such as the operations of financial institutions and procedures for raising long-term finance — into a microeconomic *positive* science centred around corporate policy decisions and addressing questions, such as: What are the effects of alternative investment, financing, and dividend policies on a firm's stock price? In this way, corporate financial decision making was formulated as an application of economic asset valuation models with reference to perfect capital markets. In this perspective, an understanding of corporate financial behavior and the behavior of capital markets (incorporating investment finance and portfolio investment) are integrated as two sides of the same investment coin.

We have noted that a capital market where prices provide meaningful signals for capital allocation is an important component of a capitalist system. In such a system, when firms issue securities to finance their activities, they can expect to obtain fair prices and, equally, when investors choose to invest in the firm's securities, they do so knowing that they are paying fair prices. The foundations of neoclassical finance theory ardently defend such a view of efficient markets (e.g., Fama, 1976, Chapter 5).

At the same time as when the basic conceptual models of efficient capital markets were being tested against databases of historical capital market price movements, the theoretical implications of the models for corporate financial decision making were being clarified.

It follows that the firm's key financial decision making nodes:

  (i) Where the firm should be making financial investments (the investment decision),
 (ii) How the firm should be financing those investments, given available sources of investment finance *vis-à-vis* debt and equity (the capital structure decision), and

(iii) At what point the firm should be returning the fruits of those investments back to the firm's investors (the dividend decision),

must be understood on the basis of providing the firm's investors with a rate of financial return that at least matched their comparable opportunities elsewhere. In other words, investors' required expectation of financial return represents *a firm's cost of financial capital*, on the basis of which all corporate financial decisions must be assessed.

The logical outcome was that firms were exhorted to justify their investment decisions on the basis of the net present value (NPV) of their expected cash flows to shareholders discounted by a cost of capital calculated from the CAPM. Notwithstanding the reluctance of practitioners to be in accord with a literal interpretation of the NPV investment criterion, researchers in management accounting and finance by the mid-1970s were generally won over by a belief in its efficacy. A great deal of activity developed around surveying and documenting the extent to which capital budgeting decision makers used, or did not use, various techniques for analyzing potential investments. The implication was always that the use of NPV revealed sophistication, whereas the use of methods such as payback and accounting rates of return (ARR) revealed ignorance of better methods or irrationality in refusing to adopt better methods. Miller (of MM) (1977) questioned why "the pay-back criterion continues to thrive despite having been denounced as Neanderthal in virtually every textbook in finance and accounting over the last 30 years" (p. 274).

MM held that just as the amount of cake cannot depend on how it is distributed, so the value of the firm cannot depend on how its ownership is distributed between shareholders and debt holders. Thus, the market value of a firm, V_{firm}, as the sum of the market value of the debt, V_D, and equity, V_E, claims on the firm is independent of its capital structure; which is to say, independent of whether the firm is funded more by debt financing or by equity financing:

$$V_{firm} = V_E + V_D = V_0, \tag{5.1}$$

where $V_0 = $ the value of the firm assuming no debt. Equation (5.1) is MM's Proposition 1.

Equation (5.1) is another way of saying that the company's weighted average cost of capital (K_{AV}) as the weighted average of the company's cost of equity (shareholders' expectation of return), K_E, and the cost of its debt, K_D (the interest rate on the debt in the case that the principal is expected to be repaid), is independent of how the company is financed between debt and equity — since if it were otherwise, the present value of the firm as the value of the firm's future cash flows would be dependent on its capital structure between debt and equity. In other words,

$$K_{AV} \equiv K_E \frac{V_E}{V_E + V_D} + K_D \frac{V_D}{V_E + V_D}, \tag{5.2}$$

is independent of leverage. With the firm's leverage, L, defined as

$$L = \frac{V_D}{V_E + V_D}, \tag{5.3}$$

Eq. (5.2) may be expressed as

$$K_{AV} \equiv K_D L + K_E (1 - L). \tag{5.4}$$

Since K_{AV} is independent of leverage, we have:

$$K_{AV} = K_U, \tag{5.5}$$

where K_U is the firm's cost of equity in the case that the firm is unlevered (no debt). Rearranging Eq. (5.2) with Eq. (5.5), we have MM's Proposition 2:

$$K_E = K_U + \frac{V_D}{V_E}(K_U - K_D), \tag{5.6}$$

which captures the idea that the reason the company is unable to reduce its overall cost of capital (K_{AV}) by substituting less costly debt in place of typically more costly equity is that, with additional debt, the firm's risk exposure (which remains unchanged) is loaded onto fewer shareholders who accordingly require a higher rate of return. The outcome is that shareholders' cost of equity as their required rate of return increases with debt as in Eq. (5.6), so that K_{AV} as determined by Eq. (5.4) remains unchanged, and hence equal to K_U (Eq. (5.5)).

MM then declared that a dollar paid by the firm as dividends to its shareholders was a dollar more in their pockets, but a dollar less in the firm (which the shareholders owned). Hence, the value of the firm was independent of its dividend policy as well as its capital structure, and managers were exhorted to ignore both, and apply themselves instead to the discovery of projects with positive NPV.[5]

Nevertheless, Modigliani and Miller later considered that these outcomes ignored a firm's corporate tax liability, as well as the tax obligations of its investors. Interest payments on debt are tax deductible at the corporate level, which means that every dollar of interest paid reduces the firm's tax liability by an amount Tc, where Tc denotes the firm's rate of corporate tax liability. For example, with a corporate tax rate of 30%, a \$1 payment of interest reduces the firm's corporate tax liability by 30 cents. Supposing that the firm holds debt equal to V_D in perpetuity with an annual interest rate, i_D, the interest liability is then $V_D \times i_D$, annually in perpetuity. This is to say, the reduction in its corporate tax liabilities, or tax savings TS, on account of the debt is

$$TS = V_D i_D Tc, \tag{5.7}$$

annually in perpetuity. Allowing that the appropriate discount rate is the rate of interest, i_D, MM accordingly determined the present value of the tax savings ($PVTS$) to the firm (consistent with Eq. (6.8), p. 77) as

$$PVTS = \frac{V_D \cdot i_D \cdot T_c}{i_D} = V_D T_c. \tag{5.8}$$

For example, if the firm's rate of corporate tax liability is 30%, a dollar of debt equates with a reduction of the firm's future tax obligations, which has a current value of 30 cents. It followed that Eq. (5.1) must be replaced with

$$V_E + V_D = V_0 + V_D T_c, \tag{5.9}$$

where V_0 denotes what the value of the company would be in the case that it held no debt. The equation appears in MM's 1963 paper, *Corporate Income Taxes and the Cost of Capital: A Correction.*

In relation to dividends, MM recognized that the tax authorities taxed a dollar of the firm's dividends in the hands of its shareholders at the

---

[5]This exhortation appears in Modigliani and Miller's 1958 paper, *The Cost of Capital, Corporation Finance, and the Theory of Investment.*

shareholder's marginal rate of income tax, which was held to be much higher than the rate of capital gains tax imposed on the dollar if it remained in the firm until the shareholder came to sell their stock. It now appeared that rather than upholding the irrelevance of the firm's capital structure and dividend policies, firms should strive to be 100% debt financed and never pay dividends to shareholders.[6]

In response to the unrealistic corner point solutions generated from such assumptions, the early leading candidates for the study of departures from the MM conditions as a justification for a firm's restricted undertaking of debt, were *bankruptcy costs* due to legal costs on transfer of assets and fire sales of assets if the firm should pass into receivership, and *financial distress*, referring to the difficulties to the firm in functioning effectively once bankruptcy is threatened. Departures from the MM conditions as a justification for a firm paying dividends, were *tax clienteles*, which considered that some investors should prefer dividends to capital gains for tax reasons; *transaction costs*, if a shareholder must consistently sell a proportion of their stocks to provide income as "homemade" dividends; and dividends as *signalling* the firm's sustained value to investors. Additionally, when the firm either takes on debt or commits itself to making regular dividend payments, the imposition on management to maintain regular visible cash flows in the form of either interest payments on debt or dividends to shareholders was viewed as mitigating the *agency* problem between the firm's management as agent and shareholders as the firm's owners. In other words, interest payments on debt and dividends discipline the firm's managers to perform in the best interests of shareholders. An explosion of models based on agency theory — with information asymmetry, the nature of implicit and explicit contracts, as well as non-pecuniary considerations, such as reputation and effort aversion — has been motivated by the need to attain reconciliation between the directives of theory and observed practice.[7]

---

[6]The Nobel Prize Committee cited the MM propositions when it awarded the Nobel Prize in Economics to Franco Modigliani in 1985 and to Merton Miller in 1990.

[7]Interestingly, Merton Miller himself chose to distance himself from these developments. His observation was that the theoretical tax savings contingent on debt financing are sufficiently significant that it cannot make sense to equate them with something as ill-defined as "financial distress" or even the costs of a restructure following bankruptcy — which for

Thus, we observe that academic contributions that acknowledge the institutional/behavioral dimensions of corporate finance are expected to confront the paradigm of perfect markets and present arguments in the language of its terms of reference. As Ross recognizes in a 1988 review of the MM propositions, "economists now do look at finance through the eyes of MM" (p. 133), thereby supporting Weston (1989) and Miller's (1988) contention (in his own review chapter of the MM propositions) that "showing what *doesn't* matter can also show, by implication, what *does*" (p. 100). Or, again, as Stiglitz (1988) puts it, "Some of the most productive responses to the MM results have come from those who did not feel able to accept the conclusion that financial policy is irrelevant. The MM results force those sceptics to identify which of the assumptions underlying the MM theorem should be modified or rejected" (p. 122).

Reconciliation of observed practice with theoretical models continues to be pursued within an MM/cost of capital framework, where mathematical coherence and integrity are a condition for contribution. The academic position is that a stream of literature has thereby been successfully generated, as a result of which the understanding of corporate financial behavior has been hugely stimulated and consequently greatly sharpened from both theoretical and empirical perspectives. A glance at the *Journal of Corporate Finance* or the *Journal of Finance*, for example, reveals the striking departure that has taken place from everyday language as a medium in which to develop concepts and ideas to that of the mathematically skilled and the academically rigorous and abstract.

5.4. A Critique of the MM Propositions

Modern corporate finance theory is founded on the proposition that financial capital is supplied to firms by investors who have an "expectation of return", and that, reciprocally, such expectation represents the firm's "cost

---

Miller, were not "that" significant (Miller, 1977). Instead, he considered that although the current supply of debt financing was indeed tax-advantaged, nevertheless — as an outcome of individual tax preferences — the marginal benefit of any *additional* dollar of debt must be zero (otherwise in efficient markets that additional dollar of debt financing would surely be forthcoming). Thereby, Merton reverted to his original proposition as to the *irrelevancy* of financial structure. An interesting case of his Miller (1977) paper offering a correction to his MM (1965) paper, which was itself a correction to his MM (1958) paper.

of financial capital". With such assumptions, it had appeared possible to construct a *positive* theory of corporate finance, aimed at prescribing rules for decision makers, which would assist managers to make decisions that were optimal from the point of view of shareholders. Nevertheless, in response to unrealistic theoretical outcomes (firms should, in principle, be 100% debt financed and pay no dividends to shareholders), theoretical development has subsequently come to be directed at providing models that are *descriptive* of the way corporate financial decisions are actually made. Thus, we might observe that, very much without debate, corporate finance theory has actually moved from its original positive MM (1958) role of offering principles of scientific management to managers to one merely of attempting to rationalize within the strictures of its theory towards why companies behave as they do.

The MM predictions are founded on a conceptualization of the firm as an investment counter held by investors who hold well diversified portfolios of such counters and who have perfect knowledge of the firm's worth. In reality, corporate managers are entrusted with maintaining the integrity and wellbeing of *their* particular firm with limited information. Shareholders may have many investment counters — and be prepared to jeopardize the firm — but managers have only one reputation. If managers care for their reputation, they must seek to manage the continued sustainability of their firm in combination with taking advantage of opportunities for long-run profit. Realistically, the firm is a response to strategic corporate decisions made at the level of senior management in the face of a plethora of unknowns. Attaining value for the firm requires the attainment of effective "productivity", which requires working through an understanding of the firm in its competitive environment and an unfolding economy, with the intent of safeguarding and potentially expanding the firm's market position, which in turn requires the exercise of a coordinated management of product improvement, marketing, and strategy — against which financial markets are unstable and evolving.

Managers are realistically unable to assess future cash flows on the basis of probability functions for possible future states, and, thereby, they encounter a problem of fundamental uncertainty in specifying the parameters in a net present value (NPV) valuation model. Managers will indeed make careful assessments of future cash flows. The point is that there is much more to such an assessment in terms of ambiguity, genuine uncertainty and strategic implication than can be captured in any kind of straight-forward NPV calculation. Even if it were possible to meaningfully attribute additional earnings to the indefinite future as they might derive from initiatives taken today, there exists the almost impossible task of estimating the cost of capital with any degree of accuracy. Shiller (1981) determines that if stock prices are allowed to move within their likely ranges on the basis of psychology, the determination of the cost of financial capital is put truly in the "nebulous regions". Fama and French (1997) concede that "estimates of the cost of equity are distressingly imprecise" (p. 178), and have concluded that project valuation is "beset with massive uncertainty" (p. 179).

When we represent the investment decision (the first pillar of corporate finance) as a mechanistic maximizing of NPV calculations, we make a gross simplification. From a management perspective, NPV calculations and projected returns are, at any rate, difficult to communicate to investors with any precision.

A stronger determinant of a company's stock price is the ability to meet quarterly targets for earnings per share (EPS), which are immediately visible to investors. The firm's profits to shareholders are leveraged by debt (the second pillar of corporate finance). Debt makes a good situation better, and a bad situation decidedly worse.[8] The implication is captured in Eq. (5.6), which reveals that provided the investment attains a rate of return that exceeds the interest rate on the debt (K_D), more debt (higher V_D/V_E) implies a greater return to shareholders (K_E), but that if the investment

---

[8]This attribute of debt is captured in the word "leverage", a lever being that which on a fulcrum allows for a small force to move a greater force (Archimedes: "Give me a place to stand and I well move the Earth"). Equally, the word "gearing" is used to denote debt financing (more a UK terminology). Again, a gear, in a car or bicycle, for example, is that which translates an input rate of revolution into a higher rate of revolution. For many of us, a house purchase is the prime example of financial leverage. You purchase a property for $100,000 with a $10,000 deposit (equity finance) and a $90,000 mortgage (debt finance). One week later, the market tells you that the property can be sold at $110,000. Ignoring all agent/legal fees, you have doubled your initial investment of $10,000. A 10% movement in house price has awarded you with a 100% return! Alternatively, an abrupt rise in interest rates leads you to realize that your property is saleable only at $90,000. Now, a 10% downward movement has wiped out your deposit (a 100% loss).

attains a rate of return that underscores the interest rate on the debt, more debt implies a lower return to shareholders. Even more than NPV calculations, a firm's management must be alert to the firm's leveraged position.

In the good times, debt allows managers to boost the earnings available to shareholders. Thereby, managers are able to boost their own reputatations and prestige and the justification for their augmented pay. The trick, of course, is not to be holding so much debt as to be caught out when the economic cycle turns against the firm. The issue of the firm's debt exposure is therefore a dynamic one, rather than a static one as assumed by the textbooks.

The role of debt in stimulating the economy and the profits of firms while simultaneously creating conditions of unsustainability that lead ultimately to collapse, was evident up to and during the global financial crisis (GFC). The economy was prime-pumped by easy borrowing, as managers responded rationally to the use of debt to leverage greater returns to their shareholders. With higher levels of debt on both corporate and individual balance sheets, asset prices rose, encouraging even more borrowing aimed at achieving purchases before prices might rise even further, encouraging even higher levels of debt. The low cost of borrowing — mortgage rates, in particular — encouraged a speculative real estate boom, until the rising roller coaster of the economy stalled before peering perilously downward. Against the ensuing uncertainty, the reliance of the system on the smooth functioning inter-relationships of its component parts (the obligations between counter parties in relation to collateralized debt obligations, swapped obligations, and insured liabilities, etc.) abruptly came into sharp relief, causing markets to blink, and for a time, simply refusing to function, as liquidity was withdrawn from the system and banks feared to lend (even to each other).

An economist who had anticipated such events was Hyman Minsky. His theories articulated the importance of debt in the economic cycle and emphasized the macroeconomic dangers of speculative bubbles in asset prices (*Stabilizing an Unstable Economy*, 1986). Minsky's work proposes theories that link financial market fragility in the economy with speculative investment bubbles endogenous to financial markets. His theories, however, were ignored by central bank policies. Rather, as the Modigliani and Miller irrelevancy propositions articulated, the individual firm's debt was allowed to be "irrelevant".[9]

Robert Shiller (2010) quotes the economist Paul Krugman as stating that the professions went astray because they mistook beauty, clad in impressive-looking mathematics, for truth. *The Economist* newspaper in reviewing the allocation of the 2013 Nobel Prize in Economics (to Eugene Fama, Lars Peter Hansen and Robert Shiller) could not help but state doubts about the standing of the prize given "how little we know about the behavior of markets". One recipient, Eugene Fama, the newspaper noted, was an ardent supporter of efficient markets,[10] while another, Robert Shiller, was known for his recognition of actual bubbles, in technology stocks in the 1990s and in housing in the 2000s (*The Economist*, 2013).

---

[9]Following Minsky, when times are good, investors take on debt (and risk); and the longer that times stay good, the more debt they take on. In such prosperous times, as corporate cash flow rises beyond what is needed to pay off debt, a speculative euphoria develops, until, inevitably, a point is reached where the cash generated by the assets acquired is no longer sufficient to pay off the mountains of debt that were taken on to acquire the assets. At this point, losses on such speculative assets prompt lenders to call in their loans. This leads to a collapse of asset values as investors are forced to sell off even their safer positions to make good on their loans. Markets spiral downward and create a severe demand for cash. The GFC was similarly triggered as, under pressure from shareholders in the good times to increase returns, banks operated with minimal equity, leaving them exposed when the downturn occurred. This slow movement of the financial system from stability to fragility, followed by crisis, means that inevitably we arrive at what has become known as a "Minsky moment". Similarly, the Asian tiger economies in the 1990s enjoyed the experience of high levels of debt fuelling a sense of wealth creation (escalating house prices, for example) and exuberance as the banks made possible ever higher debt levels to fund asset purchases (as opposed to new investments) up to the point of unsustainability and ultimate collapse.

[10]To the extent, *The Economist* notes, that in response to its own incessant warnings of bubbles in the markets, Fama had declined to renew his subscription to *The Economist*. Shame on you, Gene Fama. The *Economist* newspaper is the best thing in my life after sliced bread — it is worth the subscription cost if only for the puns in its article titles ("Xi who must be obeyed: How one man rules China", for example, cover of issue September 20–26, 2014). And I am not saying this just to make up for diddling *The Economist* out of my full subscription dues by pretending for many years to be still a student. Speaking of puns, I am told there exists an international pun contest for high-brow puns and the all-time winner is: A vulture boards an airplane, carrying two dead raccoons. The flight-attendant says, "I'm sorry, sir, we allow only one carrion per passenger." Alternatively, you might wish to share a more low-brow offering that my friend's son came home from school with: Two Mexican firemen: One is called Hosé, the other one is called Hose-B. So now you know if you are more high-brow or low-brow. I think I must be mostly low-brow, but with perhaps a suggestion of high-brow. Hmmm...

The observed dividend decision by firms (the third pillar of corporate finance) is effectively without explanation in pure finance theory. The taxes paid on dividend distributions have in market history significantly exceeded 40%. In the face of such heavy deadweight cost to shareholders, dividend clienteles, dividend signalling and agency theory (as observed in Section 5.3) can all be lined up as explanations. Nevertheless, we are reminded of Miller's (1977) observation that "the supposed trade-off between the deadweight taxes and the explanations looks suspiciously like the recipe for the fabled horse-and-rabbit stew — one horse and one rabbit" (p. 264).

In the above contexts (as was discussed in relation to the CAPM in Chapter 2), it is not a case of whether the MM propositions are "right" or "wrong". It is, rather, a case of whether they are *useful* or *not useful* in providing a conceptual framework that assists comprehension and thereby a measure of control over our environment.[11] With the MM theory (as with the CAPM), the problem is that experiences are not actually illuminated by the model's core assumptions, but by postulating exceptions to those assumptions. The broader outlooks of *strategic* corporate management, the cycles of economic growth and contraction, the importance of debt leverage in building the economy and market up-cycles before turning the cycles steeply downward, an awareness of the elements of *reputation* and *trust* underlying corporate and financial activity, and recognition of an *ethical* dimension to behavior, are all outside its domain. The model is more or less moribund.[12]

---

[11]Without such patterns of recognition, we are left confused by the data. We are unable to cope intelligently ("intelligence" is the ability to see patterns) with the data. The process is ultimately subjective in the sense that reality *is* my sense of pattern formation imposed on my sense data. On such basis, Putnam (1979) (see footnote 14, Chapter 2) argues *against* the idea that the essential *reason-to-be* of a theory is to continue to make predictions with 100% certainty, a notion on which he considers that both the Popperian deductivists and the Kuhnian inductivists, in their different ways, rely.

[12]The case is similar to the experience of building a model of the solar system with the Earth at the centre. The model has distorted what is actually central to the dynamics of the solar system and therefore cannot be extended to understanding the universe outside the solar system. Astronomers prior to Copernicus would look to discover each new planet and thereafter seek to account for its orbit in relation to the earth at the centre with additional considerations. The point is that by assigning our vantage position to the sun, *things are made much simpler.* Ultimately, we choose the sun-at-the-centre model because it is a *more useful* model. It *facilitates* advancement.

In the aftermath of the GFC, we have become more aware of the limitations of corporate financial theory developed on the MM propositions. We require not so much continued adjustments to the MM propositions but, rather, an acknowledgement of the fact that financial challenges cannot be resolved with more sophisticated mathematics of rational behavior. Progress requires that we recognize the social science nature of corporate decision making not as an add-on, but as central to an understanding of how formalized groups of people with responsibilities for outcomes actually make decisions. The broader management literature addresses these issues, which represent the context within which financial corporate decision making actually takes place. In finance, however, the social dynamic of corporations in the context of uncertainty is permitted only as required to sustain the idealized model of the firm "through the eyes of MM" (Ross, 1988, p. 133).

5.5. Recent Developments in Corporate Finance

Shefrin (2001) observes that the traditional approach to corporate finance is based on three concepts:

(1) Rational behavior,
(2) The CAPM, and
(3) Efficient markets,

but that

(a) Psychological phenomena prevent decision makers from acting in a rational manner,
(b) Security risk premiums are not determined by security betas, and
(c) Market prices are regularly at odds with fundamental values.

Thus, all three components of the traditional paradigm are effectively undermined.

The outcome of such observations has been a body of corporate financial research aimed at understanding the psychology of market participants, as financial managers and investors. Much of the impetus for these studies derives from the cognitive psychological experiments of Daniel Kahneman and Amos Tversky (1979), as well as of Griffin and Tversky (1992) and Kahneman and Lovallo (1993). For example, their experiments show how anchoring occurs during normal decision making when individuals overly rely on a specific piece of information to govern their thought processes. Once the anchor is set, there is a bias towards adjusting or interpreting other information to reflect the "anchored" information.[13]

In this work, the psychological attribute of *overconfidence* has provided a particular focus for investigation in academic finance. Shefrin makes the case for overconfidence for both markets and firms. Such "psychology of the markets" challenges the traditional view that the collective actions of market participants in setting prices are always rational.[14] In early work, Daniel, Hirshleifer, and Subrahmanyam (1998) advance a model of financial market distortions based on investor overconfidence relating to information in combination with a bias to confirm preconceived views when public information subsequently accords with the preconceived view, while remaining indifferent to such information when it challenges preconceived views. The essence of this contribution is confirmed by Rabin and Schrag (1999), who find that decision makers have a tendency to interpret new information as confirmatory of prior beliefs and expectations.[15]

The implications of *overconfidence* for specifically corporate financial decision making have subsequently received a good deal of attention. Following Shefrin (2001) are Gervais and Odean (2001, "Learning to be overconfident"), Heaton (2002, "Managerial optimism and corporate

---

[13]These biases are examined comprehensively in *Behavioral Finance: Insights into Irrational Minds and Markets* (Montier, 2002), which links the well documented biases of Kahneman and Tversky (1979) to investment behavior. After Tversky's death (the Nobel Prize in Economics in not awarded posthumously) Kahneman was awarded the prize in 2002.

[14]Although the recognition of investor confidence as a focus for recent studies is typically regarded as a recent development, investor confidence actually connects with the view of markets prior to the advent of the MM propositions. We are reminded, for example, of Keynes' animal spirits and his recognition that "speculators may do no harm as bubbles on a steady stream of enterprise. But the position is serious when enterprise becomes the bubble on a whirlpool of speculation. When the capital development of a country becomes a by-product of the activities of a casino, the job is likely to be ill-done" (*The General Theory of Employment, Interest and Money*, 1936).

[15]Could this, perhaps, be a gender thing? We say it is a woman's prerogative to change her mind; but that a man is disinclined when driving to admit the need to stop and ask for new directions. Hence, the quip as told to me by a female friend: Why did the Hebrews wander for forty years before they reached the promised land? Moses refused to stop and ask the locals for directions.

finance"), and Hilary and Menzly (2006, "Does past success lead analysts to become overconfident?"). Heaton (2002), Malmendier and Tate (2005*a*, 2005*b*, 2008), and Goel and Thakor (2008) focus on CEO overconfidence and the implications for firm corporate investment decisions, while Doukas and Petmezas (2007) (who find that overconfident mangers are liable to engage in a run of ultimately unwise acquisitions) and Ferris, Jayaraman and Sabherwal (2011) focus on CEO overconfidence in relation to mergers and acquisitions.

The application of overconfidence to a firm's financing arrangements (capital structure) has been developed by Hackbarth (2008), while Ben-David, Graham, and Harvey (2007) develop a link between overconfidence and the firm's dividend policy decisions, and Hilary and Hsu (2011) apply overconfidence to examine managers' ability to predict earnings. The application of human psychology to shareholders' assessment of dividends has, of course, long been recognized in the literature: for example, the "bird in the hand" argument for dividends — where investors are more confident about immediate dividends than future capital gains — roundly rebuked by MM (1961). Notwithstanding, Shefrin and Statman (1984) and more recently Baker and Wurgler (2004) have advanced arguments for "dividend preference" in the context of Kahneman and Tversky's (1979) prospect theory.

The implications of cognitive psychology represent a valid dimension of corporate financial decision making. Nevertheless, we observe that the scope of such contributions is restricted to a micro-level focus on understanding how the traditional elements of (1) rational behavior, (2) the CAPM, and (3) efficient markets are *perturbed* by the cognitive biases of the *individual decision maker*, about which the core paradigms remain fixed. In effect, "behavioral finance" is allowed only a narrow interpretation, which fails, for example, to incorporate the socialization of the workplace and the dynamics of decision making in groups. Thus, although following the GFC, the term *behavioral finance* is now in vogue, it would be a mistake to think that corporate finance has been liberated from its MM antecedents and that the humanity of business (as understood prior to the MM propositions) has been reinstated. We continue to observe finance through the eyes of the old paradigms. The impact of broader behavioral and dynamic strategic considerations on the conditioning of human enterprise continues to be avoided.

5.6. Time for Reflection: What Have We Learned?

The paradigm that states that investors' required rate of return identifies the firm's "cost of capital" leads naturally to the supposition that the firm can be modelled as a single investment asset in a well diversified portfolio of investment assets. Following from this proposition, corporate finance research continues to be founded on the MM proposition — that in perfect markets, the firm's capital structure and dividend policies are irrelevant. *Qualitative* research with a social–strategic dynamic as the central proposition of corporate financial activity is stubbornly resisted. Nevertheless, a theory of decision making can only be meaningful in so far as the context of its assumptions is descriptive for the individual(s) concerned of the environment in which the decision making is assumed to apply. Keasey and Hudson (2007) consider that academics who wish to better understand the beliefs and actions of managers as they dictate corporate financial activity "should leave their offices and go and talk with them" — rather than insisting on building elaborate theoretical models with limited success. They state:

> "In the context of 'traditional' finance, the research community, unfortunately, tends to act as though all important insights are already contained within the existing core of financial theory. All that remains is a protracted tidying up process whereby any remaining anomalies or puzzles are somehow reconciled with the existing core theory no matter how complex and unlikely are the manoeuvres necessary to do this. . . One way forward will be to actively engage with each set of participants and try to understand their beliefs and actions. Once the participant sets are better understood in their own terms, then interactions between them can be explored from a sound base" (p. 947).

However, it is easy to see why this does not occur. A realistic association with corporate management requires cooperation with a particular firm or organization over a number of years and is necessarily labor-intensive — the conducting of questionnaires as well as interviews with senior staff — the dissemination of which must conform to an academically acceptable mode of qualitative research that is differentiated from investigative journalism. Condensing the outcomes of all this work into the limited space allocated to a journal article represents another significant hurdle for academics.

Thus, a case study approach has never been popular in finance. And, so, the admission that ambiguity and textualisation might contribute to theory development continues to be resisted.

The onus on academics is to generate publications and subsequent citations of their work. *Quantitative* research — the running of regressions on hypothesized explanatory variables — holds out the prospect of publishing academic articles with less pain. Thus, empirical data mining continues to be aimed at whether issues in corporate finance can be related to just about anything. If, for example, "corporate governance" should be in vogue, relating capital structure to the composition of the board of directors (their age, gender, etc.) is popular. The "statistically significant" outcomes of much of this kind of research are invariably nuanced (at best) in economic significance. But this need not be of concern to the aspiring academic in finance, provided the outcome paper appears as a robust econometric exercise that can be located with reference to the prevailing academic literature. If, in addition, the published paper subsequently captures the attention of other academics and is cited in *their* publications, the original author is on the way to becoming a successful academic.

Good lecturers realize that corporate finance cannot be taught without incorporating what institutions and people actually do and that informed comment, however anecdotal, should be allowed to contribute to a meaningful exposition of the principles. Nevertheless, a theory's explanatory capability is circumscribed by the methodological approaches it adopts, with the outcome that everyday observations of markets are confined to confront the paradigm of perfect markets and present arguments within its terms of reference. For this reason, the textbooks are advancing only marginally. The GFC is accorded lip service but the subject matter continues to be based on the same static models, which are propagated as truth.

PART C

Stock Markets and Investment Choices: Growth, Asset Pricing and Portfolio Construction

Chapter 6

Mathematics of Growth

Mathematics, rightly viewed, possesses not only truth, but supreme beauty — a beauty cold and austere, like that of sculpture.

Bertrand Russell

As far as the laws of mathematics refer to reality, they are not certain; and as far as they are certain, they do not refer to reality.

Albert Einstein

A wise man should have money in his head, but not in his heart.

Jonathan Swift

October. This is one of the peculiarly dangerous months to speculate in stocks in. The others are July, January, September, April, November, May, March, June, December, August, and February.

Mark Twain

6.1. Introduction

This chapter examines the mathematics of growth. As such, the chapter provides the framework for understanding growth, which supports subsequent chapters when we seek to build a quantitative model that is capable of grasping, in some meaningful manner, the essential dimensions and dynamics of market behavior. This is because the mathematics of markets is ultimately the mathematics of probabilistic statistics. In subsequent chapters, we seek to refine what the model is capable of teaching us — both in terms of what the model is capable of revealing of itself, as well as in terms of what the model admits to being beyond its scope.

The chapter aims to provide the intuition behind the algebra that is applied in the text. The aim is sometimes restricted by space — a full discussion of the algebra would require a dedicated mathematical text. Nevertheless, the chapter should serve at least to encapsulate the mathematical framework of the text and, as such, guide the reader to areas where they may seek to consolidate a mathematical background.[1]

The theme of this chapter, roughly, is that we commence with the simple power laws for growth accumulation (Section 6.2) and proceed to examine growth as the outcome of simple interest rates, from which we establish the principle of discounting (Section 6.3). We proceed to encounter continuously compounding growth (Section 6.4). This leads to a survey of the application of logarithms (Section 6.5). The *normal distribution* of outcomes is introduced in Section 6.6, before Section 6.7 makes a connection with growth in asset prices. Section 6.8 develops the calculus of differentiation, which provides the foundation on which Section 6.9 is able to offer insight into the mathematics of the *normal distribution*. Section 6.10 proceeds to apply the statistical insights that were attained for a single investment to a portfolio of many investments, which, in turn, allows for recognition of the *central limit theorem* — or *law of large numbers* (Section 6.11). Section 6.12 provides the payoff for this chapter in that it combines the insights of the previous sections (concepts of variability, normally distributed outcomes, and the central limit theorem) to arrive at a *binomial* model that captures the variability of normally distributed continuously-compounding growth rates. This model will provide a foundation for our building of asset pricing models in subsequent chapters. The final section, Section 6.13, concludes with a brief discussion.

6.2. The Important Power Laws[2]

By x^N, we shall *mean x* multiplied by itself N times. Thus, $x^1 \equiv x, x^2 \equiv x{\cdot}x$, $x^3 \equiv x{\cdot}x{\cdot}x$, etc. And, so, for example, $x^3 \cdot x^4 \equiv (x{\cdot}x{\cdot}x){\cdot}(x{\cdot}x{\cdot}x{\cdot}x) \equiv x^7$. More generally:

$$(1) \quad \boxed{x^A x^B \equiv x^{A+B}.} \quad\quad (6.1)$$

---

[1]To give some indication of the relevance of the derivations (as well as assisting the reader to back reference the equations in later chapters), those equations that are referenced in subsequent chapters are bordered.

[2]In general, as is customary, the multiplication sign "x" (or x) in the text is either omitted or, to give clarity, is denoted by ".". We shall occasionally avail of the $\equiv$ sign to emphasize that the relation is true by definition.

It follows that

$$\boxed{(x^A)^N \equiv x^A . x^A . x^A . \ldots \equiv x^{A+A+A\cdots} (N \text{ such repetitions}) = x^{NA}.}$$

(6.2)

To see how this translates for a fraction, $1/N$, observe that with Eqs. (6.1) and (6.2):

$$\left[x^{\left(\frac{1}{N}\right)} \right]^N = x^{\frac{1}{N}} x^{\frac{1}{N}} x^{\frac{1}{N}} \ldots (N \text{ such repetitions})$$

$$= x^{\frac{1}{N}+\frac{1}{N}+\frac{1}{N}\cdots} (N \text{ repetitions}) = x. \qquad (6.3)$$

Thus, by $x^{\frac{1}{N}}$ we *mean* that number which when multiplied by itself N times is equal to x.

By x^{-A}, we shall *mean* $\frac{1}{x^A}$. Thus we have

(2) $\boxed{x^{-A} \equiv \frac{1}{x^A}.}$ (6.4)

We have $x^A \frac{1}{x^A} \equiv 1$, which with Eqs. (6.1) and (6.4), can be expressed $x^A x^{-A} = x^0$. It follows that we can write

(3) $\boxed{x^0 = 1.}$ (6.5)

6.3. Discrete Returns, Compounding, and Discounting

Consider that your bank deposit accumulates interest at, say, a rate of 10% per annum, to be added annually. Thus, if you commence with $100, after 1 year, you have

$$\$100(1.1) = \$110.$$

Now that we have grown by 10% in the first year, a further 10% growth in the second year means that at the end of the second year, your bank deposit has grown to

$$\$100(1.1)(1.1) \equiv \$100(1.1)^2 = \$121$$

and so on.

If by investing $100 today in my bank account, I can look forward to $100(1.1)^2 = $121 in two years' time, I can equate one amount with the other (that is, \$100 now can be equated with \$100$(1.1)^2$ two years from now). For example, if a friend wishes to borrow \$100 from me today and repay after two years, the amount I require after two years — if I am not to lose out by lending — is \$100$(1.1)^2 = \$121$. Thus, we say that \$100 is the *present value* of \$100$(1.1)^2$ at the end of two years. And how do we derive \$100 from \$100$(1.1)^2$? By dividing \$100$(1.1)^2$ by 1.1^2, of course; which is to say, the present value (PV) of the cash amount \$$X_2$ at the end of two annual periods is derived as

$$PV = \frac{\$X_2}{(1+i)^2},$$

where i is the annual, or per period, interest rate. More generally, the PV of amounts \$$X_1$, \$$X_2$, \$$X_3$, ..., \$$X_N$, at the end of 1, 2, 3, ..., N periods, respectively, on an interest rate, i, per period, is determined as

$$PV = \frac{\$X_1}{(1+i)} + \frac{\$X_2}{(1+i)^2} + \frac{\$X_3}{(1+i)^3} + \cdots + \frac{\$X_N}{(1+i)^N}. \qquad (6.6)$$

Or, availing of the summation sign, $\sum$, as

$$PV = \sum_{y=1}^{N} \frac{\$X_y}{(1+i)^y}. \qquad (6.7)$$

The above expression can be simplified when the amount \$$X_1$ at the end of the first period grows at a constant rate, $g\%$, in each subsequent period. We then have

$$PV = \frac{\$X_1}{(1+i)} + \frac{\$X_1(1+g)}{(1+i)^2} + \frac{\$X_1(1+g)^2}{(1+i)^3} + \cdots + \frac{\$X_1(1+g)^{N-1}}{(1+i)^N},$$

which is simplified by recognizing that by multiplying both sides of the above equation by $\frac{1+g}{1+i}$ we can express

$$PV\frac{(1+g)}{(1+i)} = \frac{\$X_1(1+g)}{(1+i)^2} + \frac{\$X_1(1+g)^2}{(1+i)^3} + \cdots + \frac{\$X_1(1+g)^N}{(1+i)^{N+1}}.$$

We now subtract the above equation from the proceeding equation to deliver

$$PV\left(1 - \frac{1+g}{1+i}\right) = \frac{\$X_1}{(1+i)} - \$X_1\left(\frac{1+g}{1+i}\right)^N \frac{1}{(1+i)}.$$

Provided the growth rate, g, is less than the interest rate, i, $(1+g)/(1+i)$ is a fraction and the right-hand term with sufficiently high value of N can be discarded; which is to say, if we consider a sequence of cash flows "growing forever" at rate g, their PV, is determined as

$$PV\left(1 - \frac{1+g}{1+i}\right) = \frac{\$X_1}{(1+i)},$$

which upon rearranging, provides the "growing perpetuity":

$$PV = \frac{\$X_1}{i - g}. \tag{6.8}$$

An even further simplification is obtained when the growth rate is zero and we have $\$X_1$ at the end of each period "in perpetuity". The PV of such a perpetuity is then derived from Eq. (6.8) with $g = 0$ as

$$PV = \frac{\$X_1}{i}. \tag{6.9}$$

6.4. Continuously Compounding Growth Rates

If in Section 6.3, the growth rate 10% is applied semi-annually, so that 5% growth is applied at the end of six months, and a further 5% applied at the end of the year, a $100 deposit grows at the end of the first year to

$$\$100(1.05)(1.05).$$

This is to say, a $100 deposit grows at the end of the first year to

$$\$100\left(1 + \frac{0.1}{2}\right)\left(1 + \frac{0.1}{2}\right) \equiv \$100\left(1 + \frac{0.1}{2}\right)^2$$
$$= \$110.25,$$

which offers a small improvement on the outcome for annualized interest ($110). If the 10% were to be applied as 2.5% quarterly, we would have

$$\$100\left(1 + \frac{0.1}{4}\right)\left(1 + \frac{0.1}{4}\right)\left(1 + \frac{0.1}{4}\right)\left(1 + \frac{0.1}{4}\right) \equiv \$100\left(1 + \frac{0.1}{4}\right)^4$$
$$= \$110.38,$$

at the end of the first year (a further improvement on the outcome for semi-annualized interest).

Extending the concept leads us to say that if a 10% growth were to be applied more or less "continuously" in the above manner, we would have

$$\$100 \left(1 + \frac{0.1}{N}\right)^N,$$

where N is a "large" number. Expanding $\left(1 + \frac{x}{N}\right)^N$ provides an expression in powers of x. For large N and x as a fraction, it turns out that we can express[3]:

$$\left(1 + \frac{x}{N}\right)^N = 1 + x + \frac{1}{2!}x^2 + \frac{1}{3!}x^3 + \frac{1}{4!}x^4 + \cdots + \frac{1}{N!}x^N. \quad (6.10)$$

More specifically, the left-hand side expression $(1+x/N)^N$ approaches (gets ever closer to) the right-hand side as we add more terms (ie, as N approaches infinity, expressed $N \to \infty$). It is not, at this stage, immediately obvious why the expansion of $\left(1 + \frac{x}{N}\right)^N$ should have the particular form of Eq. (6.10). A justification is forthcoming in Section 6.8 (p. 98) when we apply the concept of "differentiation" to continuously compounding growth. At this stage, we note simply that with x as a fraction, and increasing N, the final terms in Eq. (6.10) are increasingly insignificant. In which case, for very large N, the right-hand side of Eq. (6.10) is effectively independent of N. With x as a fraction, and large N, it is possible to express the right-hand side of Eq. (6.10) as:

$$e^x = 1 + x + \frac{1}{2!}x^2 + \frac{1}{3!}x^3 + \frac{1}{4!}x^4 + \cdots + \frac{1}{N!}x^N, \quad (6.11)$$

where e is a particular number (yet to be specified). Again, the idea is that the left-hand side identification of e^x is expressed ever more accurately as the right-hand side as $N \to \infty$. Thus, as $N \to \infty$, we have (combining Eqs. (6.10) and (6.11)):

$$\left(1 + \frac{x}{N}\right)^N = e^x. \quad (6.12)$$

---

[3] ! denotes the factorial. So $2! = 2(1) = 2$; $3! = 3(2)(1) = 6$; $4! = 4(3)(2)1 = 24$, and so on.

We can justify a unique number e independent of x as follows. For any given x, the right-hand side of Eq. (6.11) can be expressed as a^x for *some a*. If we consider an alternative value of x, say, $2x$, the right-hand side of Eq. (6.11) can again be expressed as b^{2x} for *some b*. We may then invoke the principle that by doubling the continuously compounding growth rate (from x to $2x$), the same growth outcome is achieved in half the time (a case of "double your velocity and you get there in half the time"). Thus, applying the growth rate x over two successive periods is equivalent to applying the growth rate $2x$ over a single period. That is, we must have

$$a^x \times a^x = b^{2x},$$

but (with Eq. (6.1)) the left-hand side of the above equation $= a^{2x}$, so that we have $a^{2x} = b^{2x}$, which is to say, $a = b$, and thus the unique number we choose to call e in Eq. (6.11) is justified. We may therefore determine the unique value of e simply by setting $x = 1$ in Eq. (6.11):

$$e = 1 + 1 + \frac{1}{2!} + \frac{1}{3!} + \frac{1}{4!} + \cdots,$$

$= 2.718282\ldots$ This continues to be defined more accurately (to more decimal places) as the series is expanded. The point is, whatever value of x we choose to insert in Eq. (6.11), we always arrive at the same value for the e variable as the solution!

Thus, we can say that when a growth rate of $x\%$ is applied over a period to a starting price, P_0, repeatedly as $x\%/N$ over each of N sub-periods, the outcome price at the end of the period, P_1, is determined as[4]

$$P_1 \simeq P_0 e^{\left(\frac{x\%}{100}\right)}. \tag{6.13}$$

If the growth rate $x\%$ is allowed to continue over t periods, we would have $P = P_0 e^{(x/100)} e^{(x/100)} e^{(x/100)} \ldots$ (t repetitions), in which case (with Eq. (6.1)):

$$P_t = P_0 e^{\left(\frac{x\%}{100}\right)t}. \tag{6.14}$$

---

[4]The $\simeq$ represents "approximately equal to". Strictly speaking, the outcome price P_1 approaches $P_0 e^{(x/100)}$ at the end of the period as the number N of period sub-divisions over which $x\%/N$ is applied approaches ∞. In Eq. (6.14), we allow that growth is continuously updated, in which case, the '=' sign is appropriate.

We refer to such continuous compounding growth as *exponential* growth, and e as the *exponential* number (2.718282...). Intriguingly, e is termed "irrational' on account of that e cannot be expressed precisely as a fraction — meaning that e as 2.718282... continues with additional digits for ever. In our example of a 10% growth rate applied continuously over a year to an initial deposit of \$100, we have the outcome at the end of one year (with a calculator) as

$$100e^{0.1} \simeq \$110.517\ldots$$

and at the end of, say, ten years, as,

$$100e^{10(0.1)} = 100e \simeq \$271.828\ldots.$$

To see how the calculator determines $e^{0.1}$, we can write $e^{0.1} = e^{\frac{1}{10}}$ as that number which, when multiplied by itself ten times, is equal to e (Eq. (6.3)). The calculator gave us $e^{0.1} = 1.10517\ldots$ (above). And, yes, $1.10517^{10} = 2.7183 = e$.

The infinite series Eq. (6.11) captures the effect of applying the exponential rate, x, to a dollar as equal to \$$(1 + x)$ plus an additional amount due to continuous compounding. Actually, provided x is not too big a fraction, the value of additional terms in Eq. (6.11) quickly becomes negligible. Thus, limiting ourselves to the first three terms of the series in Eq. (6.11) gives us

$$\$100 \left(1 + 0.1 + \frac{1}{2!}0.1^2 \right) = \$110.5,$$

which is a reduction of less than 0.02% from the evaluation that was obtained when we applied 10% continuously: \$100.517...(above).

The graph of e^x is represented in Fig. 6.1. We observe that as x increases, e^x increases at an increasing rate. This is because that which is the object of continuously compounding growth accumulates, or grows, not continuously with reference to an original starting valuation, but continuously with reference to the most recent valuation — it grows on itself — what is what we fundamentally mean by "exponential" growth.[5]

---

[5]The significance and potential power of exponential or continuously compounding growth is highlighted by the legend that records that a courtier Sissa Ben Dahir presented an Indian

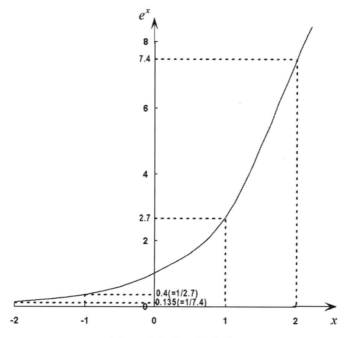

Figure 6.1. Graph of e^x.

6.5. Application of Logarithms

Suppose we require the continuously compounding — which is to say, exponential — growth rate, R, that is equivalent to compounding quarterly at 10%. In other words, suppose that we are asked to solve for R where:

$$e^R = \left(1 + \frac{0.1}{4}\right)^4 = 1.1038.$$

That is, the question becomes, given $e^R = 1.1038$, what is the value of R?

King Sharim with a beautiful, handmade chessboard. The king asked Sissa Ben Dahir what he would like in return for his gift and the courtier surprised the king by asking for one grain of rice on the first square, two grains on the second, four grains on the third, and so on. The king readily agreed and asked for the rice to be brought. All went well at first, but the requirement for 2^{N-1} grains on the Nth square demanded over a million grains on the 21st square, more than a million million (trillion) on the 41st and there simply was not enough rice in the whole world for the final squares (from Peter Swirski (2006), *Of Literature and Knowledge: Explorations in Narrative Thought Experiments, Evolution, and Game Theory*).

The answer is the natural logarithm of 1.1038 to base e. Why? Because by the natural logarithm of 1.1038 to base e — which we write as $\ln(1.1038)$ — we *mean* that number R such that $e^R = 1.1038$.

This is to say, by the natural logarithm of 1.1038, we *mean* the continuously compounding growth rate on \$1 that produces \$1.1038.

To compute the natural logarithm, we shall generally require a calculator (since we do not have a simple closed algebraic expression by which to calculate a logarithm).[6] However, it follows that the natural logarithm of e^R, $\ln(e^R)$, is that number X such that $e^X = e^R$, which is to say, $X = R$. In other words,

$$\ln(e^R) \equiv R. \qquad (6.15)$$

Similarly, expressing $e^{(\ln R)} = X$, and taking the logarithm of both sides, we have

$$\ln[e^{(\ln R)}] = \ln(X),$$

which with Eq. (6.15) provides

$$\ln(R) = \ln(X),$$

which is to say, $X = R$, so that we can say

$$e^{(\ln R)} \equiv R. \qquad (6.16)$$

Thus, to solve the above problem:

$$e^R = 1.1038,$$

we take the natural logarithm of both sides of the equation, to give (with Eq. (6.15))

$$\ln(e^R) \equiv R = \ln(1.1038)$$
$$= 0.0988(9.88\%) \text{ with a calculator.}$$

Additional properties of logarithms:

$$(1) \quad \boxed{\ln(A \times B) = \ln(A) + \ln(B).} \qquad (6.17)$$

---

[6]In the old days, two pages of log tables.

For example,

$$\ln(12 \times 80) = \ln(960) = 6.867,$$

and $\ln(12) = 2.485$ and $\ln(80) = 4.382$, which add to 6.867.[7]

$$(2) \quad \boxed{\ln(X^Y) = Y \ln(X).} \qquad (6.18)$$

For example,

$$\ln(1.5^4) = \ln(5.06) = 1.62$$

and $4 \times \ln(1.5) = 4 \times 0.41 = 1.62$ also.

As another example, consider

$$\$400 \times (1.04)^t = \$1,000,$$

which addresses the following problem: If I start with $400, how many periods of growth at 4% do I need before I accumulate $1,000? To solve, tidy up the above as

$$(1.04)^t = \frac{\$1,000}{\$400} = 2.5.$$

Now take the natural logs of both sides:

$$\ln[(1.04)^t] = \ln(2.5),$$

---

[7]Equation (6.17) is the principle of the slide rule, which has each number calibrated as its logarithm. The slide rule determines 12 multiplied by 80 by having calibrated a length 2.485 corresponding to 12 on one rule and a length 4.382 corresponding to 80 on a sliding rule, so that when they are connected, the distance 6.867 naturally appears — and the reverse calibration (the "anti-log" of 6.867) shows 960 on the rule. In the old days, when I was at school in Bolton, Lancashire, we took pride in how rapidly we could apply our slide rules — a sort of showing how fast a dude we were on the draw — a lost skill now that we have handheld electronic calculators. Ah, nostalgia is not what it used to be. The modern equivalent is young people showing how quickly they are able to transmit their phone text messages. I don't come close, of course. But I am still in position two of slide rules if anyone wishes to challenge me.

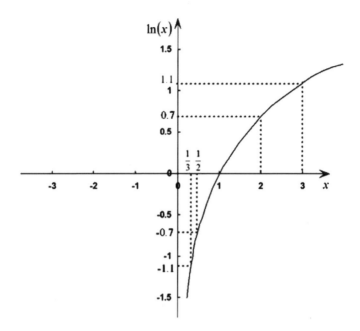

Figure 6.2. Graph of ln(x).

and with Eq. (6.18), the above provides:

$$t \times \ln(1.04) = \ln(2.5), \text{ yielding}$$

$$t = \frac{\ln(2.5)}{\ln(1.04)} = \frac{0.916}{0.0392} = 23.4 \text{ periods.}$$

$$(3) \quad \ln\left(\frac{A}{B}\right) = -\ln\left(\frac{B}{A}\right), \quad\quad\quad (6.19)$$

as illustrated in Fig. 6.2. Equation (6.19) follows from Eq. (6.18) on account of (by definition) $A/B \equiv \frac{1}{B/A} \equiv (B/A)^{-1}$, so that $\ln(A/B) \equiv \ln[(B/A)^{-1}] = $ (with Eq. (6.18)) $-\ln(B/A)$.

The graph of $\ln(x)$ is represented in Fig. 6.2. The distinctive feature of $\ln(x)$ is that it increases as x increases, but at a declining rate. We note that $\ln(x)$ is unbounded above — any value of $\ln(x)$ can be attained with a sufficiently high value of x — and that $\ln(0) = -$infinity $(-\infty)$, which follows because with exceedingly large N, we can express $\ln(0)$ as approximately equal to $\ln(1/N) \equiv \ln[(N)^{-1}]$, which (with Eq. (6.18)) $\equiv -\ln(N)$, which (exceedingly large N) is approximately equal to $-\ln(\infty) = -\infty$.

To understand growth more realistically, we need to introduce just one more concept — which is that growth rates — as in nature — are seldom fixed, but, rather, are *variable*. Introducing even the essential elements of the concept of variability in asset returns will, however, concern us to the end of Chapter 12. As Mr. Spock might respond, dead-pan, on the good ship *Enterprise*, "Fascinating".

6.6. The Normal Distribution

A normal distribution captures the idea that, although all outcomes from minus infinity ($-\infty$) to plus infinity ($+\infty$) might be strictly allowable, the more we move away from some central outcome, the lower the expectation that a particular outcome will occur. The assumption of normality is that the distribution of outcomes is symmetrical in that for any divergence from the central location, a positive or a negative divergence is equally likely. For such a distribution, we might envisage a graph with some notion of probabilities on the y-axis against possible outcomes on the x-axis as in Fig. 6.3. In Fig. 6.3, the probability curve, $p(x)$, does not actually represent the probability of each x-axis outcome. Rather, the graph works by stipulating that the area under the curve between two outcomes (on the x-axis) is the probability that the outcome occurs within that *range* on

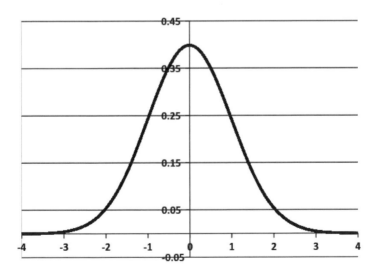

Figure 6.3. The unit normal distribution curve.

the x-axis.[8] The entire area under the $p(x)$ curve is therefore equal to 1. Note that as x approaches plus or minus infinity, the curve approaches, but never actually reaches, zero on the y-axis. Note also that the probability of an absolutely precise outcome occurring is zero (we speak only of the probability within a *range* of outcomes).

We refer to the central outcome of a normal distribution as the *mean* of the distribution (which we represent as μ). It represents the average outcome over the entire probability-weighted distribution from $-$infinity to $+$infinity ($-\infty$ to $+\infty$). The greater the divergence of the possible outcomes from the central outcome (μ) (which is to say, the "fatter" the area under the curve away from the central position), the greater what we call the *variance* or, alternatively, the *standard deviation* (σ) of the outcomes. The variance of the distribution is measured as

$$\text{variance} = \sum_{x=-\infty}^{x=+\infty} (x-\mu)^2 \times [\text{probability that } x \text{ lies within } (\Delta x)],$$

(6.20)

which captures the idea of covering the x-axis in Fig. 6.3 in small increments of x, which we call Δx, and for each small increment of Δx, measuring the probability that x lies in that segment of Δx (which is the area under the curve at that point contained by the "distance" Δx) and multiplying that probability by $(x-\mu)^2$, where x is the central value of the Δx increment. The summation sign, $\sum_{x=-\infty}^{x=+\infty}$, captures the idea that we sum or add together all such probability-weighted outcomes between $x = -\infty$ and $+\infty$. The standard deviation (σ) is then determined as the square root of the variance: $\sigma \equiv \sqrt{variance}$.[9]

Figure 6.3 actually represents a particular case of the normal distribution — called the unit normal distribution — in that the mean or central outcome (μ) is zero and the standard deviation (σ) about such an outcome is equal to 1.0. By inspection, Fig. 6.3 tells us that there is a very high probability that an outcome with such a probability distribution will occur between -3 and $+3$.

---

[8]The actual equation for the normal distribution must await our development in Section 6.9.
[9]The concept of the mean and standard deviation are presented for a distribution of *finite* outcomes as Eqs. (6.61), (6.62), and (6.63) in Sections 6.10.1 and 6.10.2.

Table 6.1 presents the area under the curve in Fig. 6.3 to the *left* of a range of numbers on the *x*-axis.[10] The number is displayed in the left-hand column with an additional significant figure along the horizontal line. Thus, the first entry for 0 is 0.5, because the area to the left of the zero point on the *x*-axis in Fig. 6.3 is one half of the total area under the curve (=1). There is, therefore, a 50% probability that the outcome will occur less than zero (and, of course, a 50% probability that the outcome will occur greater than zero). The final entry in the table tells us that the area to the left of the number 2.99 in Fig. 6.3 is already 99.86% of the total area under the curve (=1), which is to say, an outcome greater than 2.99 has probability 0.14% of occurring.

Table 6.1 considers directly only the probability that an outcome is less than a positive number (in the range of 0 to 3.0). However, due to the symmetry of the normal distribution curve, we can use the table to compute the probability of an outcome less than a negative number. For example, consider the probability that an outcome is less than −0.25. From the table, the probability of finding an outcome less than +0.25 is 59.87%. The area to the right of +0.25, is therefore 100 − 59.87% = 40.13%. But, by symmetry, this is also the area to the left of −0.25, and so 40.13% is in fact the probability of having an outcome less than −0.25.[11]

Again, as an application of Table 6.1, consider the probabilities for the unit normal distribution that are presented in Table 6.2. In Table 6.1, we note that the probability of an occurrence less than 1.0 is 84.13%. Hence the probability of an occurrence greater than 1.0 is 100% − 84.13% = 15.87%. By symmetry, the probability of an occurrence in the range of +/−1.0 from the mean of zero is, therefore, 84.13% − 15.87% = 68.26% — as depicted in Table 6.2. As another example, the probability of an occurrence less than 1.96 is 97.50% (Table 6.1). Hence, the probability of an occurrence greater than 1.96 is 100% − 97.50% = 2.5%. By symmetry, the probability of an

---

[10]As a matter of terminology, we refer to the area to the left of a general number *x* in Fig. 6.3 — which is the probability that a random selection from the unit normal distribution is less than *x* — as $N(x)$.

[11]So that the above calculation for a negative number can be avoided, some texts are kind enough to display directly the results for a negative number also. These days, the numbers are electronically available.

Table 6.1. Probability table for the unit normal distribution.

Z	0.00	0.01	0.02	0.03	0.04	0.05	0.06	0.07	0.08	0.09
0.0	0.5000	0.5040	0.5080	0.5120	0.5160	0.5199	0.5239	0.5279	0.5319	0.5359
0.1	0.5398	0.5438	0.5478	0.5517	0.5557	0.5596	0.5636	0.5675	0.5714	0.5753
0.2	0.5793	0.5832	0.5871	0.5910	0.5948	0.5987	0.6026	0.6064	0.6103	0.6141
0.3	0.6179	0.6217	0.6255	0.6293	0.6331	0.6368	0.6406	0.6443	0.6480	0.6517
0.4	0.6554	0.6591	0.6628	0.6664	0.6700	0.6736	0.6772	0.6808	0.6844	0.6879
0.5	0.6915	0.6950	0.6985	0.7019	0.7054	0.7088	0.7123	0.7157	0.7190	0.7224
0.6	0.7257	0.7291	0.7324	0.7357	0.7389	0.7422	0.7454	0.7486	0.7517	0.7549
0.7	0.7580	0.7611	0.7642	0.7673	0.7704	0.7734	0.7764	0.7794	0.7823	0.7852
0.8	0.7881	0.7910	0.7939	0.7967	0.7995	0.8023	0.8051	0.8078	0.8106	0.8133
0.9	0.8159	0.8186	0.8212	0.8238	0.8264	0.8239	0.8315	0.8340	0.8365	0.8389
1.0	0.8413	0.8438	0.8461	0.8485	0.8508	0.8531	0.8554	0.8577	0.8599	0.8621
1.1	0.8643	0.8665	0.8686	0.8708	0.8729	0.8749	0.8770	0.8790	0.8810	0.8830
1.2	0.8849	0.8869	0.8888	0.8907	0.8925	0.8944	0.8962	0.8980	0.8997	0.9015
1.3	0.9032	0.9049	0.9066	0.9082	0.9099	0.9115	0.9031	0.9147	0.9162	0.9177
1.4	0.9192	0.9207	0.9222	0.9236	0.9251	0.9265	0.9279	0.9292	0.9306	0.9319
1.5	0.9332	0.9345	0.9357	0.9370	0.9382	0.9394	0.9406	0.9418	0.9429	0.9441
1.6	0.9452	0.9463	0.9474	0.9484	0.9495	0.9505	0.9515	0.9525	0.9535	0.9545
1.7	0.9554	0.9564	0.9573	0.9582	0.9591	0.9599	0.9608	0.9616	0.9625	0.9633
1.8	0.9641	0.9649	0.9656	0.9664	0.9671	0.9678	0.9686	0.9693	0.9699	0.9706
1.9	0.9713	0.9719	0.9726	0.9732	0.9738	0.9744	0.9750	0.9756	0.9761	0.9767
2.0	0.9772	0.9778	0.9783	0.9788	0.9793	0.9798	0.9803	0.9808	0.9812	0.9817
2.1	0.9821	0.9826	0.9830	0.9834	0.9838	0.9842	0.9846	0.9850	0.9854	0.9857
2.2	0.9861	0.9864	0.9868	0.9871	0.9875	0.9878	0.9881	0.9884	0.9887	0.9890
2.3	0.9893	0.9896	0.9898	0.9901	0.9904	0.9906	0.9909	0.9911	0.9913	0.9916
2.4	0.9918	0.9920	0.9922	0.9924	0.9927	0.9929	0.9931	0.9932	0.9934	0.9936
2.5	0.9938	0.9940	0.9941	0.9943	0.9945	0.9946	0.9948	0.9949	0.9951	0.9952
2.6	0.9953	0.9955	0.9956	0.9957	0.9958	0.9960	0.9961	0.9962	0.9963	0.9964
2.7	0.9965	0.9966	0.9967	0.9968	0.9969	0.9970	0.9971	0.9972	0.9973	0.9974
2.8	0.9974	0.9975	0.9976	0.9977	0.9977	0.9978	0.9979	0.9979	0.9980	0.9981
2.9	0.9981	0.9982	0.9982	0.9983	0.9984	0.9984	0.9985	0.9985	0.9986	0.9986

The table shows the probability $N(z)$ that an occurrence, z, will be less than the number in the left-hand column (while moving from left to right on the top row to allow for an additional significant figure). Thus, consistent with the symmetry of Fig. 6.3, the probability that the outcome is less than 0.0 (the first entry in the table) is 0.5 (50% probability), and the probability that the outcome is less than 2.99, the final entry in the table is already close to 1 (99.86% probability).

occurrence in the range of $+/-1.96$ from the mean of zero is, therefore, $97.50\% - 2.5\% = 95.0\%$ (as depicted in Table 6.2).

The usefulness of Table 6.1, which applies to a unit normal distribution (with mean $\mu = 0$ and standard deviation $\sigma = 1$), is that it can be

Table 6.2. Table of selected probabilities for a unit normal distribution.

Distance from the mean	Probability that the outcome will fall in the range of column 1 (%)
1.0	68.26
1.645	90
1.960	95
2.575	99

applied readily to a general normal distribution with mean μ and standard deviation σ. This is because any normal distribution (characterized by its mean, μ, and standard deviation, σ) can readily be transformed in relation to the unit normal distribution, as we now demonstrate.

To this end, consider, firstly, that when we have a set of numbers X with mean μ^* and standard deviation σ^*, the set of numbers $a + bX$ (meaning that we take each number, x, in the set X and multiply by b and then add a) has mean $\mu = a + b\mu^*$ and standard deviation $\sigma = b\sigma^*$. In other words:

When set X has mean μ^* and standard deviation σ^*,
it follows that the set $a + bX$ has

$$\text{mean } (\mu) = a + b\mu^*$$

and $\hspace{4cm}$ (6.21)

$$\text{standard deviation } (\sigma) = b\sigma^*.$$

For any set of numbers, the above can be demonstrated with Eqs. (6.61)–(6.63) below. In reverse, we have the outcome that when we take a set of numbers that is normally distributed with mean μ and standard deviation σ, the set of numbers $(x - \mu)/\sigma$, meaning that we take each member of the set x and subtract μ before dividing by σ, is normally distributed with a mean $\mu^* = 0$ with standard deviation $\sigma^* = 1$. This insight is sufficient to relate a general normal distribution to the unit normal distribution of Fig. 6.3 and Table 6.1.

Thus, for example, in Table 6.2, we have the statement that there is a 90% probability that the outcome of a distribution with mean $\mu = 0$ and standard deviation $\sigma = 1$ will lie between -1.645 and $+1.645$; which allows us to make the statement that there is a 90% probability that the outcome x from a distribution with mean μ and standard deviation σ is contained as

$$-1.645 < (x - \mu)/\sigma < +1.645,$$

(since $(x - \mu)/\sigma$ is distributed with mean $= 0$ and standard deviation $= 1$), which is the statement (multiplying across by σ and adding μ) that there is a 90% probability that

$$\mu - 1.645\sigma < x < \mu + 1.645\sigma,$$

which, in turn, is the statement that there is a 90% probability that the variable x that is normally distributed with mean μ and standard deviation σ, lies between plus and minus 1.645 standard deviations ($1.645 \times \sigma$) from the mean (μ). In other words, we can generalize Table 6.2 as Table 6.3, which is illustrated in Fig. 6.4.

For example, if I choose randomly from a distribution with mean $\mu = 10\%$ and a standard deviation $\sigma = 20\%$, what is the probability that my outcome selection will

(i) Be greater than 15%?
and
(ii) Lie between 5% and 15%?

Solution:

(i) We have $(15\% - 10\%)/20\% = 0.25$.

The probability that a random selection from the unit normal distribution is less than 0.25, we call $N(0.25)$. We have already determined this probability as 0.5987 from Table 6.1. Hence, there is a 59.87% probability that my outcome selection (with $\mu = 10\%$, and $\sigma = 20\%$) will be *less* than 15%, and hence, a *40.13%* probability that my selection is *greater* than 15%.

Table 6.3. Table of selected probabilities for a normal distribution.

Number of standard deviations from the mean	Probability that the outcome will fall in the range of column 1 (%)
1	68.26
1.645	90
1.960	95
2.575	99

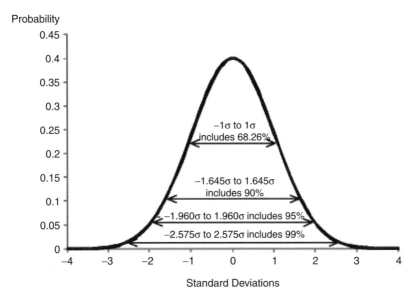

Figure 6.4. The normal distribution curve.

(ii) We have $(5\% - 10\%)/20\% = -0.25$.

The probability that a random selection from the unit normal distribution is less than -0.25, we call $N(-0.25)$. This was calculated above as 40.13%. The probability that my outcome selection falls between 5% and 15% is, therefore, $(100 - 40.13 - 40.13)\% = 19.74\%$ (note how the second 40.13 is the solution to part (i)).

6.7. The Normal Distribution and Asset Pricing

The outcome valuation for an asset at the end of a time period, $\$P$, can be expressed as the starting valuation, $\$P_0$, multiplied by $(1 + x)$ for some x. However, when the growth is compounding on its continuously updated value as opposed to its starting value, the outcome valuation is expressed as the starting valuation multiplied by e^y. Such exponential growth occurs frequently in nature where y is normally distributed.

We identify the number Z as a randomly selected value from the distribution of outcomes between $-\infty$ and $+\infty$ with attached probabilities as represented in Fig. 6.3 (with central, which is to say, mean outcome $\mu = 0$ and standard deviation $\sigma = 1.0$). As we have observed, it follows that the distribution for $\mu + Z\sigma$ — meaning that each outcome Z is multiplied by σ to which we then add μ — is distributed with mean μ and standard deviation σ.

The unknown outcome, at the end of a period, of applying a randomly selected exponential growth rate from a normal distribution with mean μ and standard deviation σ, to an asset value $\$P_0$ at the commencement of the period, can therefore be represented as $\$P_0$ multiplied by e^y, where $y = \mu + Z\sigma$. In other words:

When we invest $\$P_0$ at the commencement of a period, the outcome at the end of the period $= \$P_0 e^{\mu + Z\sigma}$

or, expressed alternatively, the value P_{t+1} at a time $t + 1$ relates to the value P_t at time t as

$$P_{t+1} = P_t e^{\mu + Z\sigma}, \qquad\qquad (6.22)$$

where μ represents the underlying mean or expected exponential growth rate for the period from time t to time $t+1$, with standard deviation σ, and Z represents a random drawing from $-\infty$ to $+\infty$ with probability determined by the unit normal distribution in Fig. 6.3. The model of stock price exponential growth and decline as Eq. (6.22) captures the fact that while stock price growth is theoretically unbounded on the upside ($e^\infty = $ infinity), prices cannot be less than zero ($e^{-\infty} = $ zero). The assumption that stock market growth can at least approximately be modeled by such a process is justified by the evidence of past stock price performance.

Consistent with the previous section, although a normal distribution of stock returns ($R_i, i = 1 \ldots N$) typically does not generally comply with $\mu = 0$ and $\sigma = 1$ as in Fig. 6.3, the distribution for $(R_i - \mu)/\sigma$, meaning that we subtract the mean of the possible outcomes μ from each possible outcome R_i, and divide that number by the standard deviation, σ, of the possible outcomes ($R_i, i = 1 \ldots N$), provides a normal distribution of outcomes $(R_i - \mu)/\sigma$ that *does* have a mean $\mu = 0$ and standard deviation $\sigma = 1$.

We have seen how this insight allows for an application for the unit normal distribution. Thus, consider that returns on your investment portfolio are normally distributed and that the mean return, μ, is again equal to, say, 10% per annum with standard deviation, σ, equal to, say, 20% per annum about such mean return. Suppose at the commencement of the year, you wish to estimate the probability that the return at the end of the year on your investment portfolio will be less than, say, 5%. This is the kind of question an investment portfolio manager may well wish to answer. The probability that the outcome return $x\%$ is less than 5% is the probability that $(x - 10)/20$ is less than $(5 - 10)/20 = -0.25$. And recognizing that $(x - 10)/20$ is normally distributed with mean $\mu = 0$ and $\sigma = 1$, the probability that $(x - 10)/20$ is less than -0.25, which we call $N(-0.25)$, is the area under the curve in Fig. 6.3 to the left of -0.25. This was calculated above with Table 6.1 as 40.13%. Thus, 40.13% is the probability that my portfolio underperforms 5% at the end of the year.

6.8. Rates of Change between Variables and their Implied Direct Relation: The Calculus

We often encounter the problem of knowing how an outcome, say y, is *changing* with respect to another variable x — but where we wish to know the direct functional relation that determines y in relation to x, which we write as $y = f(x)$. Progressing from a rate of change of a variable y with respect to x, to a direct or absolute dependence of y on x, is what we call *integration*.

As an introduction to the idea, consider that we are driving out of London on the M1 motorway north to our destination with a speed of 70 miles per hour (mph). The speed of 70 mph tells us that the *rate of change* of our distance travelled (miles) with respect to time (hours) can be expressed[12]:

$$\frac{\Delta distance}{\Delta time} = 70 \ mph. \tag{6.23}$$

So if $\Delta time = 1$ hour, $\Delta distance = 70$ miles. Suppose, however, that we wish to know not our rate of change of distance with respect to time, $\Delta distance/\Delta time$, as expressed by Eq. (6.23), but the actual *distance*

---

[12]By the symbol "Δ", we again imply "a small change in" (as was denoted by Δ in Eq. (6.20)); thus $\Delta distance/\Delta time$ expresses a small change in distance divided by the commensurate small change in time (over which the small change in distance occurs). Unless we are dealing with a summation, $\sum$ (as in Eq. (6.20)), we generally do not express a small change Δy (for some y) without stipulating the *corresponding* Δx against which the Δy occurs. Thus, $\Delta y/\Delta x$ expresses the change in y (Δy) *with respect to* x (Δx).

travelled from London as a function of time. The answer, is the *integration* of Eq. (6.23), as

$$distance \text{ (miles)} = 70 \text{ } mph \times time \text{ (hours)} + \text{a fixed number,} \quad (6.24)$$

so that, with each additional hour of elapsed *time*, we add a further 70 miles of *distance* to our journey. The fixed number in Eq. (6.24) allows us to determine *distance* as the distance from a specific point of our choosing. For example, we might decide that Eq. (6.23) does not apply as we travel, say, the first 20 miles of our journey from the start-off point of departure until we are on the M1 motorway. If we maintain our speed at 70 mph once we are on the motorway, the distance we have travelled from our start-off point of departure is determined as

$$distance \text{ (miles)} = 70 \text{ } mph \times time \text{ (hours)} + 20 \text{ miles,}$$

where *time* is the time we have been on the motorway.

We can generalize Eqs. (6.23) and (6.24) with the statement that

$$\boxed{\frac{\Delta y}{\Delta t} = A,} \quad (6.25)$$

implies the relation

$$\boxed{y = A \cdot t + \text{a constant (some fixed number).}} \quad (6.26)$$

In general, we can say that when the rate of change of y with respect to t ($\Delta y/\Delta t$) is equal to a constant (A), y is linearly related to t as $y = A \cdot t +$ a constant. Thus, if I tell you that at each point for x, $\frac{\Delta y}{\Delta x} = 3$, without specifying what either y or x actually refer to, you can, nevertheless, immediately deduce $y = 3x +$ a constant.

If we had a "quadratic" relation between y and x as

$$\boxed{y = Ax^2 + \text{a constant,}} \quad (6.27)$$

for example, as $y = 3x^2 + 4$ in Fig. 6.5, we can verify by inspection of the figure that at any point, the gradient or slope of the curve is determined as $\frac{\Delta y}{\Delta x} = 6x$. We can generalize this outcome with the statement that Eq. (6.27)

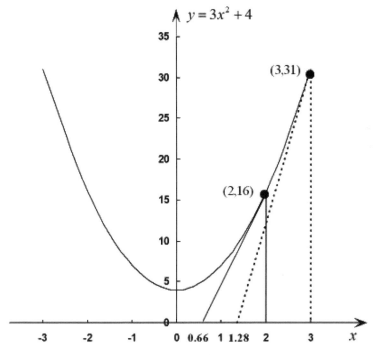

Figure 6.5. Graph of $y = 3x^2 + 4$.

implies

$$\boxed{\frac{\Delta y}{\Delta x} = 2A \cdot x.} \tag{6.28}$$

We can see this algebraically by considering that a small change in x, Δx, in Eq. (6.27), leads to some commensurate small change in y, Δy. Substituting this effect into Eq. (6.27) provides

$$y + \Delta y = A(x + \Delta x)^2 + \text{a constant},$$

giving

$$y + \Delta y = A(x^2 + 2x\Delta x + \Delta x^2) + \text{a constant},$$

then subtracting Eq. (6.27) from the above equation provides

$$\frac{\Delta y}{\Delta x} = 2Ax + \Delta x,$$

which, ignoring the Δx term as we consider ever smaller values of Δx, is Eq. (6.28).

In going from Eq. (6.27) to Eq. (6.28), we say that we have *differentiated* the function y as a function of x in Eq. (6.27). To capture the *continuity* in the change of y with respect to x, we express $\frac{\Delta y}{\Delta x}$ as $\frac{dy}{dx}$. This is to say, $\frac{dy}{dx}$ represents $\frac{\Delta y}{\Delta x}$ as $\Delta x \to$ zero.[13]

If we were to continue to consider increasing powers of x, the outcome would be the statement that the equation:

$$y = Ax^N + \text{a constant,} \tag{6.29}$$

implies the relation[14]:

$$\frac{\Delta y}{\Delta x} = ANx^{N-1}. \tag{6.30}$$

For example,

$$y = 12 + 3x^9,$$

is consistent with the relation:

$$\frac{\Delta y}{\Delta x} = 27x^8.$$

As a more exotic example, consider the relation $y = e^t$ as in Fig. 6.1 (with x replaced by t so as to identify t as the "time" variable). The interesting observation is that at each point of the curve, the slope of the curve, $\Delta(e^t)/\Delta t$, is actually equal to e^t. Thus, at $t = 0$, we have $y = e^t = e^0 = 1$ and the slope at that point is also equal to 1. At $t = 1$, we

---

[13]As is customary, we use the "$\to$" sign to denote "approaches".

[14]The result can be demonstrated algebraically following the line of argument used to demonstrate Eq. (6.28). Thus, Eq. (6.29) allows for

$$y + \Delta y = \text{constant} + A(x + \Delta x)^N,$$

which multiplying out provides

$$y + \Delta y = \text{constant} + A(x^N) + ANx^{N-1}\Delta x + \text{terms of higher order in } \Delta x.$$

Subtracting Eq. (6.29) from the above and ignoring the terms of higher order in Δx, leads to Eq. (6.30).

have $y = e^t = e^1 = e$ and the slope at that point also equals e. At $t = 2$, we have $y = e^t = e^2$ and the slope is also equal to e^2 at that point, and so on. In general, we can say that

$$y = e^t + \text{a constant,} \tag{6.31}$$

implies

$$\frac{\Delta y}{\Delta t} = e^t. \tag{6.32}$$

If, more generally, we had drawn the graph of

$$y = Ae^{Rt} \tag{6.33}$$

where R is some fixed (constant) value, we would find that at any point, the slope $\Delta y / \Delta t$ is determined as

$$\frac{\Delta y}{\Delta t} = A \cdot Re^{Rt}. \tag{6.34}$$

Thus, with Eqs. (6.33) and (6.34), we have the rate of change of y with respect to t ($\Delta y / \Delta t$) as a proportion of the contemporaneous value of y as

$$\frac{\Delta y}{\Delta t} \bigg/ y = \frac{A \cdot Re^{Rt}}{Ae^{Rt}} = R,$$

$$\frac{\Delta y}{\Delta t} \bigg/ y = R. \tag{6.35}$$

Equation (6.35) captures our understanding of exponential growth as that which occurs as a small percentage increase of the updated valuation repeated "continuously". An example helps to illustrate. Thus, consider the price P_0 of an asset at commencement of a year made subject to a growth rate of, say, 0.000038% at the end of each minute. We then have the outcome price P_t of the asset at the end of t years as (Eq. (6.1)):

$$P_t = P_0(1 + 0.00000038)^{time},$$

where *time* is the number of minutes in t years, which allowing e^x sufficiently close to $1 + x$ for very small x (Eq. (6.11)) provides (with Eq. (6.2)):

$$P_t = P_0 e^{0.00000038 \times time}.$$

By "scaling" 0.000038% per minute as $0.000038 \times (365 \times 24 \times 60)\%$ per year $= 20\%$ per year, we can express the above as

$$P_t = P_0 e^{0.20t}, \tag{6.36}$$

with t measured in years, which reproduces Eq. (6.14) (p. 79) as an example. We then have (with Eqs. (6.33) and (6.34)):

$$\frac{\Delta P_t}{\Delta t} = P_0 0.20 e^{0.20t}, \tag{6.37}$$

and hence Eq. (6.35) as

$$\frac{\Delta P}{\Delta t} \bigg/ P = 0.20, \tag{6.38}$$

where P is the (by minute) updated price and Δt is the one minute updated time period measured in years, on account of that 0.20 (20%) is per year.

Furthermore, we can now see that the functional form of e^x as Eq. (6.11):

$$e^x = 1 + x + \frac{1}{2!}x^2 + \frac{1}{3!}x^3 + \frac{1}{4!}x^4 + \cdots,$$

is appropriate, in that, on differentiating each of the above right-hand side terms (with Eqs. (6.29) and (6.30)) we have

$$\frac{\Delta e^x}{\Delta x} = 0 + 1 + \frac{2}{2!}x^1 + \frac{3}{3!}x^2 + \frac{4}{4!}x^3 + \cdots$$

$$= 1 + x + \frac{1}{2!}x^2 + \frac{1}{3!}x^3 + \frac{1}{4!}x^4 + \cdots$$

$$(\text{with Eq. (6.11)}) = e^x,$$

which confirms that the expression for e^x as Eq. (6.11) is consistent with Eqs. (6.31) and (6.32).

In Fig. 6.2, we have the function $y = \ln(x)$. By examination, we can see that the gradient or slope of the curve, which is to say, $\frac{\Delta \ln(x)}{\Delta x}$ is determined as $\frac{1}{x}$. For example, at $x = 1$, $\frac{\Delta \ln(x)}{\Delta x} = 1$, while at $x = 2$, $\frac{\Delta \ln(x)}{\Delta x} = 1/2$, and at $x = 3$, $\frac{\Delta \ln(x)}{\Delta x} = 1/3$, etc. We can generalize these outcomes as

$$\boxed{y = \ln(x) + \text{constant},} \tag{6.39}$$

implies the relation[15]

$$\boxed{\frac{\Delta y}{\Delta x} = \frac{1}{x}.}$$ (6.40)

The relation between the relation $y = \ln(x)$ and the relation $y = A.\ln(x)+$ a constant, is that in the latter case, y is increasing at A times the rate of $\ln(x)$. Hence, given

$$y = A.\ln(x) + \text{a constant},$$ (6.41)

Eqs. (6.39) and (6.40) imply

$$\frac{\Delta y}{\Delta x} = \frac{A}{x}.$$ (6.42)

With this insight, we may refer again to our example equation for exponential growth above as Eq. (6.38):

$$\frac{\Delta P_t}{\Delta t}\Big/P_t = 0.20,$$

which we may rewrite as

$$\frac{\Delta t}{\Delta P_t} = \frac{1}{0.20}\frac{1}{P_t}$$

and with our knowledge of integration (Eqs. (6.41) and 6.42), write the above as

$$t = \frac{1}{0.20}\ln(P_t) + C \text{ (a constant)},$$

so that (with Eqs. (6.15) and (6.17)):

$$0.20t = \ln(P_t) + \ln(e^{0.20C}) = \ln(P_t e^{0.20C}),$$

and, thus (with Eq. (6.16)):

$$P_t = \frac{1}{e^{0.20C}}e^{0.20t}.$$

---

[15]We can see this algebraically by considering that $y = \ln(x)$ provides (with Eq. (6.16)):

$$e^y = x, \quad \text{or,} \quad x = e^y,$$

which (with Eqs. (6.31) and (6.32)) provides $\frac{\Delta x}{\Delta y} = e^y$ or $\frac{\Delta y}{\Delta x} = \frac{1}{e^y} = \frac{1}{x}$.

With $t = 0$, we have (with Eq. (6.5)) $P_0 = 1/e^{0.2C}$, which determines the constant term $(1/e^{0.2C})$ as P_0, so that we have the outcome that

$$P_t = P_0 e^{0.20t}, \qquad (6.43)$$

is derivable from Eq. (6.38). More generally, we can state that commencing with Eq. (6.35) as

$$\frac{\Delta P_t}{\Delta t} \bigg/ P_t = x,$$

which we have derived from Eq. (6.14) (p. 79), we arrive back at Eq. (6.14):

$$P_t = P_0 e^{xt}.$$

We conclude that the above two equations are interchangeable.

Finally, we can extend the idea of differentiation to allow for the concept of a "function of a function". In simple terms, if John is working twice as fast as Peter, who is working three times faster than Jonathan, it must be that John is working $2 \times 3 = 6$ times faster than Jonathan. Suppose, then, we have

$$y = \ln(x^{10})$$

and we wish to determine dy/dx (we transfer to the notation dy/dx (from $\Delta y/\Delta x$) simply to convey a "continuous" change of y with respect to x). With Eqs. (6.39) and (6.40), we can say that y is changing with respect to x^{10} at the rate

$$\frac{dy}{d(x^{10})} = \frac{1}{x^{10}}.$$

And (with Eqs. (6.29) and (6.30)), we can say that x^{10} is changing with respect to x at the rate

$$\frac{dx^{10}}{dx} = 10x^9.$$

Thus given $y = \ln(x^{10})$, we have

$$\frac{dy}{dx} = \left(\frac{1}{x^{10}}\right)(10x^9) = \frac{10}{x}.$$

Or consider Eq. (6.31):

$$y = e^x + \text{a constant},$$

implying (Eq. (6.32))

$$\frac{dy}{dx} = e^x.$$

Then with

$$y = Ae^{Nx}, \tag{6.44}$$

we would determine

$$\frac{dy}{dx} = \frac{dy}{d(Nx)} \frac{d(Nx)}{dx}$$

$$= Ae^{Nx} \text{ (with Eqs. (6.31) and (6.32))}$$

$$\times N \text{ (with Eqs. (6.25) and (6.26))}$$

$$\frac{dy}{dx} = A \cdot Ne^N, \tag{6.45}$$

which we justified graphically above (Eqs. (6.33) and (6.34)). As another example, consider

$$\boxed{y = \ln[xe^A + (1 - x)e^B].} \tag{6.46}$$

Following the above approach, we have

$$\frac{dy}{d[xe^A + (1 - x)e^B]} = \frac{1}{xe^A + (1 - x)e^B}$$

and

$$\frac{d[xe^A + (1 - x)e^B]}{dx} = e^A - e^B,$$

so that

$$\boxed{\frac{dy}{dx} = \frac{e^A - e^B}{xe^A + (1 - x)e^B}.} \tag{6.47}$$

More generally, we can say that when y is a function of g [which we may write as: $y = f(g)$] and g itself is a function of $x[g = g(x)]$:

$$y = f[g(x)], \tag{6.48}$$

we can determine

$$\frac{dy}{dx} = \frac{df[g(x)]}{d[g(x)]} \frac{d[g(x)]}{dx}. \tag{6.49}$$

A particularly useful application of differentiation is that it allows us to determine when a function is either maximized or minimized. For example, suppose we have

$$y = 1 + 2x - x^2$$

and we wish to determine x so as to maximize y as a function of x. Figure 6.6 depicts the graph of the relation between y and x. We can

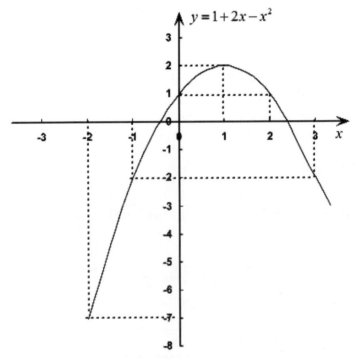

Figure 6.6. Graph of $y = 1 + 2x - x^2$.

immediately see that the maximum value of y is achieved at the point that the gradient of the curve is flat, which is to say, at the point that $dy/dx = 0$. In this case, dy/dx is determined (with Eqs. (6.25)–(6.26) and (6.27)–(6.28)) as

$$\frac{dy}{dx} = 2 - 2x,$$

which (by observation) $= 0$ when $x = 1$ (as depicted in Fig. 6.6). Thus, the maximum value of y (on substitution of $x = 1$ back into $y = 1 + 2x - x^2$) is $y = 2$. By inspection of the function, we can see that this is indeed the case (no other value of x provides a value of y greater than 2).

6.9. The Calculus of the Normal Probability Function

The equation for the probability distribution curve, $p(x)$, for normally distributed outcomes in Fig. 6.4 is given as

$$p(x) = \frac{1}{\sigma\sqrt{(2\pi)}} e^{-\frac{1}{2}[(x-\mu)/\sigma]^2}, \qquad (6.50)$$

which is generally regarded as mysterious. Well, it *does* contain the three most famous *irrational* numbers (numbers that cannot be expressed as a fraction, which is to say, to any finite end after the decimal point; and, thus, sometimes known as "vulgar" fractions): (*i*) the exponential number e (as above), (*ii*) the ratio of the circumference of a circle to the radius, 2π, and (*iii*) $\sqrt{2}$[16]; which does perhaps qualify Eq. (6.50) as mysterious!

However, we can remove some of the mystery of Eq. (6.50) by looking again at the unit normal curve in Fig. 6.3 and asking what it is about the

---

[16]When Pythagoras's student Hippasus tried to calculate the value of $\sqrt{2}$, he found that he could not achieve the outcome as a fraction. The discovery rather shattered the elegant mathematical world of Pythagoras and his followers and we are told that Hippasus was drowned for his disturbing discovery. We can show $\sqrt{2}$ is irrational by stating that it *is* rational and hence can be expressed as $\sqrt{2} = a/b$ for some integers a and b. But then, $2 = a^2/b^2$, which is to say, $a^2 = 2b^2$. But $2b^2$ is necessarily even, which dictates that a^2 is even, and hence a is even. But if a is even, $a^2/2$ is even, in which case b^2 is even, and hence, b is even. So we can divide both a and b by 2, to give $\sqrt{2} = c/d$. But then c and d must both be even, etc. A nice example of a proof by *reductio ad absurdum*.

curve that *does* appear obvious or intuitive. We might agree that the slope or gradient of the curve at the center $x = 0$ is flat, which is to say, equal to zero, and that the curve also tends to such flatness at the extremes as x approaches $+/-$infinity. In other words, the incremental change in $p(x)$ — which we designate as $\Delta p(x)$ — divided by the corresponding small change in x — which we designate as Δx — approaches zero:

$$\frac{\Delta p(x)}{\Delta x} \to 0,$$

both as $x \to 0$ and as $p(x) \to 0$. With this insight, we can consider that the curve in Fig. 6.3 complies with

$$\frac{\Delta p(x)}{\Delta x} = -kxp(x), \tag{6.51}$$

for some constant k, since $\Delta p(x)/\Delta x$ then equals zero when $x = $ zero (the centre of the curve) and when $p(x)$ approaches zero (at the extreme end of the curve at $x = +/-$ infinity).[17]

We have the function of x on the right-hand side of Eq. (6.51) looking perhaps rather complicated as $xp(x)$. The trick is to isolate this complexity so that we can apply the insights of integration developed above. Thus, we write Eq. (6.51) as

$$\frac{\Delta p(x)}{p(x)} = -kx\Delta x. \tag{6.52}$$

We solve Eq. (6.52) by setting the left-hand side of the equation equal to $\Delta y(x)$ for some function of x, $y(x)$; and the right-hand side equal to $\Delta z(x)$ for some function of x, $z(x)$. That is, we have $\Delta y(x) = \Delta z(x)$, for which we may write

$$\Delta y(x) = \frac{\Delta p(x)}{p(x)} \tag{6.53}$$

---

[17]We have inserted the negative sign in Eq. (6.51) on account of that it is evident from Fig. 6.3 that the slope of the function $p(x)$ is negative (in other words, k is positive in Eq. (6.51)).

and

$$\Delta z(x) = -kx\Delta x. \tag{6.54}$$

We can write Eq. (6.53) as

$$\frac{\Delta y(x)}{\Delta p(x)} = \frac{1}{p(x)} \tag{6.55}$$

and Eq. (6.54) as

$$\frac{\Delta z(x)}{\Delta x} = -kx. \tag{6.56}$$

But applying what we know about the derivative of a log (Eqs. (6.39) and (6.40)), Eq. (6.55) provides

$$y(x) = \ln[p(x)] + \text{constant}, \tag{6.57}$$

while with Eqs. (6.27) and (6.28), Eq. (6.56) provides

$$z(x) = -\frac{k}{2}x^2 + \text{constant}. \tag{6.58}$$

We have $\Delta y(x) = \Delta z(x)$, which is to say, the rates of change of the functions $y(x)$ and $z(x)$ are equal. It follows that the functions themselves (Eqs. (6.57) and (6.58)) must be equal plus or minus a constant:

$$\ln[p(x)] = -\frac{k}{2}x^2 + \text{constant}. \tag{6.59}$$

Taking the exponential (e to the power) of both sides of the equation, we have (Eq. (6.16)):

$$p(x) = Ae^{-(k/2)x^2}, \tag{6.60}$$

for a constant A.

Equation (6.60) provides the basic structure of the full expression of Eq. (6.50). The requirement that the curve is centered on some mean, μ, not necessarily equal to zero and that the standard deviation is equal to σ for a specified σ, together with the requirement that the area under the curve $p(x)$ is 1, leads ultimately to the full expression for the probability function for the normal distribution as Eq. (6.50)[18]:

$$p(x) = \frac{1}{\sigma\sqrt{(2\pi)}} e^{-\frac{1}{2}[(x-\mu)/\sigma]^2}.$$

6.10. Portfolio Formation: Expected Returns, Standard Deviations (Variance), Covariance, Beta, and Correlation Coefficients

So that we might progress from a consideration of growth applied to a single asset to growth applied to a portfolio of assets, we introduce the concepts of *expected return, variance and standard deviation, covariance, beta, and correlation* from basic statistics. The concepts are explained by a simple example. Thus, let us consider that we have the forward-looking estimates for the annual return performances for the "Food & Drink" and "Mining" sectors given the future states of the economy as a "recession" (25% probability), "most-likely" (50% probability), or "boom" period (25% probability), as in Table 6.4.

6.10.1 *Expected return*

By the *expected* return, $E(R)$, for an asset or sector, we shall mean the sum of the possible outcome returns, $R_i(i = 1 \ldots N)$, each multiplied by its

---

[18]We have

$$p(x) = Ae^{-(k/2)x^2}. \tag{6.60}$$

However, we still need to determine the constants, k and A. We determine A by requiring that the integration under the curve $p(x) = Ae^{-(k/2)x^2}$ is equal to 1 (i.e., $\sum_{x=-\infty}^{+\infty} Ae^{-(k/2)x^2} \Delta x = 1$). The trick here is to consider that outcomes that are less likely as we move on the x-axis away from the origin can be refigured as outcomes that are less likely as we move *radially* away from the origin. It is this insight that leads to the requirement $A = \sqrt{[(k/(2\pi)]}$. We determine k by requiring that the standard deviation is equal to σ for a specified σ, which leads to $k = 1/\sigma^2$. Substituting these values in Eq. (6.60) gives

$$p(x) = \frac{1}{\sigma\sqrt{(2\pi)}} e^{-\frac{1}{2}(x/\sigma)^2}.$$

The requirement that the mean is equal to μ for a specified μ is achieved by a horizontal shift of the curve on the x-axis, which finally provides Eq. (6.50):

$$p(x) = \frac{1}{\sigma\sqrt{(2\pi)}} e^{-\frac{1}{2}[(x-\mu)/\sigma]^2}.$$

Dan Teague fills in the details at http://courses.ncssm.edu/math/Talks/PDFS/normal.pdf.

Table 6.4. Estimated outcome returns for Food & Drink and Mining Sectors (stylized).

Probability forecast	Estimated outcome returns for Food & Drink and Mining		
	Recession (25%)	Most likely (50%)	Boom (25%)
Food and Drink	6%	7%	8%
Mining	2%	12%	22%

probability, p_i, of occurrence:

$$E(R) \equiv p_1 R_1 + p_2 R_2 + p_3 R_3 + \cdots + p_N R_N$$

or with the summation, $\sum$, sign:

$$E(R) \equiv \sum_{i=1}^{N} p_i R_i. \tag{6.61}$$

Thus, the expected annual returns for the sectors are

$$E(R_{F\&D}) = 0.25(6)\% + 0.50(7)\% + 0.25(8)\% = 7\%$$

and

$$E(R_{Mng}) = 0.25(2)\% + 0.50(12)\% + 0.25(22)\% = 12\%.$$

6.10.2 *Variance and standard deviation*

By the *variance* of a range of outcomes, *VAR(R)*, we mean that we take the expected outcome for the range of outcomes — as calculated above, $E(R)$ — and from it, subtract each possible outcome and square the outcome difference. We then add together the possible squared outcomes where each is multiplied by the probability of that outcome occurring.[19] Thus,

$$VAR(R) \equiv \sum_{i=1}^{N} p_i [E(R_i) - R_i]^2. \tag{6.62}$$

---

[19] In Section 6.6, we introduced the concept of variance in relation to continuously distributed outcomes that are subject to a normal distribution, Eq. (6.20).

Thus, the variances of the forward–looking annual returns for the sectors are

$$VAR(R_{F\&D}) = 0.25(7-6)^2 + 0.5(7-7)^2 + 0.25(7-8)^2 = \underline{0.5}$$

and

$$VAR(R_{Mng}) = 0.25(12-2)^2 + 0.5(12-12)^2 + 0.25(12-22)^2 = \underline{50.0}.$$

By the *standard deviation* of a range of outcomes, $\sigma(R)$, we mean the square root of the variance of the range of outcomes:

$$\boxed{\sigma(R) \equiv \sqrt{VAR(R)}.} \tag{6.63}$$

And hence, of course:

$$VAR(R) = [\sigma(R)]^2. \tag{6.64}$$

Thus, the standard deviations of the forward-looking annual returns for the sectors are

$$\sigma(R_{F\&D}) = \sqrt{(0.5)} = \underline{0.707\%}$$

and

$$\sigma(R_{Mng}) = \sqrt{(50.0)} = \underline{7.071\%}.$$

6.10.3 *Covariance*

The covariance of returns for a pair of assets is a measure of how the returns on the assets co-vary or move together. The calculation is similar to variance calculation; but instead of squaring the difference between the value of each outcome return and the expected return for an individual asset, we calculate the product of this difference for two different assets. Thus, the covariance, $COV(R_{F\&D}, R_{Mng})$, between the returns for the food and drink ($F\&D$) and mining (Mng) sectors is defined as

$$\boxed{COV(R_{F\&D}, R_{Mng}) = \sum_{i=1}^{3} \left\{ p_i \left[E(R_{F\&D}) - R_{F\&D,i} \right] \left[E(R_{Mng}) - R_{Mng,i} \right] \right\}}$$

$$= 0.25(7-6)(12-2) + 0.50(7-7)(12-12)$$
$$+ 0.25(7-8)(12-22) = \underline{5.00}. \tag{6.65}$$

From Eq. (6.65), we can deduce the following properties of covariances:

(i) For any variable return, R_A, if the return R_C = constant, we have $COV(R_A, R_C) = 0$.

(ii) The covariance of a return with itself is the variance of that return:

$$COV(R_A, R_A) \equiv VAR(R_A).$$

(iii) $COV(R_A, R_B) \equiv COV(R_B, R_A)$.

(iv) The covariance of the returns on an asset, say, R_A, with the returns for a portfolio of assets is the sum of the covariances of the return, R_A, with the return, R_i, of each asset, i, in the portfolio, each covariance weighted by the proportional contribution of asset, i, in the portfolio. Thus, for example, the covariance of the return on the food & drink sector, $R_{F\&D}$, with the return on a portfolio, $R_{portfolio}$, that combines the food & drink and mining sectors in proportions $\omega_{F\&D}$ and $\omega_{Mng}(\omega_{F\&D} + \omega_{Mng} = 1)$ is determined with Eq. (6.65) as

$$COV(R_{F\&D}, R_{portfolio})$$

$$= \sum_{i=1}^{3} \{p_i[E(R_{F\&D}) - R_{F\&D,i}][E(R_{portfolio}) - R_{portfolio,i}]\}$$

$$= \sum_{i=1}^{3} \{p_i[E(R_{F\&D}) - R_{F\&D,i}][\omega_{F\&D}E(R_{F\&D})$$

$$+ \omega_{mng}E(R_{Mng}) - \omega_{F\&D}R_{F\&D,i} - \omega_{mng}R_{Mng,i}]\}.$$

And hence, we see that

$$COV(R_{F\&D}, R_{portfolio})$$

$$= \omega_{F\&D}COV(R_{F\&D}, R_{F\&D}) + \omega_{Mng}COV(R_{F\&D}, R_{Mng}),$$

which confirms property (*iv*) above, and which with property (*ii*) provides

$$\boxed{COV(R_{F\&D}, R_{portfolio}) = \omega_{F\&D}VAR(R_{F\&D}) + \omega_{Mng}COV(R_{F\&D}, R_{Mng})}$$

and similarly: (6.66)

$$\boxed{COV(R_{Mng}, R_{portfolio}) = \omega_{Mng}VAR(R_{Mng}) + \omega_{F\&D}COV(R_{F\&D}, R_{Mng}).}$$

6.10.4 *Variance of portfolio returns*

The variance of the portfolio return is the sum of all pairs of covariances between the portfolio asset returns, each weighted by the product proportions of the asset pairs in the portfolio. To see this, consider that we form a portfolio with a proportion $\omega_{F\&D}$ allocated to the food & drink sector and the remaining proportion ω_{Mng} allocated to the mining sector. We then have the variance of the portfolio from the definition as Eq. (6.62) as

$$VAR(R_{portfolio})$$

$$\equiv \sum_{i=1}^{3} \left\{ p_i \left[E(R_{portfolio}) - R_{portfolio,i} \right]^2 \right\}$$

$$= \sum_{i=1}^{3} \left\{ p_i \left[\omega_{F\&D} E(R_{F\&D}) + \omega_{mng} E(R_{Mng}) \right. \right.$$

$$\left. \left. - \omega_{F\&D} R_{F\&D,i} - \omega_{mng} R_{Mng,i} \right]^2 \right\}$$

$$= \omega_{F\&D}\omega_{F\&D} COV(R_{F\&D}, R_{F\&D}) + \omega_{Mng}\omega_{Mng} COV(R_{Mng}, R_{Mng})$$

$$+ \omega_{F\&D}\omega_{Mng} COV(R_{F\&D}, R_{Mng}) + \omega_{Mng}\omega_{F\&D} COV(R_{Mng}, R_{F\&D}),$$

which with properties (*ii*) and (*iii*) above provides

$$VAR(R_{portfolio})$$
$$= \omega_{F\&D}^2 VAR(R_{F\&D}) + \omega_{Mng}^2 VAR(R_{Mng}) \qquad (6.67)$$
$$+ 2\omega_{F\&D}\omega_{Mng} COV(R_{F\&D}, R_{Mng}).$$

A comparison of Eqs. (6.66) and (6.67) shows that we can express the variance of the portfolio alternatively as

$$VAR(R_{portfolio}) = \omega_{F\&D} COV(R_{F\&D}, R_{portfolio})$$
$$+ \omega_{Mng} COV(R_{Mng}, R_{portfolio}), \qquad (6.68)$$

which is to say, the variance of a portfolio's returns is the weighted sum (by portfolio proportion) of each asset's covariance of returns with the portfolio return.

If we invest in a portfolio that includes the food & drink and mining sectors in combination with a *risk-free* asset, we would have

$$E(R_{portfolio}) = \omega_{Mng}E(R_{Mng}) + \omega_{F\&D}E(R_{F\&D})$$
$$+ (1 - \omega_{Mng} - \omega_{F\&D})r_f \qquad (6.69)$$

and with property (*i*) above, the above expressions for $COV(R_{F\&D}, R_{portfolio})$ and $COV(R_{Mng}, R_{portfolio})$ (Eq. (6.66)) and $VAR(R_{portfolio})$ (Eqs. (6.67) and (6.68)) *remain formally unchanged* (the only difference is that by allocating a proportion $1 - \omega_{Mng} - \omega_{F\&D}$ of the portfolio to the risk-free asset, we have $\omega_{Mng} + \omega_{F\&D}$ less than ($<$) 1).

6.10.5 *An example with normal distribution tables*

In Section 6.7, given estimates of a stock's mean or drift return, μ, and standard deviation, σ, we were able to apply Table 6.1 to provide probabilities for an asset's outcome return within a specific range. We can now provide similar estimates, not just for a single asset knowing its attributes, but for a portfolio of such assets.

As an example, suppose we invest: 50% in the food & drink sector, 40% in the mining sector, and 10% in a risk-free asset (with return $= 5\%$).

We have (with Eq. (6.69), and the above values):

$$E(R_{portfolio}) = 0.50(7\%) + 0.40(12\%) + 0.1(5\%) = \underline{8.80\%}$$

and (with Eq. (6.67), and the above derived determinations for $VAR(R_{F\&D})$, $VAR(R_{Mng})$ and $COV(R_{F\&D}, R_{Mng})$, p. 108):

$$VAR(R_{portfolio}) = 0.50^2(0.5) + 0.40^2(50.0) + 2(0.50)(0.40)(5.00)$$
$$= \underline{10.125}.$$

And, hence (with Eq. (6.63)):

$$\sigma(R_{portfolio}) = \sqrt{(10.125)} = \underline{3.182\%}.$$

Provided we can allow that the outcome returns are normally distributed, we are now in a position to apply Fig. 6.3 and Table 6.1.

For example, we can say that the probability is 68.26% that our portfolio return in the following year will lie between

$$8.80 - 3.182 \quad \text{and} \quad 8.80 + 3.182,$$

that is, between 5.618% and 11.982%; and the probability is 95% that the portfolio return will lie between

$$8.80 - 1.96(3.182) \quad \text{and} \quad 8.80 + 1.96(3.182),$$

that is, between approximately 2.56% and 15.04%.

6.10.6   *Beta*

The beta of an asset has been defined as the sensitivity of the asset's return to the market's return. More formally, we define the beta, β_A, of an asset, A, in relation to a portfolio, as the asset's contribution to the variance of the portfolio's returns; which is to say as the covariance of that asset's returns with the returns of the portfolio divided by the variance of the portfolio's returns. Thus,

$$\beta_A \equiv \frac{COV(R_A, R_{portfolio})}{VAR(R_{portfolio})}. \tag{6.70}$$

We have from Eq. (6.66)

$$COV(R_{F\&D}, R_{portfolio}) = \omega_{F\&D}VAR(R_{F\&D}) + \omega_{Mng}COV(R_{F\&D}, R_{Mng}),$$

$$COV(R_{Mng}, R_{portfolio}) = \omega_{Mng}VAR(R_{Mng}) + \omega_{F\&D}COV(R_{F\&D}, R_{Mng}).$$

Thus with the values for a portfolio comprising 50% in the food and drink sector, 40% in the mining sector, and 10% in the risk-free rate, in Sections 6.10.2 and 6.10.3 (p. 108) we have

$$COV(R_{F\&D}, R_{portfolio}) = 0.5(0.5) + 0.4(5.00) = 2.25,$$

$$COV(R_{Mng}, R_{portfolio}) = 0.4(50.0) + 0.5(5.00) = 22.50.$$

And, thus (with Eq. (6.70), and the portfolio variance value as 10.125 from Section 6.10.5 (p. 111)).

$$\beta_{F\&D} = \frac{2.25}{10.125} = 0.222,$$

$$\beta_{Mng} = \frac{22.50}{10.125} = 2.222.$$

From the definition of beta (Eq. (6.70)), it follows that the weighted sum by capital contribution of the betas of a portfolio is always equal to 1.0. We can see that this is so with Eq. (6.68):

$$VAR(R_{portfolio}) = \omega_{F\&D}COV(R_{F\&D}, R_{portfolio})$$
$$+ \omega_{Mng}COV(R_{Mng}, R_{portfolio}),$$

by dividing throughout by $VAR(R_{portfolio})$. We then have

$$1 = \omega_{F\&D}\frac{COV(R_{F\&D}, R_{portfolio})}{VAR(R_{portfolio})} + \omega_{Mng}\frac{COV(R_{Mng}, R_{portfolio})}{VAR(R_{portfolio})}.$$

With the definition of beta (Eq. (6.70)), the right-hand side of the equation is the weighted sum of the asset betas in the portfolio (the beta of the risk-free rate is zero). Therefore

$$\sum_{i=1}^{N} \omega_i \beta_i = 1. \tag{6.71}$$

Thus, for the above example, we have

$$\beta_{portfolio} = 0.5\beta_{F\&D} + 0.4\beta_{Mng}$$
$$= 0.5(0.222) + 0.4(2.222) = 1.0.$$

6.10.7 *Correlation*

An additional useful concept is that of the *correlation* between return outcomes. We can illustrate by considering the correlation between the returns for the food & drink and mining sectors, $CORR_{F\&D,Mng}$. The correlation between two sets of possible returns is calculated by taking the covariance between the two return outcomes, $COV(R_{F\&D}, R_{Mmg})$, as above, and dividing by the product of the standard deviations of the two returns. Thus:

$$CORR_{F\&D,Mng} \equiv \frac{COV(R_{F\&D}, R_{Mng})}{\sigma_{F\&D}\sigma_{Mng}}. \tag{6.72}$$

Clearly, we have the property that

$$CORR_{F\&D,Mng} = CORR_{Mng,F\&D}.$$

Thus, we calculate the correlation coefficient between the food & drink and mining sectors (with the above standard deviation values, p. 108), $CORR_{F\&D,Mng}$, as

$$CORR_{F\&D,Mng} = \frac{5}{(0.707)(7.071)} = 1.0,$$

which expresses the fact that the outcome returns for the food & drink and mining sectors in the above example move in lockstep (Table 6.4: $R_{F\&D}$: 6%, 7%, 8%, corresponding with R_{Mng}: 2%, 12%, 22%, respectively). More precisely, there is an exact *linear* relation between the returns for the food & drink and mining sectors, which in this case is expressed as

$$R_{F\&D} = 5.8 + 0.1R_{Mng}.$$

In effect, the return on either the food & drink or mining sectors determines the return on the other sector. Similarly, if the relation between the two sectors had been a negative linear relation ($R_{F\&D}$: 6%, 7%, 8%, corresponding with R_{Mng}: 22%, 12%, 2%, respectively), so that we have

$$R_{F\&D} = 8.2 - 0.1R_{Mng},$$

we would have calculated the correlation coefficient between the returns on the two assets as -1. Thus, the correlation coefficient must always have a value between -1 and $+1$. If in Table 6.4, the return on the mining sector in a boom period had been set equal to 2% (while maintaining the other entries as in the table), we would have calculated a correlation coefficient between the two sets of returns as exactly zero (since, in this case, we have the outcome that a 1% change in return for the food & drink sector can correspond with *either* a $+10\%$ *or* a -10% change in the return for the mining sector).

6.11. The Central Limit Theorem

When a set of numbers has mean (μ) and variance (*VAR*), the mean and variance of the *addition* of random pairs from the set (with replacement of the initial selection) are, respectively, 2μ and $2VAR$. To see this, consider the (randomly chosen) numbers:

$$2, 4, 6, 20,$$

each with equal probability of being drawn. The mean of these numbers (with Eq. (6.61)) $= 1/4 \, (2+4+6+20) = \underline{8}$ and the variance is accordingly determined (with Eq. (6.62)) as

$$\frac{1}{4}\left\{(8-2)^2 + (8-4)^2 + (8-6)^2 + (8-20)^2\right\} = \underline{50}.$$

A combination of two drawings provides the possible outcomes as follows (with equal probability):

$$
\begin{array}{llll}
4[2+2] & 6[2+4] & 8[2+6] & 22[2+20] \\
6[4+2] & 8[4+4] & 10[4+6] & 24[4+20] \\
8[6+2] & 10[6+4] & 12[6+6] & 26[6+20] \\
22[20+2] & 24[20+4] & 26[20+6] & 40[20+20],
\end{array}
$$

for which (i.e., for 4, 6, 8, 22, 6, 8, 10, 24, 8, 10, 12, 26, 22, 24, 26, 40) the mean and variance are, respectively, 16 and 100 (standard deviation = 10). And we note that these outcomes (16 and 100) are, respectively, twice the mean (8) and twice the variance (50) of the two sets of numbers from which they have been constructed as pairs (i.e., 2, 4, 6, 20). (And, thus, the standard deviation of the pairs (10) is $\sqrt{2}$ times the standard deviation of the original set $(\sqrt{50}) = 7.071$.)

Generalizing, we can say that the mean of the addition of two outcomes from different sets A and B, $\mu(A + B)$, is determined as

$$\boxed{\mu(A + B) = \mu(A) + \mu(B),} \tag{6.73}$$

where $\mu(A)$ and $\mu(B)$ are, respectively, the mean of sets A and B. Equation (6.73) is consistent with Eq. (6.61). Consistent with Eq. (6.67) (with Eq. (6.72)), the variance (*VAR*) of such addition is determined as

$$VAR(A + B) = VAR(A) + VAR(B) + 2\sigma(A)\sigma(B)CORR_{A,B}, \qquad (6.74)$$

where $CORR_{A,B}$ is the correlation coefficient between the first drawing and the second drawing. In the above example, the two selections are drawn *independently* from the *same* set (the selected drawing of the first number give us no information as the drawing of the second number), and hence we have both $CORR_{A,B} = 0$ and $VAR(A) = VAR(B)$. In this case, Eq. (6.73) tells us that the mean of the sum of the two selections is twice the sample mean, and Eq. (6.74) tells us that the variance of the sum of the two selections is twice the sample variance. This is what we demonstrated above.

Further generalizing from our example, if we were to make combinations of N numbers from the set of 2, 4, 6, 20 (with replacement), and calculate their addition, the mean of the additions would be equal to N times the mean of the set (2, 4, 6, 20) and the variance of the additions would be equal to N times the variance of the set (2, 4, 6, 20). Accordingly, the standard deviation of the additions would be equal to $\sqrt{N}$ times the standard deviation of the set. For example, if we were to randomly make combinations of 100 selections (with replacement) from the set 2, 4, 6, 20, the mean addition, μ, of the combinations would have a value $= 100$ times the mean of 2, 4, 6, 20 $(=8) = 800$ with standard deviation $\sigma = \sqrt{100} (=10)$ times the standard deviation of 2, 4, 6, 20 $(=\sqrt{50} = 7.071) = 70.71$.

However, while many combinations of 100 selections are likely to cluster around the value, 800, we expect to encounter decreasing numbers of combinations that add to numbers increasingly removed from 800. Thus, it is possible (but unlikely) to have a combination of 100 selections whose addition is as high as 2,000 — this number can only be attained by selecting the value 20 in each of our 100 selections. Similarly, it is possible (but unlikely) to have a combination that provides an addition as low as 200 — which can only be attained by selecting the value 2 as each of our 100 selections. Due to symmetry, we can imagine that the gradient of the probability distribution will be as in Fig. 6.4; which is to say, it is flat at the mean and will tend to flatten to zero as we approach increasingly less likely (high and low) combinations of the numbers away from the mean. In other words, we can visualize that the distribution of 100 combinations is *normally* distributed with mean $(\mu) = 800$ ($100 \times$ mean outcome of a single drawing) and standard deviation $= 70.71$ ($\sqrt{100}\times$ the standard deviation of the outcome of a single drawing). This is *the central limit theorem*, or *law of large numbers*.

6.12. The Binomial Representation of Normally Distributed Exponential Growth Rates

Consider that an asset grows exponentially over a short interval with *either* rate $\mu + \sigma$ or rate $\mu - \sigma$ with equal probability. Thus, from an initial wealth investment, W_0, the up-wealth outcome, S_u, and down-wealth outcome, S_d, are determined, respectively, as

$$\boxed{S_u = W_0 e^{\mu + \sigma} \quad \text{and} \quad S_d = W_0 e^{\mu - \sigma},} \tag{6.75}$$

which is represented in Fig. 6.7.

The outcomes in Fig. 6.7 represent a *binomial* distribution in that only two possible exponential growth rates are allowed. In this case, we have:

the mean of $\mu + \sigma \quad$ and $\quad \mu - \sigma = \mu$

and

the standard deviation of $\mu + \sigma \quad$ and $\quad \mu - \sigma = \sigma$.[20]

Thus, Fig. 6.7 represents binomial exponential growth over the interval with a mean rate, μ, and standard deviation, σ.

$\$ W_0$

$\$W_0 e^{\mu + \sigma}$

$\$W_0 e^{\mu - \sigma}$

Figure 6.7. Exponential binomial growth outcomes.

---

[20]This follows (with Eq. (6.62)) as $\sqrt{\{0.5[\mu - (\mu + \sigma)]^2 + 0.5[\mu - (\mu - \sigma)]^2\}} = \sigma$.

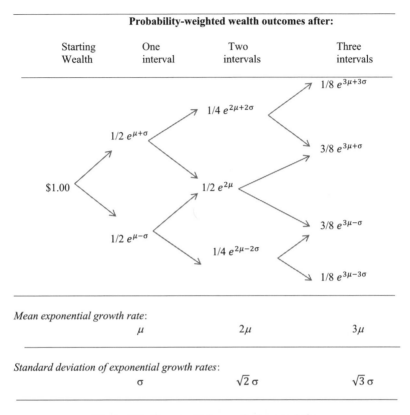

	Probability-weighted wealth outcomes after:		
Starting Wealth	One interval	Two intervals	Three intervals

Mean exponential growth rate:

| | μ | 2μ | 3μ |

Standard deviation of exponential growth rates:

| | σ | $\sqrt{2}\,\sigma$ | $\sqrt{3}\,\sigma$ |

Figure 6.8. Exponential growth charcteristics.

Successive applications of the growth process of Fig. 6.7 are represented in Fig. 6.8. With Eq. (6.1) as

$$e^{\mu+/-\sigma} \cdot e^{\mu+/-\sigma} \cdot e^{\mu+/-\sigma} \cdots = e^{\sum \mu+/-\sigma+\mu+/-\sigma+\mu+/-\sigma+\cdots},$$

we can see that successive drawings of the exponential growth rate as either $\mu+\sigma$ or $\mu-\sigma$ are *additive*. In other words, in Fig. 6.8, the outcome growth rate of the process over N intervals is the summation of N random selections from the set $(\mu + \sigma, \mu - \sigma)$. In this case, the central limit theorem tells us that the outcome distribution of the binomial exponential growth rates after N intervals (large N) is *normally* distributed with

$$\boxed{\text{mean} = N\mu} \tag{6.76}$$

and

$$\boxed{\text{standard deviation} = \sqrt{N}\sigma,} \qquad (6.77)$$

where μ and σ, respectively, are the mean and standard deviation of the process over a single interval as in Fig. 6.7.

As an example, consider that the distributed outcomes at the end of the second interval in Fig. 6.8 are determined as

$$e^{2\mu+2\sigma} \text{ with probability } \frac{1}{4},$$

$$e^{2\mu} \text{ with probability } \frac{1}{2}, \text{ and}$$

$$e^{2\mu-2\sigma} \text{ with probability } \frac{1}{4}.$$

Thus, the mean exponential return outcome at the end of the second interval (with Eq. (6.61)) is

$$\frac{1}{4}(2\mu + 2\sigma) + \frac{1}{2}(2\mu) + \frac{1}{4}(2\mu - 2\sigma) = 2\mu,$$

which is consistent with Eq. (6.76); with standard deviation determined (with Eqs. (6.62) and (6.63)) as

$$\sqrt{\left\{ \frac{1}{4}[(2\mu + 2\sigma) - 2\mu]^2 + \frac{1}{2}[(2\mu) - 2\mu]^2 \right.}$$
$$\left. + \frac{1}{4}[(2\mu - 2\sigma) - 2\mu]^2 \right\}} = \sqrt{2}\sigma,$$

which is consistent with Eq. (6.77). Progressively, for the third interval, the mean exponential return outcome is 3μ with standard deviation determined as $\sqrt{3}\sigma$, and so on.

With the insight of Eqs. (6.76) and (6.77), we can see that we can generalize Eq. (6.22):

$$P_{t+1} = P_t e^{\mu+Z\sigma},$$

to provide the relation between the price of an asset, P_{t+N} following N intervals of time from its price, P_t, at time t, as

$$P_{t+N} = P_t e^{N\mu + \sqrt{N}Z\sigma}, \tag{6.78}$$

where μ is the asset's mean exponential growth rate over each time interval, σ is the per interval standard deviation about such rate, and Z is normally distributed with mean zero and unit standard deviation.

Alternatively, in reverse, the central limit theorem tells us that if, over a period, an asset is subject to normally distributed exponential grow rates with mean rate μ^* and standard deviation about such mean σ^*, the process can be modeled as in Fig. 6.8 by setting

$$\mu = \mu^*/N \tag{6.79}$$

and

$$\text{standard deviation } \sigma = \sigma^*/\sqrt{N}, \tag{6.80}$$

over a large number N of sub intervals of the period.

In Fig. 6.8, the exponential rate over a sufficiently long period of time, can ultimately vary between $-\infty$ and $+\infty$. Nevertheless, *price* outcomes are constrained to move between zero and $+\infty$ (on account of that whereas $p_0 e^{-\infty} = 0$, we have $p_0 e^{+\infty} = \infty$). Thus, as an example of exponential growth, consider Fig. 6.7 with $\mu = 0$ and $\sigma = 0.693147$ per interval, as depicted in Fig. 6.9. We then have $e^{0.693147} = 2$ and $e^{-0.693147} = \frac{1}{2}$.[21] In this case, the asset value either doubles or halves over each interval, with the result that the outcome price is unbounded above but is bounded below by zero, as depicted in Fig. 6.10.

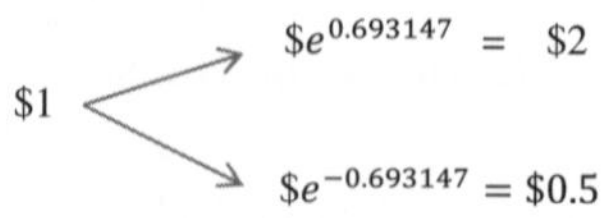

$$\$1 \begin{cases} \nearrow & \$e^{0.693147} = \$2 \\ \searrow & \$e^{-0.693147} = \$0.5 \end{cases}$$

Figure 6.9. Exponential binomial growth outcomes.

---

[21]This is an example of Eq. (6.4): if $e^{+X} = N$, then $e^{-X} = 1/N$.

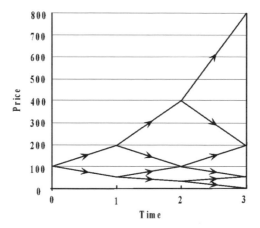

Figure 6.10. Price outcomes of exponential growth (as depicted in Fig. 6.8). The outcome pattern is of possible prices when an asset commences with a value of $100 and proceeds to either double or halve its value over each interval.

6.13. Time to Reflect: What Have We Learned?

In the following chapters of this text, we seek to address the question: To what extent does the mathematics of growth, as outlined in the present chapter, provide an essential recognition and understanding of asset price formation? If, for example, we assume that asset prices are subject to normally distributed exponential growth rates, the pattern of growth possibilities can be represented as in Figs. 6.8 and 6.10 for some mean, μ and standard deviation, σ. The mathematics of normal distributions can then be brought to bear on asset pricing with some force. For example, as was observed in Section 6.10.5, the possible outcomes for portfolio selections may be predicted with well-defined confidence intervals. Our enquiry over the following chapters will therefore be that of clarifying when the model of Fig. 6.8 appears to be applicable as well as inapplicable to our experience of stock markets.

Chapter 7

The Statistical Growth of Asset Portfolios

When you're first thinking through an idea, it's important not to get bogged down in complexity. Thinking simply and clearly is hard to do.

Richard Branson

The concept of a general equilibrium has no relevance to the real world (in other words, classical economics is an exercise in futility).

George Soros

Truth is to be found in the simplicity, and not in the multiplicity and confusion of things.

Isaac Newton

The teacher who is indeed wise does not bid you to enter the house of his wisdom but rather leads you to the threshold of your mind.

Klalil Gibran

7.1. Introduction[1]

This chapter considers the nature of asset growth that is subject to normally distributed compounding growth rates. As such, the model represents a straightforward development of Chapter 6. Nevertheless, the mathematical development is able to shed light on the economy — and the market of asset claims on the economy — as an organic process of growth and decline; the small firm size effect in the Fama and French three-factor (FF-3F) model; and reported observations that portfolios of stocks with high individual volatility appear to outperform the market.

The chapter is arranged as follows. Section 7.2 considers the case for a normal distribution as an acceptable model of asset price formation.

---

[1]This chapter develops ideas that were presented in the journal *Financial Analyst Journal* (Dempsey, 2002). I am indeed grateful and indebted to the editors and reviewers of this journal for supporting and publishing this work notwithstanding its unorthodoxy.

Section 7.3 considers the essential mathematical implications of normally distributed growth rates, before Section 7.4 adapts the findings for asset price formation. Section 7.5 progresses to consider the implications of normally distributed continuously compounding growth rates for the small firm size effect in the FF-3F model, before a final section, Section 7.6, concludes with a discussion.[2]

7.2. Normally Distributed Growth Rates as a Foundation for Asset Price Formation

When the philosopher Réne Descartes wished to build his philosophy of knowledge on a foundation that could not be disputed, he arrived, by a process of continually questioning backwards from any supposition he made, at *I think therefore I am*. The very act of doubting one's own existence, he argued, serves to establish the reality of one's own existence, or at least of one's thought. In Latin, *Cogito ergo sum*, or as he actually first wrote it in French, *je pense, donc je suis*.[3] In seeking the same for finance, we are prompted to ask how we might commence an understanding of asset price formation and growth from such a reliable foundation.

In nature, the growth response, of an organism's population (of flies, or locusts, or bacteria, etc.) does not hold still for a month or a year, and then review the past to determine how it must respond. Rather, the process of growth and decline is continuous in occurring from the position of that organism's ever-updated population.

Such continuously compounding growth was captured for our bank deposit in Chapter 6.4 (p. 78) by applying a growth rate $x\%$ per period as $(x/100)/N$ over many N sub-intervals, which with large N was identified as the growth factor e^x per period. However, such continuously compounding growth fails to capture organic growth in one most essential

---

[2]Equations that are referenced in subsequent chapters are bordered.

[3]I know this because I once tried it as a chat-up line in a French nightclub (I don't speak very much French): Without success, by the way. My niece actually offered me the following, "How much does a polar bear weigh?" "I don't know, how much *does* a polar bear weigh?" "About a ton. That should be enough to break the ice. How would you like to come home with me?" Which I now couple with my other standby: "What winks and makes love like a tiger?" "I don't know, what *does* wink and make love like a tiger?" At which point I try winking at the girl. Hmm, maybe I am getting too old for this kind of thing.

manner: Whereas the bank deposit growth was assumed to be riskless, in nature, very little is riskless. The exponential growth of our organism *can vary.*

Even in chaos, however, nature typically enforces a form of stability. Thus, nature tends to insist that the greater the deviation of the rate of growth or decline from the mean, or expected growth rate, μ, the *less* likely it is to occur. As we saw in Chapter 6.6, the *normal* probability distribution identifies such a process, as captured by the growth rate, μ and standard deviation, σ, of possible growth outcomes about μ.

As observed in Chapter 6.11, the central limit theorem implies that repeated independent sampling from a distribution (with replacement) leads to a *normal distribution* of outcomes. Thus, if stock price movements occur as new information is forthcoming, with independent impacts accumulating to update the stock price in an unforeseen manner, we must anticipate that stock returns are normally distributed. The assumption that such a process represents at least an approximation of stock price movements has been justified based on the evidence of past stock price performance (for example, Fama, 1976, Chapter 2).

We must bear in mind, however, that in accepting the normal distribution as indicative of stock price growth formation, a key assumption is that each updating of the stock price is *independent* from either previous or subsequent updates. If stock prices are subject to cascades of either euphoria or pessimism, leading to self-fuelling price movements, the assumption of independent stock prices changes is violated. Studies in fact indicate that stock returns are more accurately described as exhibiting leptokurtosis, meaning that values of the exponential growth rate, x, both near to the mean and highly divergent from the mean appear more likely than predicted by a normal distribution for x (Jackwerth and Rubinstein, 1996). Such leptokurtosis is consistent with recognition that the market is prone to periods of self-generated growths and declines, with the outcome that the volatility of stock prices is unstable through time.

Nevertheless, in developing the present chapter's arguments, we shall, for the present, hold to the simplifying assumption that stock price changes are independent in time and that the volatility or standard deviation, σ, of stock returns is fixed in time. The reality of "bubbles" and "bursts" will, however, concern us in subsequent chapters.

7.3.   The Mathematics of Normally Distributed Growth Rates

As observed in Eq. (6.22) (p. 92), when an asset is subject to normally distributed exponential growth rates, the unknown outcome at the end of a period can be expressed as the asset value $\$X_0$ at the commencement of the period multiplied by e^y, where $y = \mu + Z\sigma$:

> The end-of-the-period outcome of investing $\$X_0$
>
> at the commencement of the period $= \$X_0 e^{\mu + Z\sigma}$,

where μ represents the underlying mean or drift exponential growth rate for the period with standard deviation σ, and Z represents a stochastic (random) drawing from $-\infty$ to $+\infty$ with probability determined by the unit normal distribution in Fig. 6.3 (p. 85).

For such growth, we now define a key concept of return, namely, the "exponential growth rate per period", R, by

$$\$X_0 e^R \equiv \text{expected wealth outcome of investing } \$X_0 \\ \text{for a single period} \tag{7.1}$$

or, alternatively (with Eq. (6.15), p. 82) as

$$R \equiv \ln [\text{expected wealth outcome of investing \$1 for a single period}] \tag{7.2}$$

where ln represents the natural log function. If returns are distributed with drift or mean growth rate, μ, and standard deviation, σ, we might expect that R must be equal to μ. Intriguingly, however, this is not the case. In fact, we have the statistical relation[4]:

$$R = \mu + \frac{1}{2}\sigma^2. \tag{7.3}$$

To see why Eq. (7.3) is so, consider a binomial process as represented in Fig. 6.9 (p. 120), which represents a $1 investment that can grow with

---

[4]On substituting the definitions for R (Eq. (7.2)), μ, and σ, in Eq. (7.3), Eq. (7.3) may alternatively be expressed: ln[expected wealth outcome] = expected value of [ln(wealth outcome)] + $\frac{1}{2}$ variance of [ln(wealth outcome)].

equal probabilities to $e^{0.693147} = 2$ or $e^{-0.693147} = \frac{1}{2}$. We then have (with Eq. (6.61), p. 107):

$$\mu = \text{(for 0.69315 and } -0.69315) = 0$$

and (with Eqs. (6.62) and (6.63), p. 107–108):

$$\sigma \text{ (for 0.69315 and } -0.69315) = 0.69315.$$

Since $e^{0.69315} = 2$, whereas $e^{-0.69315} = \frac{1}{2}$, the expected outcome (of the \$1 investment) is $\$(2 + \frac{1}{2})/2 = \$1.25$, which implies (Eq. (7.2)): $R = \ln(1.25) = 0.2231$, or 22.31%.

Notwithstanding that Eq. (7.3) applies to a normal distribution (as opposed to the binomial distribution of Fig. 6.9), it is instructive to apply:

$$R = \mu + \frac{1}{2}\sigma^2,$$

to the above binomial example. We then have

$$R = 0 + \frac{1}{2}0.69315^2$$
$$= 0.2402 \quad \text{or} \quad 24.02\%,$$

which is not such a bad estimate of the value for R in the binomial example (22.31%, above).

Alternatively, we can see how Eq. (7.3) comes about algebraically by expressing the exponential growth rate, R, that delivers the expected wealth outcome in Fig. 6.7 (p. 117) as

$$\$e^R = \$[e^{\mu+\sigma} + e^{\mu-\sigma}]/2. \tag{7.4}$$

With Eq. (6.11) (p. 78), we express Eq. (7.4) as

$$\$e^R = \$\left[1 + \mu + \sigma + \frac{1}{2}(\mu + \sigma)^2 + \cdots + 1\right.$$
$$\left. + \mu - \sigma + \frac{1}{2}(\mu - \sigma)^2 + \cdots\right]/2$$
$$= \$\left(1 + \mu + \frac{1}{2}\mu^2 + \frac{1}{2}\sigma^2 + \cdots\right). \tag{7.5}$$

Allowing that the binomial representation captures the exponential process over small time intervals, the exponential growth rate, μ, and standard deviation, σ, in Eq. (7.4) relate to the exponential return, μ^*, and standard deviation, σ^*, for the actual duration as $\mu = \mu^*/N$ and $\sigma = \sigma^*/\sqrt{N}$, respectively, for large N (Eqs. (6.79) and (6.80), p. 120). Thus, in Eq. (7.5), in the limit of continuous growth rates (large N), we are justified in dropping the $\frac{1}{2}\mu^2$ term (which diminishes as $1/N^2$), while maintaining the $\frac{1}{2}\sigma^2$ term (which diminishes as $1/N$). Similarly, allowing that R also diminishes as $1/N$, we have for large N:

$$e^R \simeq 1 + R. \tag{7.6}$$

And, hence, in the limit of a small time interval, Eq. (7.4) is expressed:

$$1 + R = 1 + \mu + \frac{1}{2}\sigma^2,$$

which is Eq. (7.3).

7.4. The Outcome of Normally Distributed Growth Rates

Investors assess stock prices not in terms of their potential exponential growth characteristics, but in terms of their "expected periodic return", by which we mean the expected percentage increase in wealth generated over some *discrete* period (a month, a year). Such return is expressed:

expected periodic return $\equiv$ [expected wealth outcome of investing

$$X_0 \text{ for a single period} - X_0]/X_0, \tag{7.7}$$

where X_0 is the initial investment. In order to generalize the relationship between the above *periodic* return — which is to say, the "surface" return that market participants seek to measure — and the "sub-surface" *continuously applied* parameters μ and σ (which generate the surface periodic return), we combine Eqs. (7.1) and (7.7):

$$1 + \text{expected periodic return} \equiv e^R. \tag{7.8}$$

Equation (7.8) (with Eq. (7.3)) then provides

$$1 + \text{expected periodic return} = e^{\mu + \frac{1}{2}\sigma^2}, \tag{7.9}$$

or (with Eq. (6.11))

$$
\boxed{\text{expected periodic return} \simeq \mu + \frac{1}{2}\sigma^2.}
\qquad (7.10)
$$

Since $\frac{1}{2}\sigma^2$ is necessarily positive, Eq. (7.10) is the statement that the volatility of returns (σ) in an exponential growth process acts to *increase* the expected periodic return. This is in contra-distinction with classical Markowitz (1952) portfolio theory, which holds that random variations in a portfolio must tend to *cancel* with each outer.

7.5. Normally Distributed Growth Rates and the Small Firm Size Effect in the FF-3F Model

It is possible that the additional term $\frac{1}{2}\sigma^2$ in Eq. (7.10) adds significantly to a portfolio's returns. For example, Malkiel and Xu (1997) construct portfolios as a function of the time-varying idiosyncratic volatility (the volatility of stocks that does not relate to market movements) of the portfolio's stocks measured individually. Their average annual returns range from a low of close to 12% for the portfolio with the lowest idiosyncratic volatility (5% per month) to a high close to 19% for the portfolio with the highest idiosyncratic volatility (13% per month).

The outcome is considered by Malkiel and Xu as "surprising". This is because the conventional view holds that the idiosyncratic or non-market movement of stocks within a large portfolio of stocks should cancel out by diversification. This would be the case if discrete positive deviations from the expected mean return are equally likely as discrete negative deviations.

However, as captured by Eq. (7.10), if exponential — as opposed to discrete — returns are distributed symmetrically about a mean, μ, we do not have diversification in the sense of cancelling of overall effects. Rather, the periodic return benefits from the diversification of outcome returns as $\frac{1}{2}\sigma^2$ where σ is the standard deviation of the individual asset outcomes in the portfolio. Thus, with Eq. (7.9), an idiosyncratic volatility of asset returns of 5% per month contributes $e^{\frac{1}{2}0.05^2} - 1 = 0.125\%$ to the expected monthly periodic return of a portfolio of such assets (annualized $= 1.50\%$), while an idiosyncratic volatility of asset returns of 13% per month, contributes $e^{\frac{1}{2}0.13^2} - 1 = 0.85\%$ to the expected monthly periodic return (annualized $= 10.20\%$). The difference of 8.7% ($10.20\% - 1.50\%$) is actually greater than Malkiel and Xu's measured difference of 7% ($19\% - 12\%$).

Malkiel and Xu observe further that the volatility of their stocks is correlated closely with the inverse of their firm size. They note thereby that their results are consistent with the FF-3F model of Chapter 3, which predicts that portfolios of smaller firms provide rates of return that are greater than the returns from portfolios of larger firms. Thus, the small firm size effect of the FF-3F model is, on the face of it, explained by the statistical attributes of a normal distribution. However, our interpretation of the small firm size effect is vastly different from that of Fama and French, in that Eq. (7.10) interprets the additional small firm size return *not* as the outcome of investors "setting prices" in accordance with risk-return expectations, but rather as a straightforward statistical outcome of the idiosyncratic price movements of assets themselves.

7.6. Time for Reflection: What Have We Learned?

We have considered asset growth as subject to normally distributed continuously compounding growth rates. With no additional assumptions, the mathematics of such growth has provided a first model of asset growth. Contradicting classical Markowitz (1952) portfolio theory, the model predicts that when assets are subject to an exponential growth process, random asset variations in a portfolio of assets act to *increase* the portfolio's expected periodic return.

The model suggests that the small firm size effect in the FF-3F model may be due to the fact that portfolios comprising higher asset volatilities are *statistically* more likely to generate a higher periodic return. The essential insight is that the outcomes are not due to investors setting prices in accordance with risk-return expectations, as is generally supposed, but rather a straightforward statistical outcome of idiosyncratic asset price volatility itself. We may note that the prediction is maintained even when continuously compounding returns are not normally distributed, provided they are symmetrically distributed about the mean.

Chapter 8

The Fundamentals of Growth, Asset Pricing, and Portfolio Allocation

Do you know the only thing that gives me pleasure? It's to see my dividends coming in.

John D. Rockefeller

Fear is a far more dominant force in human behaviour than euphoria — I would never have expected that or given it a moment's thought before, but it shows up in the data in so many ways.

Alan Greenspan

Investing should be more like watching paint dry, or watching grass grow. If you want excitement, take $800 and go to Las Vegas.

Paul Samuelson

Money can't buy you happiness but it does bring you a more pleasant form of misery.

Spike Milligan

8.1. Introduction[1]

In this chapter, we build on the model of stock price formation developed in Chapter 7, in which the market economy and the market of asset claims on the economy was modelled as an organic — which is to say, an exponential — growth process. We extend the model by considering how an investor might choose to allocate investment resources between such a market and an alternative risk-free asset. To this end, we consider a log-wealth utility function as representative of an investor's sensitivity to changes in wealth accumulation. We progress to consider that the market risk premium is derived as that which balances supply and demand across risky and risk-free assets.

---

[1]This chapter develops ideas that have appeared in *Financial Analyst Journal* (Dempsey, 2002). I am grateful and indebted to the editors and reviewers of this journal for supporting and publishing this work notwithstanding its unorthodoxy.

To these ends, Section 8.2 examines the dynamics of growth of a portfolio that comprises a risky asset in combination with a risk-free asset. Section 8.3 introduces the concept and justification of a log-wealth utility function. Section 8.4 considers an investor's portfolio selection between the risky market and a risk-free asset. Section 8.5 considers the role of the market risk premium as that which balances the relative supply of risky and risk-free assets. Section 8.6 considers the role of regular dividend payments as a stabilizing contribution of an asset's cash flow to shareholders. The final section, Section 8.7, concludes with a discussion.[2]

8.2. Portfolio Formation with One Risky Asset and One Risk-Free Asset

In Chapters 6 and 7, we observed how a normal distribution of exponential growth rates with mean, μ^*, and standard deviation, σ^*, over a period of time can be modelled as the outcome of a simple two-step or *binomial* distribution of exponential growth rates imposed over a sufficiently large set of time sub-intervals. In each sub-interval, the exponential growth rate is either $\mu + \sigma$ or $\mu - \sigma$ with equal probability; where $\mu = \mu^*/N$ and $\sigma = \sigma^*/\sqrt{N}$, where N is the number of time sub-intervals accorded per period. Figures 6.8 and 6.10 (pp. 118 and 120) highlight the structure of the binomial process through time.

The next step is to extend the model of Fig. 6.8 to allow for a portfolio that is able to distinguish between the risky market and a risk-free asset. Thereafter, we shall complement the model with a model of an investor's propensity to undertake the risk implied by the model. Ultimately, we are seeking to comprehend the nature of market growth coupled with investor preferences as to the opportunities offered by such growth.

We consider the investment of a dollar that is long in both the market of risky assets and a near-riskless asset, such as government securities. In our binomial framework, the investment has equally likely wealth outcomes at the end of each single time interval (S_u and S_d), which may be represented as

$$S_u = \omega e^{\mu_M + \sigma_M} + (1 - \omega)e^{r_f} \quad \text{and} \quad S_d = \omega e^{\mu_M - \sigma_M} + (1 - \omega)e^{r_f}, \quad (8.1)$$

---

[2]Equations that are referenced in subsequent chapters are bordered.

where ω identifies the proportion of the $1 portfolio allocated to the risky market (as opposed to the riskless asset), μ_M and σ_M, respectively, are the mean exponential growth rate per interval and volatility (standard deviation) of the growth rate for the risky market, and r_f identifies the risk-free exponential growth rate. The above outcomes can be expressed:

$$S_u = e^{\mu+\sigma} \quad \text{and} \quad S_d = e^{\mu-\sigma}, \tag{8.2}$$

which, combining Eqs. (8.1) and (8.2), provides

$$\mu = \frac{1}{2}\left\{\ln\left[\omega e^{\mu_M+\sigma_M} + (1-\omega)e^{r_f}\right] + \ln\left[\omega e^{\mu_M-\sigma_M} + (1-\omega)e^{r_f}\right]\right\}, \tag{8.3}$$

$$\sigma = \frac{1}{2}\left\{\ln\left[\omega e^{\mu_M+\sigma_M} + (1-\omega)e^{r_f}\right] - \ln\left[\omega e^{\mu_M-\sigma_M} + (1-\omega)e^{r_f}\right]\right\}. \tag{8.4}$$

Allowing that the investor's portfolio is rebalanced at the end of each time interval to maintain the proportion of the portfolio in risky assets as ω, the above outcomes S_u and S_d per dollar of investment are repeated over successive intervals. Furthermore, with μ_M, σ_M, r_f, and ω assumed to be fixed across time, μ and σ are also fixed across time. The significance of these observations is that the growth behavior of a portfolio of the market of risky assets combined with a risk-free asset continues to be characterized across time by the binomial framework of Fig. 6.8 with μ and σ determined by Eqs. (8.3) and (8.4).

The usefulness of Eqs. (8.3) and (8.4) lies in the fact that for any portfolio combination of μ_M, σ_M, r_f, and ω, we can simply substitute the values into these equations, calculate μ and σ, and substitute in Fig. 6.8. Thus, *Fig. 6.8 with Eqs. (8.3) and (8.4)* represents *our model of portfolio price behavior for a general combination of risky and risk-free assets.*

To illustrate the choices of a portfolio of risky and riskless assets, consider an investment opportunity that over each investment period either increases wealth by 1/3 or decreases it by 1/4 with equal likelihoods. Because $e^{0+0.28768} = 1\frac{1}{3}$ and $e^{0-0.28768}$ equals 3/4, these outcomes can be modeled as binomial exponential growth with mean exponential growth rate $\mu = 0$ and standard deviation $\sigma = 0.28768$.[3] For simplicity, allow that the riskless asset has zero growth ($r_f = 0$). Now consider an investor who is contemplating choosing between the following three investment portfolios (A, B and C):

Portfolio A —   Investment wealth is 100% in the riskless asset
 100% riskless assets: (with zero growth).

Portfolio B —   Investment wealth is 100% in the risky
 100% risky assets: investment opportunity that with equal
                          likelihood, either increases wealth by 1/3 or
                          decreases it by 1/4 in each period.

Portfolio C —   50% of investment wealth is in the riskless asset
 50% risky/50%   as portfolio A, and 50% is in the risky
 riskless assets: investment opportunity as portfolio B.

Comparing the three portfolios, we make the following observations. With an initial investment of, say, $12, the outcome wealth for portfolio A "riskless" remains at $12 over subsequent periods. The outcome wealth possibilities are represented for portfolios B "100% risky" in the left-hand side of panel A of Fig. 8.1, and for portfolio C "50% risky/50% riskless" in the right-hand side of panel A.

To see how the numbers emerge, consider, for example, that commencing with an initial investment of $12, the upper outcome of $14 at the end of the first period for portfolio C "50% risky" is calculated as the outcome of $6 invested at 0% in the riskless asset $= $6, in conjunction with $6 that increased by $1/3 = $8, yielding $6 + $8 = $14. The entry $16\frac{1}{3}$ at the

---

[3]This particular example has been considered by Kritzman (1994) and by Kritzman and Rich (1998). Interestingly, however, these authors choose not to draw attention to the example as one of binomial exponential growth (with $\mu = 0$, $\sigma = 0.28768$). The outcome is that both Olsen and Khaki (1998) and Van Eaton and Conover (1998) interpret the numbers 1/3 and 1/4 as being merely opportunistic in Kritzman's (1994) argument that a log-wealth utility function implies non-increasing utility with an extended investment horizon. Again, Bierman (1998) uses the example of a $100 investment with equally likely outcomes $130 and $76.9 (to illustrate investor portfolio allocations), but does not draw attention to the example as one of binomial exponential growth (with $\mu = 0$, $\sigma = 0.262364$, so that $e^{0.262364} = 1.3$, and $e^{-0.262364} = 0.769$).

Portfolio *B*: 100% in a risky investment, which has equal probability per period of increasing by 1/3 or decreasing by 1/4.

Portfolio *C*: 50% in a risky investment (as portfolio *B*) and 50% in the riskless asset (with zero growth rate).

$\mu = 0; \; \sigma = 0.28768$

$\mu = 0.01031; \; \sigma = 0.14384$

Panel A: Wealth outcomes

Starting Wealth	One period	Two periods	Starting Wealth	One period	Two periods

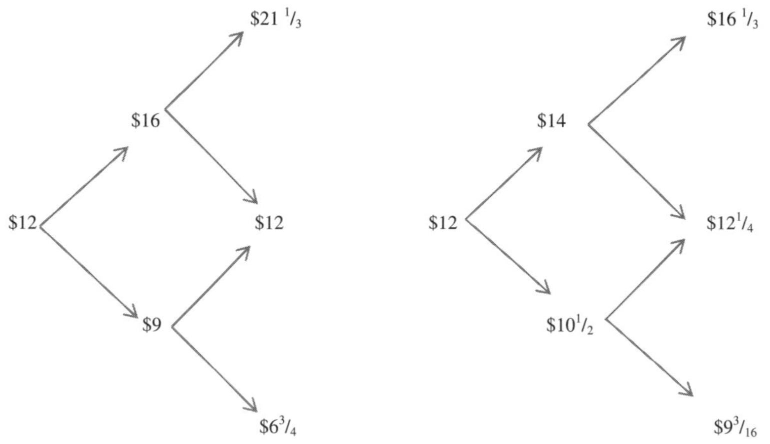

Panel B: Expected wealth, $E(W_N)$ at end of period

$12	$12.50	$13.021	$12	$12.25	$12.505

Panel C: Periodic return = $[E(W_N) - E(W_{N-1})]/E(W_{N-1})$

4.167%		2.083% (=4.167/2)

Panel D: Change in log-wealth utility per period (%)

0		1.03%

Figure 8.1. Exponential growth characteristics.

end of the second period is then calculated as the outcome of $7 invested at 0% in the riskless asset $= \$7$, in conjunction with $7 that increased by $\frac{1}{3} = \$9\frac{1}{3}$, yielding $\$16\frac{1}{3}$.[4]

The expected wealth outcomes, $E(W_N)$ — that is, the probability-weighted sum of wealth outcomes — at the end of period N for portfolios B and C are presented in panel B of Fig. 8.1. The expected periodic return over the period is then calculated as: $[E(W_N) - E(W_{N-1})]/E(W_{N-1})$, yielding the constant expected periodic returns, 4.17% and 2.08%, respectively, for portfolios "100% risky" and "50% risky" in panel C. For comparison, note that for portfolio A "riskless", the expected periodic return is trivially zero. In addition, we observe in panel A that the wealth outcomes for portfolio B "100% risky" remain "centered" through time on the initial investment outlay, $12. This is because the sequence of a gain of 1/3 followed by a loss of 1/4, and of a loss of 1/4 followed by a gain of 1/3, both bring us back to $12. In the case of portfolio C "50% risky", however, the sequences have created an upward drift, meaning that the centered or median outcome

---

[4]It is interesting to note how Eqs. (8.3) and (8.4) reproduce the outcomes for portfolios B and C in Fig. 8.1. Thus, in Eq. (8.2) for portfolio B "100% risky" ($\omega = 1$), we have $\mu = \mu_M = 0$ and $\sigma = \sigma_M = 0.28768$ (since $e^{0.28768} = 1.33$ and $e^{-0.28768} = 0.75$). As an example in Fig. 8.1, the central outcome at the end of two periods, is then derived as

$$\$12e^{\mu+\sigma}e^{\mu-\sigma} = 12e^{2\mu}$$
$$= \$12 \text{ (since } \mu = 0).$$

Thus, we have the observation that the condition for centered growth as observed in Portfolio B is that the mean exponential growth rate, μ, equals zero. However, for portfolio C "50% risky" $\left(\omega = \frac{1}{2}\right)$ with $\mu_M = 0$, $\sigma_M = 0.28768$, and $r_f = 0$, Eqs. (8.3) and (8.4) determine $\mu = 0.01031$ and $\sigma = 0.14384$. Thus, the upper outcome in Fig. 8.1 ($\$16\frac{1}{3}$) at the end of the second period for portfolio C "50% risky" is derived as

$$\$12e^{\mu+\sigma}e^{\mu+\sigma} = \$12e^{2(\mu+\sigma)}$$
$$= \$12e^{2(0.01031+0.14384)}$$
$$= \$16\frac{1}{3}.$$

And, again for Portfolio C, the central outcome at the end of two periods is derived as

$$\$12e^{\mu+\sigma}e^{\mu-\sigma} = 12e^{2\mu}$$
$$= \$12.25 \text{ (since } \mu = 0.01031).$$

has increased to an outcome value of \$12.25 at the end of the second period.

8.3. The Log-Wealth Utility Function

The question remains as to how an investor might be expected to choose between such investment choices. In order to answer this question, we must complement our model of stock behavior (Eqs. (8.1) and (8.2)) with a model of investor propensity for risk.

In his introduction of Brownian motion as a model of stock price behavior, Osborne (1964) introduced the Weber–Fecher law, which states that equal *ratios* of physical stimulus — for example, of sound frequency, or of light or sound intensity — correspond to equal *intervals* of subjective sensation, such as pitch, brightness or noise. When equal *ratios* of wealth correspond to equal *intervals* of investor "wealth sensation", which we call "utility", the investor is subject to a log-wealth utility function, U:

$$U = \ln(W). \tag{8.5}$$

To see this, consider that we commence with wealth \$$W_0$ that grows repeatedly by a factor e^R at the end of each time period, so that the outcome wealth after N periods (with Eq. (6.1)) is \$$W_0 e^{NR}$, where N is the number of time periods. Log-wealth utility implies that at each stage, the utility of the investment U is determined as

$$U = \ln\left(W_0 e^{NR}\right),$$

which (with Eqs. (6.15), (6.17) and (6.18), p. 82–83) gives

$$U = \ln\left(W_0\right) + N \cdot R. \tag{8.6}$$

Thus, as wealth either accumulates or declines by a *factor* e^R (wealth declines if R is negative) over successive time periods, utility either increases or declines by the *rate of change*, R, in wealth over each time period, independently of wealth accumulation at this point. In other words, the investor is sensitive to change in wealth as a *proportion* of wealth. As an outcome, we say that a log-wealth utility investor has "constant relative risk aversion".

We can see this alternatively by differentiating the utility of wealth U as Eq. (8.5) with regard to wealth, W (with Eqs. (6.39) and (6.40), pp. 98–99):

$$\frac{\Delta U}{\Delta W} = \frac{1}{W}, \tag{8.7}$$

which captures the idea that the utility of wealth provided with each additional unit of wealth declines with increased wealth (increases with decreasing wealth). So we can say that a log-wealth utility investor has "decreasing absolute risk aversion", meaning that equal absolute losses decline in importance as wealth increases.[5] Copeland and Weston (1988) in their text *Financial Theory and Corporate Policy*, state:

> "A decreasing marginal utility of wealth is probably genetically coded because without it we would exhibit extreme impulsive behaviour. We would engage in the activity with the highest marginal utility to the exclusion of all other choices. Addictive behaviour would be the norm" (p. 88).

As the inverse of the exponential function of growth, a natural log-utility function has the effect of balancing the instinct to pursue growth opportunities with the need to safeguard current wealth. Thus, on the one hand, while Keynes observed: "When the capital development of a country becomes the by-product of the activities of a casino, the job is likely to be ill-done", Peter Bernstein in his *Against the Gods: the remarkable story of risk* (1998) observes:

> "Yet the world would be a dull place if people lacked conceit and confidence in their own good fortune. Keynes had to admit that 'If human nature felt no temptation to take a chance . . . there might not be much investment merely as a result of cold calculation.' Nobody takes a risk in the expectation that it will fail. When the Soviets tried to administer uncertainty out of existence through government fiat and planning, they choked off social and economic progress" (p. 12).

---

[5]Although economists generally agree that investors have decreasing absolute risk aversion, there is less consensus that investors maintain strict constant relative risk aversion at the prospect of an increasingly severe loss at an increasingly low probability: "Prospect theory" suggests that investors are typically *less* averse to such downside losses than is implied by log-wealth utility. Nevertheless, we shall in the remainder of his chapter take it as a worthwhile hypothesis that investors can be described by a natural log-wealth utility.

The implications of a log-wealth utility for the investment outcomes depicted in Fig. 6.8 can be derived by application of the Von Neumann and Morgenstern (1947) theorem, which states that the utility, U, derived from an investment's possible outcomes is determined as

$$U = \sum_{i=1}^{N} p(x_i)u(x_i),$$

(8.8)

where $p(x_i)$ is the probability of each possible wealth outcome, x_i, $u(x_i)$ is the corresponding utility, and the summation sign, $\sum$, indicates that we sum over all probability-weighted utility outcomes.[6] Thus, for example, the natural log-wealth utility offered by an investment of \$1 over two periods in the exponential growth process modeled in Fig. 6.8, is determined as

$$\frac{1}{4}\ln\left(e^{2\mu+2\sigma}\right) + \frac{1}{2}\ln\left(e^{2\mu}\right) + \frac{1}{4}\ln\left(e^{2\mu-2\sigma}\right),$$

which (with Eq. (6.15), p. 82) gives:

$$= 2\mu,$$

which is to say, the natural log-wealth utility offered by an investment of \$1 over two periods is the mean exponential growth rate over two periods, 2μ. More generally, it is clear on inspection that the utility offered by an investment of \$1 over N periods U_N remains as the mean exponential growth rate over N periods, $N\mu$. That is, for such an investor:

$$U_N = N\mu.$$

(8.9)

Which is to say, the investor enjoys per period utility:

$$U = \mu,$$

(8.10)

from investment in exponential growth *quite independently* of the *dispersion* of possible outcomes at the termination of each stage of the

---

[6]It can be demonstrated that the Von Neumann and Morgenstern (1947) theorem is consistent with the most fundamental axioms of rational ranking and addition of utilities (for example, the above text by Copeland and Weston (1988), *Financial Theory and Corporate Policy*, Chapter 4).

investment process. Only the mean exponential growth rate per period, μ, is important.

It follows that the per period utility offered by an investment's expected periodic return as it derives from the per period continuously applied parameters μ and σ as given in Eq. (7.9):

$$\text{expected period return} = e^{\mu + \frac{1}{2}\sigma^2} - 1,$$

is equal to μ independent of σ. In other words, the contribution to the expected periodic return generated by the dispersion of outcomes, $\frac{1}{2}\sigma^2$, is precisely sufficient to compensate the investor for bearing such dispersion. In a fundamental sense, for a log-wealth utility investor:

risk has created its own reward.

Equations (8.3), (8.4), and (8.10) constitute our joint model of stock market behaviour and investor utility in the context of risk. Before progressing to discuss the implications for stock market performance generally, we first highlight the way in which the model resolves the issue of how an investor might choose between portfolios A "100% riskless", B "100% risky", and C "50% risky" above. Thus, for portfolio A "100% riskless", the utility remains as $\ln(12) = 2.4849$ at the end of each period. The per period utility gain is therefore zero. For portfolio B "100% risky" in the left-hand side of Fig. 8.1, we have $\mu = 0$. With Eq. (8.10), the per period utility, U, is therefore zero. For portfolio C "50% risky", we have $\mu = 0.0103$. With Eq. (8.10), the per period utility, U, is therefore equal to 0.0103, or 1.03%.[7] Thus, we observe that the per period utility of 1.03% offered by the *hybrid* portfolio C "50% risky/50% riskless" actually *exceeds* the utility offered by either portfolio A "100% riskless"

---

[7]The designation "percent" for utility $\times$ 100 is arbitrary. The effect of employing the designation here is that the per period utility from investing an amount $\$W$ in a risk-free investment with per period exponential growth rate, r_f is normalized as r_f percent. To see this effect, observe that if we have an initial investment of $\$W_0$ subject to exponential growth rate, r_f, the outcome at the end of the period is $\$W_0 e^{r_f}$. Hence the gain in log-wealth utility is $\ln[W_0 e^{r_f}] - \ln(W_0) = \ln(W_0) + \ln[e^{r_f}] - \ln(W_0)$ (with Eq. (6.17), p. 82) $= r_f$ (with Eq. (6.16)). Representing utilities as "percentages" thereby allows utilities to be directly compared with the utility that would be derived if the asset was risk-free.

(per period utility $= 0$) or portfolio B "100% risky" (per period utility $= 0$). Portfolio C "50% risky" is therefore the preferred portfolio.[8]

8.4. Optimal Portfolio Selection

A question we might ask at this stage is: Does some other portfolio combination of the risky and riskless asset offer a log-wealth utility investor an even greater utility than that offered by a 50% risky/50% riskless split? For an answer, observe that the per period log-wealth utility, U, offered by a portfolio with proportion ω in the risky asset of Fig. 6.8 may be expressed (with Eqs. (8.3), (8.8), and (8.10)) as

$$ U = \frac{1}{2} \left\{ \ln\left[\omega e^{\mu_M + \sigma_M} + (1 - \omega)e^{r_f} \right] + \ln\left[\omega e^{\mu_M - \sigma_M} + (1 - \omega)e^{r_f} \right] \right\}. $$

(8.11)

The value of U is maximized with respect to ω at the point that $dU/d\omega = 0$ (Chapter 6.8). With Eqs. (6.46) and (6.47) (p. 101), we have on differentiating Eq. (8.11):

$$ \frac{dU}{d\omega} = \frac{1}{2} \left[\frac{e^{\mu_M + \sigma_M} - e^{r_f}}{\omega e^{\mu_M + \sigma_M} + (1 - \omega)e^{r_f}} + \frac{e^{\mu_M - \sigma_M} - e^{r_f}}{\omega e^{\mu_M - \sigma_M} + (1 - \omega)e^{r_f}} \right]. \quad (8.12) $$

---

[8]We could, had we wished, chosen to demonstrate these outcomes from first principles. Thus, for example, for Portfolio B "100% risky" (left-hand side panel, Fig. 8.1) we have

original wealth utility $= \ln(12)$	$= 2.4849,$
end-of-period 1 utility $= 0.5 \ln(16) + 0.5 \ln(9)$	$= 2.4849,$
end-of-period 2 utility $= 0.25 \ln\left(21\frac{1}{3}\right) + 0.5 \ln(12) + 0.25 \ln\left(6\frac{3}{4}\right)$	$= 2.4849.$

For portfolio "100% risky", the per period utility gain is therefore zero (consistent with the derivation in the text above with application of Eqs. (8.3) and (8.10)); whereas for Portfolio C "50% risky" (right-hand side panel, Fig. 8.1) we have

original wealth utility $= \ln(12)$	$= 2.4849,$
end-of-period 1 utility $= 0.5 \ln(14) + 0.5 \ln(10.5)$	$= 2.4952,$
end-of-period two utility $= 0.25 \ln\left(16\frac{1}{3}\right) + 0.5 \ln\left(12\frac{1}{4}\right) + 0.25 \ln\left(9\frac{3}{16}\right)$	$= 2.5055.$

For portfolio C "50% risky", the utility gain is therefore $= 2.5055 - 2.4952 (= 0.0103)$ in the first investment period and $2.4952 - 2.4849 (= 0.0103)$ in the second period, which is to say, 1.03% per period (again consistent with the derivation in the text with application of Eqs. (8.3) and (8.10)).

In the case that $\mu_M = r_f$, we determine by inspection that the right-hand side of the above equation $=0$ when $\omega = \frac{1}{2}$. Thus, we conclude that in the case that the drift exponential market growth rate, μ_M, is equal to the risk-free rate, r_f, a log-wealth utility investor continues to invest in a portfolio comprising 50% in the risky market and 50% in the riskless asset in preference to any other combination. We note that this result is retained independent of the standard deviation, σ_M, of the market returns. We have, therefore, a powerful mathematical argument that even allowing economic and markets downturns to the point that investment appreciation as μ appears no greater than the risk-free rate, investors will continue to invest 50% of their portfolios in the risky market: The market will come back.

We may represent the above outcome for $\mu_M = r_f$ graphically as in Fig. 8.2. The solid gradient line in the lower part of the figure joining the combination $[0, r_f]$ and the combination $[\sigma_M, R_M]$ is the capital market line (CML) in continuous time for a single period. It is the locus of portfolios that combine the risk-free asset (with standard deviation $\sigma = 0$ and risk-free return $R = r_f$) and the market portfolio with standard deviation $\sigma = \sigma_M$

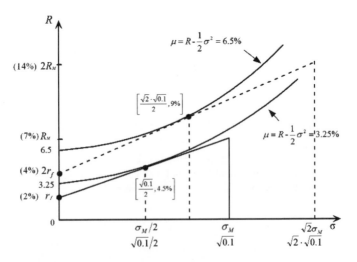

Figure 8.2. The CML for one and two period investments.

x-axis:	0	$0.5\sqrt{0.1}$	$\sqrt{0.1}$	$\sqrt{2}\sqrt{0.1}$
lower utility curve:	3.25	4.5	8.25	13.25
high utility curve:	6.5	7.75	11.5	16.5

and market expected return $R = R_M$, where R_M is defined in relation to the market's mean exponential growth rate μ_M with standard deviation, σ_M, as in Eq. (7.3):

$$R_M = \mu_M + \frac{1}{2}\sigma_M^2.$$

In the figure, the per period market expected return (R_M) has been set at 7% and the per period risk-free rate (r_f) at 2% (arbitrary numbers).

Equation (7.3) determines the per period standard deviation for the market, σ_M, in relation to R_M and μ_M as

$$\frac{1}{2}\sigma_M^2 = R_M - \mu_M, \tag{8.13}$$

so that, for the particular case $\mu_M = r_f$ (with the above inputs), we have in Fig. 8.2:

$$\frac{1}{2}\sigma_M^2 = 0.07 - 0.02 = 0.05 \ (5\%),$$

yielding $\sigma_M = \sqrt{0.1}$ (as depicted on the x-axis in Fig. 8.2).

In Fig. 8.2, the utility curves join portfolios that offer equal utility, U, for combinations of expected return (R) and standard deviation (σ). With Eq. (8.10), we have:

$$U = \mu,$$

for a log-wealth utility investor. Thus, for such an investor, the utility curves for a single period are identified (with Eq. (7.3)) as

$$U = \mu = R - \frac{1}{2}\sigma^2 = \text{constant}, \tag{8.14}$$

which is to say, at each point on a utility curve $(U = \text{constant})$, R relates to σ as

$$R = U + \frac{1}{2}\sigma^2. \tag{8.15}$$

Since the higher the U value in Eq. (8.15), the higher is the required R for any value of σ, it is clear that higher utility curves in Fig. 8.2 represent higher utilities, and, thus, the maximum utility attained by a portfolio on the CML occurs at the point that a utility curve is tangential to the CML.

In Fig. 8.2, we have drawn the utility curve that is tangential to the CML (with $\mu_M = r_f$) at the midpoint of the CML. To see that the midpoint is indeed the correct location, observe that the gradient of the utility curve is determined as $dR/d\sigma$, which with Eq. (8.15) (with Eqs. (6.27) and (6.28)) is determined as

$$\frac{dR}{d\sigma} = \sigma. \tag{8.16}$$

The gradient of the CML over a single period in Fig. 8.2 is determined as $(R_M - r_f)/\sigma_M$, which, with Eq. (7.3), is expressed:

$$\frac{R_m - r_f}{\sigma_M} = \frac{\mu_M + \frac{1}{2}\sigma_M^2 - r_f}{\sigma_M}. \tag{8.17}$$

On equating Eqs. (8.16) and (8.17), the utility curve is tangent to the CML when

$$\sigma = \frac{\mu_M + \frac{1}{2}\sigma_M^2 - r_f}{\sigma_M}, \tag{8.18}$$

which, in the particular case $\mu_M = r_f$, provides

$$\sigma = \frac{r_f + \frac{1}{2}\sigma_M^2 - r_f}{\sigma_M} = \frac{1}{2}\sigma_M, \tag{8.19}$$

which in Fig. 8.2 is the midpoint on the x-axis between $\sigma = 0$ (the riskless asset) and $\sigma = \sigma_M$ (the market portfolio). The standard deviation $\sigma = \frac{1}{2}\sigma_M$ identifies the portfolio comprising 50% in the market and 50% in the risk-free asset,[9] precisely as was determined with Eq. (8.12). For this portfolio, the return, R, is determined as $R = \frac{1}{2}R_M + \frac{1}{2}r_f = (7\% + 2\%)/2 = 4.5\%$, with $\sigma = \frac{1}{2}\sigma_M = \sqrt{0.1}/2$. With such a portfolio, investor log-wealth utility,

---

[9]This follows from Eq. (6.67) as

$$\sigma_{portfolio}^2 = \omega_{market}^2\sigma_M^2 + \omega_{risk\text{-}free}^2\sigma_{rf}^2 + 2\omega_{market}\omega_{risk\text{-}free}\,COV(R_{market}, R_{risk\text{-}free})$$

$$= \omega_{market}^2\sigma_M^2 + 0 + 0;$$

and hence $\sigma_{portfolio} = \omega_{market}\sigma_M$.

U_1, per period is determined with Eq. (8.14) as

$$U_1 = \mu = R - \frac{1}{2}\sigma^2$$

$$= 0.045 - \frac{1}{2}(\sqrt{0.1}/2)^2 = \underline{3.25\%}.$$

Over N periods, the slope for the CML of opportunity portfolios is determined similarly to Eq. (8.17) (with Eqs. (6.76) and (6.77), pp. 118–119) as

$$\frac{NR_m - Nr_f}{\sqrt{N}\sigma_M} = \frac{\sqrt{N}(\mu_M + \frac{1}{2}\sigma_M^2 - r_f)}{\sigma_M}, \tag{8.20}$$

where μ_M, r_f, and σ_M, as above, relate to a single period. In this case, the assumption $\mu_M = r_f$ implies that the requirement of being tangent to the utility curve (combining Eqs. (8.16) and (8.20)) is

$$\sigma = \frac{\sqrt{N}\frac{1}{2}\sigma_M^2}{\sigma_M} = \frac{1}{2}\sqrt{N}\sigma_M, \tag{8.21}$$

which is again the statement that for a log-wealth utility investor, utility is maximized by holding a portfolio that is at the point midway between the riskless asset (with $\sigma = 0$) and the market portfolio (with $\sigma = \sqrt{N}\sigma_M$), which is, again, a portfolio comprising 50% the market and 50% the risk-free asset.

Over two periods in Fig. 8.2, we have the return on the market $= 2R_M = 2(7\%) = 14\%$, with standard deviation $= \sqrt{2}\sigma_M = \sqrt{2}\sqrt{0.1}$, and the risk-free rate $= 2r_f = 2(2\%) = 4\%$. The midpoint portfolio on the dashed CML, therefore, occurs at $R = (14\% + 4\%)/2 = 9\%$ with standard deviation $\sqrt{2}\sqrt{0.1}/2$, so that the utility, U_2, over two periods is determined with Eq. (8.14) as

$$U_2 = \mu = R - \frac{1}{2}\sigma^2$$

$$= 0.09 - \frac{1}{2}\left[\sqrt{2}\sqrt{0.1}/2\right]^2 = 6.5\%,$$

precisely twice that accorded for a single period investment (3.25% above).

Comparing Eq. (8.17) with Eq. (8.20) confirms that for an N-period investment, the gradient of the CML has increased by a factor of $\sqrt{N}$; which is to say, the market's ratio of expected return over and above the risk-free rate divided by the market standard deviation of returns $= [R_M - r_f]/\sigma_M$ — *the price of risk* — has increased by a factor $\sqrt{N}$. Of itself, this result would appear to imply that multi-period investment is necessarily more favorable than shorter period investment. The explanation is that although the price or reward for risk is indeed increasing with additional periods of investment, the utility afforded per additional unit of expected wealth is also decreasing, so that utility per investment period remains unchanged.

8.5. Portfolio Allocation and the Market Risk Premium

The question now is: Does the equality of μ_M and r_f — with the implication that log-wealth utility investors allocate their portfolios 50% in the risky market and 50% in riskless assets — represent actual market equilibrium? To begin to answer, we note first that the market has historically been unable to offer riskless participation in equal measure with risky participation, with the result that equity assets have historically constituted the greater proportion of asset portfolios. Equilibrium requires that investors choose to allocate their portfolios between the market of risky assets and a riskless asset so as to be consistent with the *relative availability* of these asset classes. For this reason, the risky market has historically been priced so that μ_M is greater than r_f.

In attempting to model an investment portfolio with just two asset classes (risky market/riskless asset), we shall consider that investors, institutional and individual, have tended historically to have something close to two-thirds of investment portfolios dominated by risky equity investments with high quality bonds typically representing a perceived secure component.[10] Interestingly, it is possible without actually being very much more specific, to specify in terms of the model, fairly close constraints on the market risk premium. The reason, as we shall see, is that quite modest shifts in the premium predict fairly large shifts in the proportions of risky and risk-free assets held in an investment portfolio.

---

[10]The distinction between "risky equity markets" and "riskless assets" is not clear-cut. Investors choose to allocate their portfolios not only to risky equity markets and risk-free securities, but also to municipal and corporate bonds, and other types of assets. Such distinctions are accommodated in Chapter 9.

Table 8.1. The per period log-wealth utility offered by a portfolio of risky and riskless assets as a proportion, ω, of the portfolio assigned to the risky asset.

					Proportion in Risky Assets, ω							
0	0.1	0.2	0.3	0.4	0.5	0.6	0.7	0.8	0.9	1.0	1.2	1.5
A. Base case: Utility with $\mu_M = 2.0\%$; $r_f = 2.0\%$; $\sigma_M = 15\%$												
2.0	2.1	2.2	2.2	2.3	2.3	2.3	2.2	2.2	2.1	2.0	1.7	1.1
B. Utility with $\mu_M = 2.5\%$; $r_f = 2.0\%$; $\sigma_M = 15\%$												
2.0	2.2	2.3	2.4	2.5	2.5	2.6	2.6	2.6	2.6	2.5	2.3	1.9
C. Utility with $\mu_M = 3.0\%$; $r_f = 2.0\%$; $\sigma_M = 15\%$												
2.0	2.2	2.4	2.5	2.7	2.8	2.9	3.0	3.0	3.0	3.0	2.9	2.7
D. Utility with $\mu_M = 3.0\%$; $r_f = 2.0\%$; $\sigma_M = 20\%$												
2.0	2.3	2.6	2.8	3.0	3.1	3.2	3.2	3.2	3.1	3.0	2.7	1.8
E. Utility with $\mu_M = 3.5\%$; $r_f = 2.0\%$; $\sigma_M = 20\%$												
2.0	2.3	2.7	2.9	3.1	3.3	3.4	3.5	3.6	3.6	3.5	3.3	2.6
F. Utility with $\mu_M = 4.5\%$; $r_f = 2.0\%$; $\sigma_M = 30\%$												
2.0	2.7	3.2	3.7	4.1	4.4	4.6	4.7	4.7	4.7	4.5	3.9	2.4

This is demonstrated in Table 8.1, which, in relation to Eqs. (8.3) and (8.10), provides the per period utility offered by a portfolio of risky and riskless assets as a proportion, ω, of the portfolio assigned to risky (as opposed to the riskless) assets. As a base case, in the first row, we maintain the underlying exponential growth rate for the risky market, μ_M, equal to that of the riskless asset. We set $r_f = 2.0\%$ (annualized, reflecting a real return on government bonds) and standard deviation (volatility) of market returns, $\sigma_M = 15\%$ (annualized, reflecting an historical performance of US stocks). In this case, the value of U in the first row of Table 8.1 is maximized when the investment portfolio is divided equally between the risky market and a riskless asset ($\omega = 0.5$), consistent with the outcome derived above.

Setting μ_m for the risky market equal to 2.5% while maintaining $r_f = 2.0\%$ leads to the outcomes in panel B of Table 8.1. A portfolio invested 100% in a riskless asset ($\omega = 0$) has utility equal to r_f ($= 2.0\%$), while a portfolio constituted 100% in the market now has utility equal to μ_M ($= 2.5\%$). In this case, the utilities offered in the range of ω equal to 55–90% remain essentially flat at 2.6%. That is, investors with log-wealth utilities now choose to hold between 10% and 45% of their portfolio in the riskless asset. Thus, an important observation is that the "flatness" of the resulting utilities allows for a fair degree of investment flexibility consistent with log-wealth utility. Setting μ_M equal to 3.0%, while maintaining r_f at 2.0%, leads to the outcomes in panel C of Table 8.1. In this case, the utilities offered in the range of ω equal to 65–100% remain essentially flat at 3.0%, implying that investors with log-wealth utility choose to hold between 0 and 35% of their portfolio in the riskless asset. In which case, we determine that the underlying mean exponential growth rate of investments in risky markets need be as little as 1% above that offered by riskless assets, such as government bonds, before log-wealth utility investors are induced to allocate the greater portions of their portfolios to the risky markets rather than to riskless assets.

However, the difference between μ_M and r_f depends on the market's volatility, σ_M. To see this, consider market annualized volatility $\sigma_M = 20\%$ (reflecting equity volatility over market history, 1926–1994). To achieve the same profiles for investor allocations between risky and riskless assets as in panels B and C of Table 8.1, we need to increase the spread between μ_M and r_f. Thus, setting μ_m equal to 3.0% (while maintaining r_f at 2.0%) generates the utilities in panel D of Table 8.1. Again, the utilities remain essentially flat in the range of ω equal to 55–90% (as for $\sigma_M = 15\%$ in panel B), implying that investors will again invest 10–45% of their investment portfolios in the riskless asset. Setting $\mu_M = 3.5\%$ generates the utility pattern in panel E, where the utilities remain essentially flat in the range of ω equal to 65–100% (as for $\sigma_M = 15\%$ in panel C), implying that investors again choose to invest between zero and 35% in the riskless asset. Finally, if we consider a market annualized volatility as high as 30% (a value closer to the 33.6% actually measured for US stock returns over the 1926–1939 Depression period) and again set the return on government bonds at 2.0% (it was close to 1.85% during the Depression), we estimate that the risky market must be priced to offer a mean exponential growth rate of 4.5% before investors will choose to allocate their portfolios to the risky market in the 65–90% range (panel E of Table 8.1).

The above considerations suggest the possibility of a scenario whereby an increase in market volatility, due, for example, to adverse events signaling renewed economic exposure, induces investors, consistent with Table 8.1, to reduce their exposure to risky market assets as a proportion of their portfolios, which must lead to falling prices, which of itself raises the market's equity premium, until a new equilibrium position is achieved at the new market volatility consistent with Table 8.1. The possibility, of course, is that if the fall in prices of itself generates a further increase in volatility, consistent with the model, markets must fall even further. However, the downward spiral must eventually be curtailed as even lower prices at some point hold out *at least the possibility* of a rebound and upside potential, so that there is some symmetry as to upside and downside market directions. At this stage, the model predicts that even when market growth expectations are distributed no more optimistically than symmetrically about the risk-free rate, investors will choose to invest 50/50% in the risky market and risk-free assets. At this point, prices stabilize and, commensurate with a reduced volatility, investors return to the market to increase their stock holdings. Such action further reduces volatility and simultaneously raises prices until an equilibrium position that is more closely related to the original one is reinstated.[11]

We define the market risk premium, *MRP*, consistent with the capital asset pricing model (CAPM) (Eq. 2.1):

$$MRP = \text{the expected periodic market return} - \text{periodic risk-free return} \tag{8.22}$$

With Eq. (7.9):

$$1 + \text{expected periodic return} = e^{\mu + \frac{1}{2}\sigma^2},$$

we then have

$$MRP = \left[e^{\mu_M + \frac{1}{2}\sigma_M^2} - 1 \right] - [e^{r_f} - 1]$$

$$= e^{\mu_M + \frac{1}{2}\sigma_M^2} - e^{r_f}. \tag{8.23}$$

Or, allowing that the market exponential growth rates are sufficiently small, we have Eq. (7.10):

$$\text{expected periodic return} \simeq \mu + \frac{1}{2}\sigma^2,$$

---

[11]Increases in market prices tend to be associated with a reduction in market volatility; decreases in prices with increases in market volatility.

we have

$$MRP \simeq \mu_M + \frac{1}{2}\sigma_M^2 - r_f. \qquad (8.24)$$

In terms of Eq. (8.24), the implication for the market risk premium can be generalized as follows. With an annualized volatility of market returns equal to 15.0% and a real rate on government bonds of 2.0%, we have estimated the annualized growth rate for the risky market as 3.0% to induce investors to allocate between 0 and 35% of their portfolio in such risk-free assets as government bonds (panel C of Table 8.1). That is, in order to induce investors to allocate their portfolios between the risky market and risk-free assets in a way that reflects the actual market proportions of these assets, $\mu_M - r_f$ is estimated at 1.0%. However, the market investor also enjoys the additional expectation of return $\frac{1}{2}\sigma_M^2$ that is generated by the riskiness of the market itself, which with $\sigma_M = 0.15$, is also approximately 1.0%. The required annualized market risk premium over and above the rate offered by government bonds is then estimated (with Eq. (8.24)) as $\mu_M - r_f + \frac{1}{2}\sigma_M^2 = 1.0\% + 1.0\% = 2.0\%$.

By setting the market volatility, σ_m, equal to 20.0%, while maintaining r_f at 2.0%, however, we have estimated a μ_M of 3.5% to be necessary to induce investors to allocate 0–35% of their portfolio to risk-free assets (panel E of Table 8.1). In this case, $\mu_M - r_f$ is estimated as 1.5%, whereas the expectation of return generated by volatility $\frac{1}{2}\sigma_M^2$ is approximately 2.0%, so that the annualized market risk premium is estimated as $\mu_M - r_f + \frac{1}{2}\sigma_M^2 = 1.5\% + 2.0\% = 3.5\%$.

Such market risk premiums are much smaller than those that have been supposed on the basis of the historical performance of US stocks. For example, average premiums for US stocks over government bonds in the 1966–1991 period were closer to 8.0%.[12] By setting the market volatility (σ_M) as high as 30% (it was 33.6% over the period 1926–1939) while maintaining r_f at 2.0%, we have calculated a mean exponential growth rate (μ_M) of 4.5% to be necessary to induce investors to allocate 10–35% of their portfolio to risk-free assets (see panel F of Table 8.1). The expectation of return generated by the riskiness of the market itself

---

[12]Table 2.1, p. 24.

is then approximately 4.5% $\left(\frac{1}{2}\sigma_M^2, \sigma_M = 0.30\right)$. Under such conditions, the annualized market risk premium is estimated as $\mu_M - r_f + \frac{1}{2}\sigma_M^2 = 2.5\% + 4.5\% = 7.0\%$.

Thus, we observe that quite large variations in the market risk premium (2–7%) are implied by the historical variation of stock market volatility (15–30%). Nevertheless, the kind of returns actually enjoyed by US investors in the years prior to the global financial crisis appears more consistent with a risk premium commensurate with the stock market volatility (close to 30%) of the Depression years of 1926–1939.

Schwert (1991) has observed that although the data might now indicate that by the late 1980s and early 1990s, the volatility of US stock market returns had come closer to 15%, the widespread impression at this time remained that of especially volatile stock prices. Thus, we might consider that investors attach a higher probability to the possibility of a steep market decline than that which is captured by a distribution of market returns over a period of historical market stability. If investors allow a market down performance to "build on itself" with an additional increase in volatility, the downside distribution of market returns will indeed exhibit a "fatter tail" than is predicted by a normal distribution, and it may be that we indeed need to "compensate" for this tail in the model by imposing a larger standard deviation, which, in turn, implies a higher market risk premium.[13]

Alternatively, the high level of historical US stock market returns may be interpreted as the phenomenon that US stocks have continued to surpass investor expectations (Jorion and Goetzmann, 1999). That is to say, historical US market returns have outperformed against investor expectations in the long-run.[14]

---

[13]Historical returns do indeed exhibit fatter tails than predicted by a normal distribution.

[14]Recall also that in Table 2.1, the proposed null hypothesis model allowed for the interpretation of a market outperformance of 8.0% over the risk-free rate over the period 1966–1991 (as recorded by Black, 1993) as the outcome of investor expectations for the market to outperform above the risk-free rate by 6.0%, in combination with the outcome market's outperformance over investor expectations as 2.0%. (Nevertheless, even a 6.0% risk premium appears high in our model if we maintain a market volatility (standard deviation) less than 20% per annum.)

8.6. The Case for Stable Dividends

Since the days of Lintner (1965) it is well known that firms endeavour to maintain a policy of stable dividends. This is despite the fact that dividends have historically been subject to much higher rates of investor tax than would be the case if the cash were retained and allowed to contribute to a capital gain, or if the firm were to engage in buybacks of its shares from shareholders (again, for the majority of its shareholders, subjecting the cash to a much lower rate of capital gains tax).

Lintner's fieldwork suggested that managers focus on the *change* in the rate of dividend payout, and that most managers seek to avoid making changes to their dividend rates that might have to be reversed within a year or so. And, contradicting the Modigliani and Miller prescription (Chapter 5), that the firm should distribute its cash flows to shareholders on the basis that they are surplus to its investment intentions, Lintner reported that investment requirements generally had little effect on modifying the firm's pattern of dividend behavior. As an outcome, the "dividend clientele", "signaling", and "agency" hypotheses have been developed to account for the tendency of firms to maintain stable dividend policies. The difficulty with these explanations (described briefly in Chapter 5) is that they are external to the fundamental model, as well as not compensating altogether convincingly for the high costs induced when the firm chooses to distribute cash subject to high rates of tax on dividends rather than as capital gains.

Here, we offer an alternative explanation. By providing a stable cash flow, the firm is mimicking the risk-free rate component that investors seek in their portfolios when they maximize investment utility (Eq. 8.11), and thereby, is making its stocks attractive to investors as a *greater proportion* of their portfolios. It may be that by allowing its dividend policy to adjust more optimally with its investment policy needs, the firm achieves a positive net present value in cash terms, but, by destabilizing its dividend policy thereby, it induces investors to *decrease* their stockholdings at the current price.[15]

---

[15]It yet remains intriguing why firms do not seek to minimize their shareholder tax liabilities by converting wholesale to making *regular* buy-backs as opposed to paying regular dividends. A proposed explanation is that unlike other costs, the firm's avoidance of taxes is not necessarily achieved with impunity. The tax authorities hold the trump card of simply

Thus, it is not a case of whether investors are induced or not induced to hold the stock by virtue of the firm's dividend policy but, rather, the *extent* to which investors are induced to hold the stock as a proportion of their portfolios. For example, in times of stock market volatility, when investors are disposed to move their investment holdings to less volatile assets, the stable dividend component of the stock works to induce investors to maintain a holding of the firm in their portfolio at a greater proportion than would be the case otherwise.

8.7. Time for Reflection: What Have We Learned?

We have been led to some interesting observations. A first observation is that the market risk premium — the market's expectation of return above the risk-free rate — is not to be understood as that which is required to induce investors to *enter* the market, which is to say, to assume market risk in an absolute sense. Rather, it is the premium required to induce investors to allocate their portfolios between the risky market and a risk-free asset in the proportion that represents the *available* proportions of these assets. Such availability is, of course, reciprocally influenced by the risk premium itself. Thereby, the premium equates supply and demand and clears the market. A second observation is that greater market volatility induces investors to rationally reduce their market exposure, so that in periods of increased market volatility, investors are (rationally) seeking to reduce the proportion of their portfolios exposed to the market simultaneously with each other. At this point, the market has created a condition under which "everyone is selling" — until with sufficiently lower prices there exists the potential for higher returns. At this stage, the prospects of further declines in the stock market must be balanced with the prospect of gains. Our model suggests that at the point that upside and downside market prospects can be considered symmetrical about a mean expectation, log-wealth utility investors require only that the mean expectation be equal to the risk-free rate to justify investment of 50% of their assets in the risky market. This

---

being able to change the rules. For example, they have it at their call to tax buy-backs to shareholders as equivalent dividends. The firm is then exposed to the adverse publicity and opprobrium of having attempted to deny the tax authorities (and broader society) their rightful due.

observation suggests a significant hypothesis, namely that as an upturn in the market appears viable, a platform is established from which markets are able to recover. At this point, market volatility reduces and prices begin to rise to their original positions as investors reinstate their original portfolio proportions between the risky market and riskless assets. If the good news is that falling prices and a suppressed economy must eventually self-correct, the not-so-good news is the turmoil endured in the meantime.

A third observation is that the distribution of outcome returns likely has "fatter tails" (more extreme outcomes) than is predicted by a normal distribution. This will be the case if, for example, the market is capable of building on itself in bull and bear runs of self-sustaining price changes. The input value for the standard deviation of market returns in the models must accordingly be assigned greater than that which is indicated by market volatility in times of relative market stability. We have determined that an annualized market volatility of 20% in the model, requires a market risk premium of 3.5% to induce investors to invest 65% or more of their investment portfolio in the risky market; whereas with an annualized market volatility of 30%, investors require a market risk premium closer to 7.0% to induce investment to this extent in the risky market. The former volatility (20%) reflects historical equity volatility in more normal times, whereas the latter volatility (30%) may represent a "fear" factor for more extreme stock price declines.

A final observation is that the proposed framework provides a case for the observed tendency of firms to maintain stable dividend patterns.

Chapter 9

A Model of Asset Pricing and Portfolio Allocation

Bubbles go up very slowly as euphoria builds. Then fear hits, and it comes down very sharply. When I started to look at that, I was sort of intellectually shocked. Contagion is the critical phenomenon which causes the thing to fall apart.

Alan Greenspan

We simply attempt to be fearful when others are greedy and to be greedy only when others are fearful.

Warren Buffett

Money was never a big motivation for me, except as a way to keep score. The real excitement is playing the game.

Donald Trump

Ever wonder why fund managers can't beat the S&P 500? 'Cause they're sheep, and sheep get slaughtered.

Gordon Gekko

9.1. Introduction

Investors choose to allocate their portfolios not only to risky equity markets and risk-free securities, but also to municipal and corporate bonds, and other types of assets. The outcome is that the distinction between a "risky" equity market and a "riskless" asset is not clear-cut. The risk in holding assets may even depend on how they are integrated strategically in the investor's portfolio: A long-term bond may be held short-term as a risky capital exposure to interest rate movements, or, alternatively, may be held until maturity as a secure source of income. Or, again, the bonds held may be risky in their own right, but their inclusion is regarded as reducing a portfolio's overall risk by providing a hedge against market risk.

A further restriction on our analyses in the previous chapter is the imposition of a log-wealth utility function. Although we justified the choice of log-wealth utility in Chapter 8, we wish to allow a wider range of possibilities so that we might choose between them on the basis of the historical evidence of investors' exposure to the markets.

155

Accordingly, in this chapter, we extend the analysis of the previous chapter to allow (1) a more general utility function (Section 9.2) and (2) risky assets as stocks and risky bonds (Section 9.3). We show that the formulation implies the capital asset pricing model (CAPM) (Section 9.4). Section 9.5 generalizes the fundamental utility function for extended investment periods. Section 9.6 applies the model to specific market data and portfolio optimization. The example serves to illustrate the significance of the capital market line (CML) as well as the CAPM as logical outcomes of the setup. Section 9.7 considers the case for maintaining the assumption of log-wealth utility. Section 9.8 generalizes our findings to multiple assets and thereby advances a final model of asset pricing and portfolio allocation. Section 9.9 concludes the chapter with a discussion.[1]

9.2. A Generalized Utility Function

The log-wealth utility function of Chapter 8, from Eqs. (8.5) and (8.7),

$$U = \ln(W),$$

has the feature that

$$\frac{\Delta U}{\Delta W} = \frac{1}{W},$$

which captures the idea that the utility of wealth provided with each additional unit of wealth declines with increased wealth. This feature is maintained by utility functions of the more general class:

$$\frac{\Delta U}{\Delta W} = \frac{1}{W^\gamma}, \tag{9.1}$$

where γ is Pratt's measure of relative risk aversion. The introduction of γ allows for flexibility in identifying investor responses to gains and losses. A higher value of γ suppresses the utility of additional wealth. Integrating Eq. (9.1) (with Eqs. (6.29) and (6.30), p. 96) provides

$$\boxed{U(W) = \frac{W^{1-\gamma}}{1-\gamma}.} \tag{9.2}$$

---

[1]Equations that are referenced in subsequent chapters are bordered.

Equation 9.2 provides a generalization of log-wealth utility, which we can apply to exponential growth as a repetition of the exponential binomial operator in Fig. 6.8 (p. 118). Over each such sub-interval, we express the up-outcome, S_u, and down-outcome, S_d, as in Fig. 6.7, from Eq. (6.75), p. 117:

$$S_u = W_0 e^{\mu+\sigma}$$

and

$$S_d = W_0 e^{\mu-\sigma},$$

where W_0 is wealth at the start of the interval. Thus, applying the utility function of Eq. (9.2) to the above binomial process, we have the utility, U, per interval provided by the investment as (with Eq. (8.8), p. 139):

$$U = \frac{1}{2}\frac{1}{1-\gamma}\left[(W_0 e^{\mu+\sigma})^{1-\gamma} + (W_0 e^{\mu-\sigma})^{1-\gamma}\right] - \frac{W_0^{1-\gamma}}{1-\gamma}, \qquad (9.3)$$

which (with Eqs. (6.1) and (6.2), p. 74–75) can be expressed as

$$U = \frac{1}{2}\frac{1}{1-\gamma}\left[W_0^{1-\gamma} e^{(\mu+\sigma)(1-\gamma)} + W_0^{1-\gamma} e^{(\mu-\sigma)(1-\gamma)}\right] - \frac{W_0^{1-\gamma}}{1-\gamma}.$$

Equation (9.3) can therefore be written (with Eq. (6.11), p. 78) as

$$U = \frac{1}{2}\frac{W_0^{1-\gamma}}{1-\gamma}\left\{ \begin{aligned} &1 + [(1-\gamma)(\mu+\sigma)] + \frac{[(1-\gamma)(\mu+\sigma)]^2}{2} \\ &+1 + [(1-\gamma)(\mu-\sigma)] + \frac{[(1-\gamma)(\mu-\sigma)]^2}{2} + \cdots \end{aligned} \right\}$$

$$- \frac{W_0^{1-\gamma}}{1-\gamma}. \qquad (9.4)$$

Allowing that the binomial formation of Fig. 6.7 is in the limit of a short time interval, μ acts as the exponential growth rate for the period (μ^*) divided by N, and σ acts as the standard deviation for the period (σ^*) divided by $\sqrt{N}$, where N is the number of sub intervals accorded to the period (Eqs. (6.79) and (6.80), p. 120). Thus, in the limit of a short time interval, we can write

Eq. (9.4) for the utility of engaging in the investment as

$$U = W_0^{1-\gamma}\left[\mu + \frac{1-\gamma}{2}\sigma^2\right].\tag{9.5}$$

We can relate μ and σ in Eq. (9.5) to the exponential return, R, defined as Eq. (7.1):

$\$W_0 e^R \equiv$ expected wealth outcome of investing $\$W_0$ for a single period

by observing (Eq. (7.3)):

$$R = \mu + \frac{1}{2}\sigma^2.$$

Thus, we can express Eq. (9.5) as

$$U = \left[R - \frac{1}{2}\gamma\sigma^2\right]W_0^{1-\gamma}.\tag{9.6}$$

We might consider three stylized determinations of γ in Eq. (9.6) as

$$\gamma > 1, \quad \gamma = 1, \quad \gamma = 0.$$

(1) An investor with $\gamma > 1$ receives utility, U, per period of investment as Eq. (9.6) (on rearranging the $W_0^{1-\gamma}$ term with Eq. (6.4), p. 75):

$$U = \frac{R - \frac{1}{2}\gamma\sigma^2}{W_0^{\gamma-1}},$$

implying that investor utility as $\left(R - \frac{1}{2}\gamma\sigma^2\right)$ *diminishes* with increasing endowed wealth, W_0 (the greater the wealth, the less the inclination to subject the wealth to risk).

(2) An investor with $\gamma = 1$ (a log-wealth utility investor) receives utility, U, per period of investment as Eq. (9.6) (with Eq. (6.5), p. 75, Eq. (7.3) and Eq. (8.10)) as:

$$U = \mu,$$

implying that investment utility is dependent on the investment's exponential growth rate (μ), but is independent of either risk (σ) or endowed wealth, W_0.

(3) An investor with $\gamma = 0$ (a risk neutral investor) receives utility, U, per period of investment as Eq. (9.6) (with $\gamma = 0$) as:

$$U = R \cdot W_0,$$

which is consistent with $\gamma = 0$ in Eq. (9.2):

$$U = W,$$

implying that investment utility depends only on the expected generation of wealth $(R \cdot W_0)$.

In seeking to maximize utility, investors cannot control their initial wealth, W_0. It follows that the bid to maximize utility as Eq. (9.6) is the attempt to maximize:

$$\boxed{U = R - \frac{1}{2}\gamma\sigma^2.} \tag{9.7}$$

The equation states that investors seek a higher expected return R, but a lower variance σ^2, with sensitivity to variance denoted by γ.

A practical difficulty with Eq. (9.7) is that the exponential growth rate, R, for a portfolio's performance does not lend itself directly to a decomposition in terms of component assets, which is more readily handled by the discrete-time return. For this reason, with a view to implementing empirical observed data (in Section 9.6), it is useful to refigure Eq. (9.7) in discrete time. Because we are considering growth as compounding successively over short periods of time, this is readily accomplished. Thus, for the expected *discrete* return, $E(R)$, defined as

$$\$W_0[1 + E(R)]$$

$\equiv$ expected wealth outcome of investing $\$W_0$ for a single period,

we have (with e^R as Eq. (7.1))[2]:

$$1 + E(R) \equiv e^R. \tag{9.8}$$

---

[2]Strictly, we should not use the notation R to represent both the *exponential* return R (defined by Eq. (7.1)) *and* the expected *discrete* return, $E(R)$ (similarly, we have retained σ to denote the standard deviation of returns about $E(R)$). However, allowing ourselves to remain with R in $E(R)$ — rather than introducing an alternative symbol — allows for a more agreeable continuation in notation.

Allowing that R over such a short time period is small, we can express the above identity (with Eq. (6.11)) as:

$$E(R) \simeq R, \tag{9.9}$$

and similarly equate the standard deviation about $E(R)$ with the standard deviation of exponential returns, σ. Over a reasonably short time interval, we can therefore express Eq. (9.7) (approximately) as

$$\boxed{U = E(R) - \frac{1}{2}\gamma\sigma^2.} \tag{9.10}$$

9.3. Portfolio Optimization

To see how investors might maximize Eq. (9.10), we commence by restricting ourselves to a model of the market comprising three asset classes — equity stocks (with expected return, $E(R_E)$, and standard deviation, σ_E), bonds (with expected return, $E(R_B)$, and standard deviation, σ_B), and a risk-free asset (with return, r_f). Thus, Eq. (9.10) (with Eq. (6.69), p. 111, and Eq. (6.67), p. 110) for the utility of a portfolio, U_P, can be expressed as:

$$U_P = \omega_E E(R_E) + \omega_B E(R_B) + (1 - \omega_E - \omega_B)r_f$$

$$- \frac{1}{2}\gamma\left(\omega_E^2\sigma_E^2 + \omega_B^2\sigma_B^2 + 2\omega_E\omega_B\sigma_{E,B}\right), \tag{9.11}$$

where ω_E is the proportion of the investor's portfolio allocated to equity stocks, ω_B is the proportion allocated to bonds, and $(1 - \omega_E - \omega_B)$ is the proportion allocated to the risk-free asset; and where, for ease of expression in this chapter, we have replaced the notations of Chapter 6:

$$\sigma_E = \sigma(R_E),$$

$$\sigma_E^2 = VAR(R_E),$$

$$\sigma_{E,B} = COV(R_E, R_B).$$

Differentiating Eq. (9.11) with respect to first ω_E and then ω_B, and equating outcomes to zero (to maximize U_P as in Chapter 6.8), we obtain (with Eqs. (6.25)–(6.26) and (6.27)–(6.28), pp. 94–95) for equities:

$$\boxed{E(R_E) - r_f - \gamma\left(\omega_E\sigma_E^2 + \omega_B\sigma_{E,B}\right) = 0.} \tag{9.12}$$

And similarly for bonds:

$$E(R_B) - r_f - \gamma\left(\omega_B \sigma_B^2 + \omega_E \sigma_{B,E}\right) = 0. \tag{9.13}$$

Which are alternatively expressed:

$$E(R_E) - r_f = \gamma \sigma_{E,M}, \tag{9.14}$$

$$E(R_B) - r_f = \gamma \sigma_{B,M}, \tag{9.15}$$

where (with Eqs. (6.66), p. 109):

$$\sigma_{E,M} = \omega_E \sigma_E^2 + \omega_B \sigma_{E,B}, \tag{9.16}$$

$$\sigma_{B,M} = \omega_B \sigma_B^2 + \omega_E \sigma_{E,B}, \tag{9.17}$$

are, respectively, the covariances of equity and bond returns with the market (that includes equities, bonds, and a risk-free asset) return.[3] Provided estimates are available for the remaining parameters, Eqs. (9.12) and (9.13) can be solved to determine the optimal portfolio allocations for equity and debt (ω_E, ω_B) for a given investor utility, γ.

9.4. The CAPM

Equations (9.12) and (9.13) imply the standard CAPM. To see this, we multiply Eq. (9.14) by ω_E and Eq. (9.15) by ω_B, and add the equations together to obtain (with Eq. (6.68), p. 110):

$$E(R_M) - r_f = \gamma \sigma_M^2, \tag{9.18}$$

where $E(R_M) = \omega_E E(R_E) + \omega_B E(R_B) + (1 - \omega_E - \omega_B)r_f$. Using Eq. (9.18) to eliminate γ in Eqs. (9.14) and (9.15), we obtain

$$E(R_i) = r_f + \beta_i[(E(R_M) - r_f](i = E, B), \tag{9.19}$$

where (with Eq. (6.70), p. 112):

$$\beta_i = \left(\sigma_{i,M}/\sigma_M^2\right)(i = E, B), \tag{9.20}$$

which is the CAPM with the market portfolio inclusive of bonds and the risk-free asset. And, so, intriguingly, the principle of the CAPM is with us again.

---

[3] Equations (9.14) and (9.15) comply with Merton (1973).

9.5. Repeated Investment Periods

With Eq. (9.7), we have the utility, U_N, over N investment periods for a portfolio (with Eqs. (6.76) and (6.77), pp. 118–119) as

$$U_N = N \cdot R_P - \frac{1}{2}\gamma\left(\sqrt{N}\sigma_P\right)^2$$

or

$$U_N = N\left[R_P - \frac{1}{2}\gamma\sigma_P^2\right]. \qquad (9.21)$$

Equation (9.21) confirms that with repeated number of periods, N, the utility per period remains unchanged. In this case, the solution for an investor's chosen portfolio proportions (ω_E, ω_B) is independent of the number of investment periods, N, over which the investment is held.

9.6. A Worked Example

This section provides an example of portfolio allocation in the context of empirically observed market data. In this context, we clarify the contribution of the capital market line (CML), as well as revealing the CAPM as an algebraic consequence of the CML set-up.

9.6.1 *Investors Risk Aversion and Required Equity Return*

We consider a realistic representation of the market following Sharpe (2007). Thus, we allow that the market portfolio, M, can be modeled as $\omega_E = 62.0\%$ and $\omega_B = 31.0\%$ (a ratio of equity to bonds $= 2{:}1$) with 7.0% cash (short-term investments, such as the money markets or treasury bills). As Sharpe, we also take it that

Cash provides an annualized risk-free return, r_f $= 5.0\%$,

Bonds have an annualized expected return, $E(R_B)$ $= 6.4\%$,

With annualized standard deviation, σ_B $= 5.6\%$,
and that

Stock returns have an annualized standard deviation, σ_E $= 17.5\%$,
with

Correlation between stock and bond returns, $CORR_{E,B}$ $= 0.65$.

The solution of Eqs. (9.12) and (9.13) as

$$E(R_E) - 0.05 - \gamma[\omega_E.0.175^2 + \omega_B.0.65(0.175)(0.056)] = 0, \quad (9.22)$$

$$0.064 - 0.05 - \gamma[\omega_E.0.65(0.056)(0.175) + \omega_B.0.056^2] = 0, \quad (9.23)$$

with $\omega_E = 0.62$ and $\omega_B = 0.31$, then determines that the representative investor has risk aversion[4]:

$$\gamma = 2.845$$

and expectation of return on equity: $\quad E(R_E) = 10.96\%$ (annualized)

In other words, the model of Eqs. (9.12) and (9.13) in combination with the market characteristics observed empirically by Sharpe (2007) imply that investors can be represented with risk aversion $\gamma = 2.845$ with an expectation for annualized equity returns $= 10.96\%$. The following calculations for the market portfolio (M), which are used subsequently in the chapter, then follow:

The outcome market portfolio, M, has expected return, $E(R_M)$:

$$E(R_M) = \omega_E E(R_E) + \omega_B E(R_B) + (1 - \omega_E - \omega_B)r_f$$
$$= 0.62(10.96\%) + 0.31(6.4\%) + (1 - 0.62 - 0.31)(5.0\%)$$
$$= \underline{9.13\%}$$

$$(9.24)$$

and variance, σ_M^2 (with Eq. (6.68)):

$$\sigma_M^2 = \omega_E \sigma_{E,M} + \omega_B \sigma_{B,M}, \quad (9.25)$$

---

[4]We might note that values of γ greater than 1 (log-wealth utility) quickly become severe on investor risk aversion. Thus, given an investment opportunity that either doubles or halves wealth with equal probability, an investor with $\gamma = 2$ would require a probability, p, of doubling wealth, determined (with Eqs. (8.8), p. 139 and (9.2)) by

$$p(2X)^{-1} + (1-p)\left(\frac{1}{2}X\right)^{-1} = X^{-1},$$

which solves for the investor's required probability of doubling as $p = 66.67\%$, whereas an investor with $\gamma = 3$ would require a probability p of doubling wealth, determined by

$$p\frac{(2X)^{-2}}{2} + (1-p)\frac{\left(\frac{1}{2}X\right)^{-2}}{2} = \frac{X^{-2}}{2},$$

which solves for the investor's required probability of doubling as $p = 80\%$.

for which (with Eq. (6.66)), we have the covariance of equity returns with the market, $\sigma_{E,M}$, as

$$\sigma_{E,M} = \omega_E \sigma_E^2 + \omega_B \sigma_{E,B}, \tag{9.26}$$

which (with Eq. (6.72), p. 114):

$$= \omega_E \sigma_E^2 + \omega_B CORR_{E,B} \sigma_E \sigma_B$$
$$= 0.62(0.175)^2 + 0.31(0.65)(0.175)(0.056) = \underline{0.021}$$

and, similarly, for the covariance of bond returns with the market, $\sigma_{B,M}$:

$$\sigma_{B,M} = \omega_B \sigma_B^2 + \omega_E \sigma_{E,B} \tag{9.27}$$
$$= \omega_B \sigma_B^2 + \omega_E CORR_{E,B} \sigma_E \sigma_B$$
$$= 0.31(0.056)^2 + 0.62(0.65)(0.175)(0.056) = \underline{0.0049}.$$

Thus Eq. (9.25) provides

$$\sigma_M^2 = 0.62(0.022) + 0.31(0.0049) = \underline{0.0145}$$

and market standard deviation, $\sigma_M = 0.1205$ (12.05%).

The locations of the risk-free asset, bonds, and equity, as well as the above market portfolio, are represented schematically in Fig. 9.1.

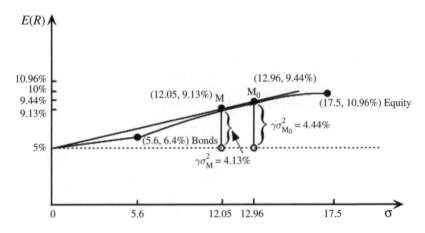

Figure 9.1. The CML for equity and bonds.

9.6.2 *The CML*

When we derive an optimal portfolio solution of Eqs. (9.12) and (9.13) across equity, bonds, and the risk-free rate — in the above case, $(\omega_E, \omega_B, 1-\omega_E-\omega_B) = (62\%, 31\%, 7\%)$ — then all other portfolio allocations $(\omega_E, \omega_B, 1 - \omega_E - \omega_B)$ that hold ω_E/ω_B in the same ratio as the above optimal portfolio — in this case, $62\%{:}31\% = 2{:}1$ — are also optimal portfolios. This follows by inspection of Eqs. (9.12) and (9.13). We can see that any portfolio for which $\omega_E/\omega_B = 2{:}1$, is also a solution of Eqs. (9.12) and (9.13) by a rescaling of the risk aversion parameter, γ. As an example, the portfolio, M_O, of equity and bonds in the ratio 2:1, but which excludes the riskless asset — which is to say, the portfolio $(\omega_E, \omega_B, 1 - \omega_E - \omega_B) = (66.666\%, 33.333\%, 0\%)$ — must offer an optimal portfolio allocation for investors with risk aversion $(\gamma) = 2.845$ (the previous γ) multiplied by $0.93 = 2.65$.

In Fig. 9.1, the straight line joining the risk-free asset with the portfolio M_0 that holds the two risky assets (equity and bonds) in their market proportions (in this case: $62\%{:}31\% = 2{:}1$) — but excluding the risk-free asset — is called the *capital market line*, which was introduced in Fig. 8.2. The line represents all combinations of the market portfolio, M_O, with the risk-free asset.

The above inspection of Eqs. (9.12) and (9.13) has revealed that provided M_O is an optimal allocation solution of the equations, all portfolio combinations of M_O with the risk-free asset are also optimal portfolios as solutions of the equations. Thus, the CML — which by construction represents combinations of the market portfolio M_O with the risk-free asset — is also the line of optimal portfolios for investors with different levels of risk-aversion, γ. And, thus, the market portfolio M — to which we allocated 7.0% cash as $(\omega_E, \omega_B, 1 - \omega_E - \omega_B) = (62\%, 31\%, 7\%)$ — is also located on this line, as depicted in Fig. 9.1.

Having established that the portfolios on the CML are optimal portfolios, it follows that — with the exception of portfolio M_0 itself — portfolios that represent alternative combinations of equity and bonds with no risk-free asset must all lie *below* the CML, as depicted by the curve joining the bond and equity clusters in Fig. 9.1. We therefore have the outcome that efficient portfolio choices are actually restricted to the portfolio M_0 in some combination with the risk-free asset; which is to say, all efficient portfolio choices comprise equity and bonds in the same ratio (2:1 in this case).[5]

The following additional calculations for the optimal market portfolio, M_O (which excludes the risk-free asset), follow as for the calculations for portfolio M above.

For the portfolio M_0, we have expected return, $E(R_{M0})$:

$$E(R_{M0}) = \omega_E E(R_E) + \omega_B E(R_B) \tag{9.28}$$
$$= 0.66(10.96\%) + 0.33(6.4\%) = \underline{9.44\%}$$

and variance, σ_{M0}^2 (with Eq. (6.68)):

$$\sigma_{M0}^2 = \omega_E \sigma_{E,M0} + \omega_B \sigma_{B,M0}, \tag{9.29}$$

for which (with Eqs. (6.66) and (6.72)):

$$\sigma_{E,M0} = \omega_E \sigma_E^2 + \omega_B CORR_{E,B} \sigma_E \sigma_B$$
$$= 0.666(0.175)^2 + 0.333(0.65)(0.175)(0.056) = \underline{0.0225}.$$

And, similarly

$$\sigma_{B,M0} = \omega_B \sigma_B^2 + \omega_E CORR_{E,B} \sigma_E \sigma_B$$
$$= 0.333(0.056)^2 + 0.666(0.65)(0.175)(0.056) = \underline{0.0053},$$

leading with Eq. (9.29) to

$$\sigma_{M0}^2 = 0.666(0.0225) + 0.333(0.0053) = \underline{0.01675},$$

so that $\sigma_{M0} = 0.1296(\underline{12.96\%})$.[6]

---

[5]To move to the right of the market portfolio, M_0 (assets with greater standard deviation), we must either borrow at the investment risk-free rate so as to remain on the CML, or move along the efficient frontier towards the equity cluster itself.

[6]Since portfolio M differs from M_0 only by the inclusion of the risk-free asset (as 7.0% of the portfolio M), it follows that (see footnote 9, Chapter 8):

$$\frac{\sigma_M}{\sigma_{M0}} = 0.93,$$

which is verified by the above values ($\sigma_M = 12.05\%$, $\sigma_{M0} = 12.96\%$).

9.6.3 *The CAPM and Roll's Critique*

The CAPM (Eqs. (9.19) and (9.20)) was presented in relation to $E(R_M)$ — the expected return on the market portfolio, M, of equity, bonds, and the risk-free asset. In this case, we have (with values above):

$$\beta_{\text{equity}} = \frac{\sigma_{E,M}}{\sigma_M^2} = \frac{0.021}{0.0145} = 1.443$$

and

$$E(R_M) - r_f = 9.13\% - 5\% = 4.13\%,$$

giving with the CAPM (Eq. (9.19)):

$$E(R_E) = 5.0 + 1.443(4.13) = 10.96\%,$$

which is precisely consistent with the value for $E(R_E)$ determined above.

Equally, however, we could have designated $E(R_M)$ as *any* efficient portfolio — which is to say, any portfolio on the CML. To see this, suppose we had designated the expected return, $E(R_{M0})$, for the portfolio, M_0, of equity and bonds only as representing the market portfolio for the CAPM. In this case, we would derive (with the above values):

$$\beta_{\text{equity}} = \frac{\sigma_{E,M0}}{\sigma_{M0}^2} = \frac{0.0225}{0.01675} = 1.343$$

and

$$E(R_M) - r_f = 9.44\% - 5\% = 4.44\%,$$

given with the CAPM:

$$E(R_E) - r_f = 5.0 + 1.343(4.44) = 10.96\%,$$

which again is precisely consistent with the value determined for $E(R_E)$ above.[7]

---

[7] Similarly, for bonds, with the market folio identified as M, we have

$$\beta_{\text{bonds}} = \frac{\sigma_{B,M}}{\sigma_M^2} = \frac{0.0049}{0.0145} = 0.338$$

and

$$E(R_M) - r_f = 9.13\% - 5\% = 4.13\%.$$

The above outcomes confirm Roll's (1977) hypothesis that provided the portfolio designated as the "market" portfolio in the CAPM is efficient with regards to the total set of assets considered (which is to say, no other portfolio of assets from the set with the same standard deviation as the designated "market" portfolio has a superior expectation of return to the designated "market" portfolio), the CAPM can be applied to recapture the original risk-return relations of the assets that constitute the market portfolio in the first place. In effect, the CAPM is an algebraic convolution that does not require empirical justification. Conversely, it is obvious that[8] in using

giving

$$E(R_B) - r_f = 5.0 + 0.338(4.13)$$
$$= 6.40\%,$$

the input value above. Or, alternatively, with the market defined as M_0, we have

$$\beta_{bonds} = \frac{\sigma_{B,M0}}{\sigma^2_{M0}} = \frac{0.0053}{0.01675} = 0.3164$$

and

$$E(R_{M0}) - r_f = 9.44\% - 5\% = 4.44\%$$

giving

$$E(R_B) - r_f = 5.0 + 0.3164(4.44)$$
$$= 6.40\%,$$

again as above.

We can also apply the results to confirm Eq. (9.18). Thus, we have

$$E(R_M) = \gamma \sigma^2_M + r_f$$
$$= 2.845(0.0145) + 0.05 = 9.13\%$$

as above, and

$$E(R_{M0}) = \gamma \sigma^2_{M0} + r_f$$
$$= 2.65(0.01675) + 0.05 = 9.44\%,$$

as above.

[8]"It is obvious that . . ." There is a story relating to G. H. Hardy, professor of mathematics at Oxford in the 1940s — the self-same who is quoted at the commencement of Chapter 5 — who while developing one of his mind-bending mathematical proofs for his students (chalk and blackboard in those days) at one point indicated flatly, "It is therefore obvious that," and began to chalk up the next line of the mathematical proof. At which point, he hesitated,

the CAPM to reconstruct expectations of return for risky assets, we cannot adopt as a market portfolio, a portfolio that does *not* lie on the CML. Roll (1977) goes so far as to argue that when the selected market portfolio does *not* lie on the true CML, any outcome prediction for stock returns is strictly possible.

Nevertheless, we might observe that the degree of error due to misallocating the true market portfolio is not determined by how far removed the "chosen market portfolio" is from the "true market portfolio", but rather by how far removed it is from the CML. If, for example, we had chosen to estimate investor expectations for *bond* returns with the CAPM with a market portfolio identified as *equity* (which, we might observe, lies significantly removed from both the true market portfolio (M_0) and *bonds*, but may not be so significantly removed from the CML), we would proceed as follows. We have (with the values above) the covariance of bonds with equity, $\sigma_{B,E}$:

$$\sigma_{B,E} = \text{CORR}_{B,E}\sigma_B\sigma_E$$
$$= 0.65(0.056)(0.175) = 0.00637$$

and

$$\sigma_E^2 = 0.175^2 = 0.0306,$$

which together imply that beta for bonds, β_{bonds}, is estimated as

$$\beta_{\text{bonds}} = 0.00637/0.0306 = 0.208,$$

and investors' expectation of return on bonds is then calculated with the CAPM as

$$E(R_B) = 0.05 + 0.208(0.1096 - 0.05) = 6.24\%,$$

which may be considered not too far removed from the actual input value (6.4% above).

---

bowed his head in consideration for some minutes, before walking out of the lecture room in thought to return some minutes later to his baffled students, and repeat in the same flat tone "It is therefore obvious that," and proceed to complete the next line of the mathematical argument.

9.7. Can We Retain Log-Wealth Utility?

If we were to impose a log-wealth utility function ($\gamma = 1$) in the example of Section 9.6, and solve Eqs. (9.12) and (9.13), we would find that we calculate investors' required expectation of return on equity $= 7.1\%$ and the return on bonds $= 5.5\%$ (other inputs as above). Comparing these returns with the input risk-free rate for cash ($=5.0\%$), we are left with an equity risk premium of about 2.0%, which is consistent with our findings in Chapter 8.

Alternatively, we can insist on a log-wealth utility function in combination with a risk premium of equity over the risk-free rate close to 6% and solve for the implied standard deviations of equity and bonds. We then determine standard deviations close to 30% for equity and close to 10% for bonds, conforming with our findings for equity in Chapter 8.

Thus, although the numbers can be made to "slide around" somewhat, we determine either a market equity risk premium of approximately 2% as commensurate with a log-wealth utility function (as was determined in Chapter 8); or an equity risk premium of 6% (as conforms with historical data), which requires either that (1) investors have a risk aversion, γ, close to 2.65, or, if we wish to retain a log-wealth utility, that (2) the standard deviations of historical asset returns, as implemented in Eqs. (9.12) and (9.13), fail to sufficiently capture investment risk exposure, and that standard deviations for equity and bonds close to 30% and 10%, respectively, are appropriate.

We recall that in Chapter 8, we considered that the assumption that stock returns are normally distributed may have led us to significantly underestimate the actually much fatter tails in the distribution that investors must face. For example, if investors perceive that the possibility of a cascading fall in prices — as, say, stock price declines create an atmosphere of uncertainty and subsequent further declines in a self-fuelling bear market — is greater than is as captured by the standard deviation of market returns measured under stable conditions, we can imagine that higher standard deviations for risky assets are required in Eqs. (9.12) and (9.13) than those that are measured under more stable market conditions. Thus, it is possible to conjecture that investors can be described as conforming to a log-wealth utility function, but that apparently high implied standard deviations for equity (30%) and bonds (10%) are required in Eqs. (9.12) and (9.13) to capture investors' awareness of the downward risk exposure not captured in a normal distribution.

9.8. Generalization of the Equations of Portfolio Choice

Equations (9.12) and (9.13) are expressed in matrix form as

$$\begin{bmatrix} E(R_E) - r_f \\ E(R_B) - r_f \end{bmatrix} = \gamma \begin{bmatrix} \sigma_E^2 & \sigma_{E,B} \\ \sigma_{B,E} & \sigma_B^2 \end{bmatrix} \begin{bmatrix} \omega_E \\ \omega_B \end{bmatrix}, \tag{9.30}$$

which generalizes as the solution for the asset risk premiums as a function of the portfolio selection weights (ω_i) for N available risky assets as

$$\begin{bmatrix} E(R_1) - r_f \\ E(R_2) - r_f \\ \vdots \\ \vdots \\ \vdots \\ E(R_N) - r_f \end{bmatrix} = \gamma \begin{bmatrix} \sigma_1^2 & \sigma_{1,2} & \cdot & \cdot & \cdot & \sigma_{1,N} \\ \sigma_{2,1} & \sigma_2^2 & & & & \\ \sigma_{3,1} & \sigma_{3,2} & \sigma_3^2 & & & \\ \cdot & \cdot & \cdot & \cdot & & \\ \sigma_{N,1} & \sigma_{N,2} & & & & \sigma_N^N \end{bmatrix} \begin{bmatrix} \omega_1 \\ \omega_2 \\ \vdots \\ \vdots \\ \vdots \\ \omega_N \end{bmatrix} \tag{9.31}$$

or, alternatively, as

$$\boxed{R = \gamma \Omega W,} \tag{9.32}$$

where the vector R represents the vector of the expected excess returns, $E(R_i) - r_f$, γ is Pratt's measure of relative risk aversion, Ω represents the covariance matrix, $[\sigma_{i,j}]$, of the variances and covariances between the expected returns, $E(R_i)$, and W is the vector of optimal weights ($\omega_1, \omega_2, \ldots \omega_N$) of the asset allocations in the portfolio.

Equation (9.32) is the solution to the optimization of utility as Eq. (9.7), which is time invariant (Section 9.5). In transferring from exponential to discrete time returns in Eq. (9.32), the assumption is that the inputs to Eq. (9.32) are measured over a sufficiently short time period that they can be scaled though time as Eqs. (6.76) and (6.77) so as to retain the time invariance of the equation. With this qualification, Eq. (9.32) represents *our model of asset pricing and portfolio allocation*. It represents asset pricing and portfolio allocations as mutually dependent. As observed in Section 9.4, the CAPM then represents a simplified outcome of the equations.

To achieve an expression for rational portfolio construction given the expected returns, $E(R_i)$, on individual assets, we express Eq. (9.32) as

$$W = \Omega^{-1}R/\gamma, \tag{9.33}$$

where Ω^{-1} represents the inverse of the covariance matrix.[9]

9.9. Time to Reflect: What Have We Learned?

We have postulated a model of market growth (with mean exponential growth, μ, and standard deviation, σ, as Fig. 6.8) and investor propensity to engage in such growth (determined by utility as Eq. (9.7)). The derivations follow from the proposition that exponential or continuously-compounding growth rates are normally distributed, in conjunction with a utility function that has generalized the salient features of a log-wealth utility function (investors respond not to absolute changes in wealth status, but to proportionate changes in wealth status). This has led to Eq. (9.32) as our joint model of capital asset pricing and portfolio allocation. The CAPM — as the statement that risk and return are consistently related — is revealed naturally in the model.

The fact that the CAPM is not revealed in the history of stock prices has many possible explanations (summarized in Chapter 2). The notion that tests of the CAPM are inadequate as encapsulated in Roll's (1977) critique has provided a recurring explanation as to empiricists' lack of success in identifying beta in the data of past stock prices. Consistent with Roll, we have demonstrated that provided a portfolio lies on the CML, it is eligible as a proxy for the total market, in making predictions consistent with the CAPM, but that when we choose a portfolio that is not on the CML, incorrect

---

[9]Equation (9.33) conforms with Merton's (1969) Eq. 60. An unsatisfactory feature of the "portfolio asset allocation" form of Eq. (9.33), is the sensitivity of the outcome portfolio allocations in practice to the input assumed expected returns for the individual assets. For example, in the worked example above, changing the risk-free rate from 5% to 4.5% (while retaining other inputs, particularly, the return on the bonds as 6.4% with standard deviation 5.6%) works to distort the allocation ratio of equity:bonds as 2:1 in the example, to a ratio of equity:bonds that is closer to 1:2.

predictions may be generated. Roll's critique insists that the complete market of investment opportunities (which must include the career potential of investors, their real estate holdings, their social security, etc., for example) is effectively unknowable. Nevertheless, Fig. 9.1 has demonstrated that provided the "true" complete market portfolio lies sufficiently close to the chosen CML, such CML leads to reasonable estimates of the expected returns for assets consistent with the true CAPM. In this case, Roll's critique may not be as significant in invalidating tests of the CAPM as is generally supposed by empiricists when data fails to support the model.[10]

Equation (9.33) reveals the logical portfolio allocation across assets consistent with asset expected outcomes. Just as we can justify the CAPM as a rational cost of equity equation for the firm, so Eq. (9.33) represents a valid model in principle for investor asset allocation preferences, assuming knowledge of the required inputs in the model. However, care must be taken with the model. It must not be taken too literally. We have found that the model as Eq. (9.32) is generally robust in predicting asset expected returns consistent with empirically observed allocations (as demonstrated with Eqs. (9.12) and (9.13), as was also noted to be the case in Chapter 8 with a two-assets model comprising a risky market and a riskless asset). In reverse, however, the model of Eq. (9.32) is sensitive to the inputs when addressed in the form of Eq. (9.33) aimed at determining investors' optimal portfolio allocations. Thus, we have observed that quite modest shifts in input asset returns imply large shifts in predicted portfolio allocations. Furthermore, in practice, the ability to meaningfully attribute the (likely unstable) variances and co-variances as required in the model diminishes rapidly with increasing number of asset allocations. We need to accept that mathematical finance can take us only so far. In fact, for portfolio management, an understanding of investor sentiment and an appreciation of markets in the economic cycle are always likely to be more important than a determination of the mathematical outcomes of the inputs in Eq. (9.33).

---

[10]After all, if indeed an asset class does exist that lies significantly above the CML — that is, an asset class that provides an exceptionally high expectation of return in relation to its market exposure — it is rather surprising that it has never been explicitly revealed as such.

In the context of Eq. (9.32) as Eqs. (9.12) and (9.13), our analysis has suggested a value for investors' measure of relative risk aversion, γ, in the range of 2.5–3.0. This is to say, investors are significantly more risk-averse than is captured by a log-wealth utility (with $\gamma = 1$). Flexibility, however, must be allowed before interpreting the above measure of investors' risk aversion (γ in the range of 2.5–3.0) literally. An alternative possibility is that the standard deviations of assets as input to the model are failing to fully capture the volatility that is implied in the downside distribution tail, which is the outcome of increases in volatility with falling prices, which trigger an increase in the equity risk premium consistent with Eqs. (9.12) and (9.13). It is generally recognized that markets fall more steeply than they climb (consider falling in the elevator and climbing on the escalator), which may be due to the fact that news brings with it an uncertainty of interpretation, so that good news is tempered by uncertainty until implications are confirmed, whereas bad news is reinforced by heightened uncertainty. Thus, the value of γ close to 2.65 required to benchmark the capital market model of Eqs. (9.12) and (9.13) to empirical observations, might be not so much the outcome of investor risk aversion greater than that captured by log-wealth utility, but rather might be the model's "compensation" allowing that the tail of negative growth outcomes is fatter than indicated by the standard deviation of market returns measured under more stable market conditions.

Allowing the need for such "benchmarking", Eqs. (9.12) and (9.13) generalized as Eq. (9.32) constitute our joint model of asset pricing and portfolio allocation.

Chapter 10

Stock Mispricing

Whether we're talking about socks or stocks, I like buying quality merchandise when it is marked down.	*The worse a situation becomes, the less it takes to turn it around, and the bigger the upside*
Warren Buffett	George Soros
We had a bubble in housing.	*History may not repeat itself, but it does rhyme a lot.*
Alan Greenspan	Mark Twain

10.1. Introduction[1]

In this chapter, we derive a theoretical framework of mispricing, and show how the fundamental models of asset price growth (Eq. (6.78), p. 120) and portfolio asset allocation (Eq. (9.32), p. 171) must be adjusted. In this way, mispricing is introduced as a significant dimension of asset pricing. We proceed to demonstrate how mispricing can be manipulated to outperform a capital-weighted index of stocks. Thereafter, we present evidence that the outperformance of portfolios of stocks of either high book-to-market (B/M) or of small firms in the Fama and French (1993, 1996) three-factor (FF-3F) model can be attributed to these portfolios capturing, on aggregate, stocks that are underpriced.

Accordingly, Section 10.2 introduces a model of mispricing. In Section 10.3, we show, with an example, how mispricing impacts a portfolio's valuation. Section 10.4 generalizes the example in terms of our

---

[1]This chapter develops ideas that were presented in *Journal of Investment Management* (Dempsey, 2012; Shi, Dempsey and Irlicht, 2015). I am indeed grateful and indebted to the editors and reviewers of this journal for supporting and publishing this work.

175

model of mispricing. This leads us to consider that an investment strategy of equal-weighted portfolio asset allocations is capable of "immunizing" mispricing so as to outperform a conventional capital-weighted index (Section 10.5). In Section 10.6, we propose a quite general portfolio of non-capital-weighted assets as an "immunizing" investment strategy. Section 10.7 progresses to advance mispricing as an explanation of stock behavior as described by the FF-3F model. Section 10.8 concludes with a brief discussion.[2]

10.2. The Model

We make a distinction between the observed market price of an asset, p_t, and the notion of the asset's fundamental or intrinsic value, p^*, by expressing

$$\boxed{p_t = p_t^* e^{Z\varepsilon},} \tag{10.1}$$

where Z represents a random selection from the normal distribution with mean zero and unit standard deviation (as presented in Fig. 6.3, p. 85) with the outcome multiplied by ε, so that ε represents the standard deviation of the mispricing growth/decline exponential rates that impact the asset's fundamental valuation. In Eq. (6.22), we considered the market price, p_{t+1}, of an asset at time $t + 1$ in relation to its market price, p_t, at time t as

$$p_{t+1} = p_t e^{\mu + Z\sigma},$$

where μ is the asset's mean exponential growth rate for the period from t to $t + 1$ with Z as above with the outcome multiplied by σ, so that σ represents the standard deviation of the potential growth rates about μ. We now consider Eq. (6.22) as representing the *fundamental* or *intrinsic* progression of the firm's stock price, p^*, so that

$$p_{t+1}^* = p_t^* e^{\mu + Z\sigma}. \tag{10.2}$$

The difference between the exponential growth operator, $e^{\mu + Z\sigma}$, in Eq. (10.2) and the mispricing operator, $e^{Z\varepsilon}$, of Eq. (10.1), is that p_{t+1}^* in Eq. (10.2) is the outcome at time $t + 1$ of the operator $e^{\mu + Z\sigma}$ applied to the asset's fundamental valuation p_t^* at time t, by which process the asset's

---

[2]Equations that are referenced in subsequent chapters are bordered.

fundamental growth or decline is advanced, whereas p_t in Eq. (10.1) is the outcome market price of the mispricing operator $e^{Z\varepsilon}$ applied at the contemporaneous time t to the fundamental value, p_t^*.

With Eq. (10.1), we can write

$$\frac{p_{t+1}}{p_t} = \frac{p_{t+1}^*}{p_t^*} \frac{e^{Z_{t+1}\varepsilon}}{e^{Z_t\varepsilon}}, \tag{10.3}$$

which provides (with Eqs. (6.1) and (6.4), p. 74–75):

$$\frac{p_{t+1}}{p_t} = \frac{p_{t+1}^*}{p_t^*} e^{(Z_{t+1}-Z_t)\varepsilon} \tag{10.4}$$

or

$$p_{t+1} = p_t \frac{p_{t+1}^*}{p_t^*} e^{(Z_{t+1}-Z_t)\varepsilon}, \tag{10.5}$$

which provides (with Eq. (10.2)):

$$p_{t+1} = p_t e^{\mu+Z\sigma} e^{(Z_{t+1}-Z_t)\varepsilon} \tag{10.6}$$

or (with Eq. (6.1)):

$$p_{t+1} = p_t e^{\mu+Z\sigma+(Z_{t+1}-Z_t)\varepsilon}. \tag{10.7}$$

In the above equations, the term $e^{(Z_{t+1}-Z_t)\varepsilon}$ represents a random selection from the distribution, Z, multiplied by ε at $t+1$ minus a random selection from the distribution Z multiplied by ε at time t. The $e^{(Z_{t-1}-Z_t)\varepsilon}$ term therefore captures the observed change in price from time t to $t+1$, as an outcome of mispricing at both the commencement and end of the period. With Eq. (6.74) (p. 116), we have the outcome that the variance of a process that subtracts two outcomes (in this case, each with variance, ε^2) from a normal distribution has variance $VAR(Z_{t+1}\varepsilon - Z_t\varepsilon)$ as

$$VAR(Z_{t+1}\varepsilon - Z_t\varepsilon) = VAR(Z_{t+1}\varepsilon) + VAR(Z_t\varepsilon)$$
$$- 2\sigma(Z_{t+1}\varepsilon)\sigma(Z_t\varepsilon)CORR(Z_{t+1}, Z_t). \tag{10.8}$$

Provided the time period over which the asset is held is sufficient for the mispricing of an asset at the end of the period to be independent of its mispricing at the commencement of the period, the correlation coefficient, $CORR(Z_{t+1}, Z_t)$, in Eq. (10.8) is zero, and we have

$$VAR\left[(Z_{t+1} - Z_t)\varepsilon\right] = \varepsilon^2 + \varepsilon^2 = 2\varepsilon^2. \tag{10.9}$$

If, however, the asset is held for a shorter period, the correlation coefficient in Eq. (10.8) is greater than zero and the variance is reduced accordingly.

Similarly, the assumption that the mispricing growth/decline exponential rates applied to an asset are independent of its fundamental valuation allows us to write (again with Eq. (6.74)):

$$VAR\left[Z\sigma + (Z_{t+1} - Z_t)\varepsilon\right] = \sigma^2 + 2\varepsilon^2. \tag{10.10}$$

Over N periods, the fundamental variance is $N\sigma^2$ (Eq. (6.77), p. 119), whereas the variance due to mispricing remains maximized as $2\varepsilon^2$ (which occurs when the asset is held sufficiently long for the mispricing of the asset at the end of N periods to be independent of its mispricing at the commencement of the initial period). Under such conditions, over N periods, the standard deviation, sd, of the growth process is expressed:

$$sd = \sqrt{N\sigma^2 + 2\varepsilon^2}, \tag{10.11}$$

so that, with mispricing, the fundamental model of growth as Eq. (6.78):

$$p_{t+N} = p_t e^{N\mu + Z\sqrt{N\sigma^2}},$$

becomes

$$\boxed{p_{t+N} = p_t e^{N\mu + Z\sqrt{N\sigma^2 + 2\varepsilon^2}}.} \tag{10.12}$$

10.3. Mispricing and Portfolio Valuation

As an introduction to the impact of mispricing on portfolio valuation, consider the binomial operator of Fig. 6.7 and applied as in Fig. 10.1 to four stocks, each of which has fundamental or intrinsic value $100

Figure 10.1. The binomial mispricing operator (with $\varepsilon = 0.693$).

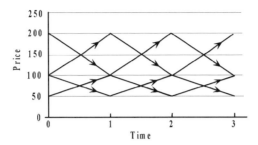

Figure 10.2. The binomial mispricing operator with $\varepsilon = 0.693$ applied to four stocks.

as in Fig. 10.2. Thus, the $200 stock is the outcome of $100e^{0.693147} = \$100 \times 2 = \$200$, the $50 stock is the outcome of $\$100^{-0.693147} = \$100 \times \frac{1}{2} = \$50$, and the two $100 stocks are made subject in the following period to mispricing as Fig. 10.1. The scenario is that of zero fundamental growth through time as market prices fluctuate about their fundamental value ($100).

Now consider that we purchase each of the four stocks in the figure at time 0, so that we invest $200 in one stock priced at $200, $100 in each of two stocks priced at $100, and $50 in one stock priced at $50 (each of which is intrinsically worth $100) for a total of $450. We have paid $450 for stocks with fundamental value $400. At the end of a subsequent time period, the stocks have changed their market value in a sort of musical chairs while maintaining their collective market value at $450. Thus, when the stocks come to be sold, the overpricing is "reclaimed" in the selling price. In the meantime, however, the overpricing is bound up as additional investment.[3]

So much may appear unsurprising. But consider that two distinct and highly noteworthy effects have taken place, which, in effect, have canceled each other. The first effect of note is that the average growth rate generated by mispricing: Two stocks double, while two stocks half in value = (100%+ 100% − 50% − 50%)/4 = 25%, is actually positive. The second effect of note is that we have invested *more* ($200) in the *overpriced* asset, which is more likely to *decrease* in value, and invested *less* ($50) in the *underpriced* asset, which is more likely to *increase* in value.

---

[3]If, for example, at any time, stocks are typically over- and underpriced with standard deviation $\varepsilon = 0.2(20\%)$, Eq. (10.15) (below) tells us that we are paying approximately $\frac{1}{2}0.2^2 = 2\%$ more than would be the case if stocks were correctly priced.

Thus, we observe that the expected individual outperformances of stocks on aggregate due to mispricing have *exactly cancelled* with the outcome of over- (under-) investment in the over- (under-) priced stocks.

10.4. The Model for Mispricing and Portfolio Valuation

To see how the above effects are revealed in the model of Eqs. (10.1) and (10.12), we first observe that the range of possibilities for the mispricing exponential rate in Fig. 10.2 (that is, 0.693147, 0, 0, −0.693147) has standard deviation (with Eqs. (6.62) and (6.63), pp. 107–108) $\varepsilon = 0.49$. With this insight, we illuminate the key equations Eqs. (10.1) and (10.12) in relation to Fig. 10.2 as follows.

(i) Eq. (10.1):

$$p_t = p_t^* e^{Z\varepsilon}.$$

In relation to Eq. (10.1), we can write the expectation for $e^{Z\varepsilon}$, $E(e^{Z\varepsilon})$, as

$$E(e^{Z\varepsilon}) = e^R, \tag{10.13}$$

where R is determined as (Eq. (7.3), p. 126):

$$R = 0 + \frac{1}{2}\varepsilon^2, \tag{10.14}$$

so that Eq. (10.1) allows us to write the expected market price for a stock, $E(p_t)$, in relation to its fundamental price, p_t^*, as

$$E(p_t) = p_t^* e^{\frac{1}{2}\varepsilon^2}, \tag{10.15}$$

so that with $\varepsilon = 0.49$ (above) in Fig. 10.2, we have the theoretical outcome $E(p_t)/p_t^* = e^{\frac{1}{2}0.49^2} = 1.128$, which captures closely the overpricing factor in the figure: $450/400 = 1.125$.[4]

---

[4]We do not expect an exact correspondence since Eqs. (10.1) and (10.13) assume that the mispricing exponential growth/decline rates are normally distributed (as opposed to binary distributed, which is the case in Fig. 10.2).

(ii) Eq. (10.12):

$$p_{t+N} = p_t e^{N\mu + Z\sqrt{N\sigma^2 + 2\varepsilon^2}}.$$

In relation to Eq. (10.12), we can write

$$E\left[e^{N\mu + Z\sqrt{N\sigma^2 + 2\varepsilon^2}}\right] = e^R, \tag{10.16}$$

where (Eq. (7.3)):

$$R = N\mu + \frac{1}{2}(N\sigma^2 + 2\varepsilon^2) \tag{10.17}$$

so that we have (with Eq. (6.11), p. 78):

$$E\left[e^{N\mu + Z\sqrt{N\sigma^2 + 2\varepsilon^2}}\right] \simeq 1 + N\mu + \frac{1}{2}(N\sigma^2 + 2\varepsilon^2), \tag{10.18}$$

where we have ignored higher powers of σ^2 and ε^2. With $\mu = \sigma = 0$, Eq. (10.18) provides

$$E\left[e^{Z\sqrt{2\varepsilon^2}}\right] \simeq 1 + \varepsilon^2. \tag{10.19}$$

With Eq. (10.12) (with $\mu = \sigma = 0$), Eq. (10.19) implies in Fig. 10.2, an expected stock return due to mispricing $= \varepsilon^2 = 0.49^2 \simeq 24\%$, which is consistent with the above direct observation of Fig. 10.2, which revealed the average growth rate generated by mispricing as 25%.[5]

10.5. Equal Weighting of Assets

The challenge is to avoid the adverse effect of over- (under-) investment in over- (under-) priced stocks due to mispricing, while taking advantage

---

[5]In Fig. 10.2, when assets 1 to 4 are subjected, respectively, to the mispricing factor as $e^{0.693147}$, e^0, e^0, $e^{-0.693147}$ (as, for example, at time 0 in the figure), the assets in a further period are typically subjected to the mispricing factor, respectively, as, e^0, $e^{0.693147}$ $e^{-0.693147}$, e^0 (as, for example, at the end of time period 1 in the figure). It is straightforward (with Eqs. (6.65), p. 108 and (6.72), p. 114) to show that the correlation coefficient between the set (0.693147, 0, 0, −0.693147) and the set (0, 0.693147, −0.693147, 0) is zero. Thus, we are justified in allocating $CORR(Z_{t+1}, Z_t) = 0$ in Eq. (10.8), and, thereby, applying Eq. (10.12) (with $\mu = \sigma = 0$) in Fig. 10.2. However, we do not expect an exact correspondence of Eq. (10.19) with Fig. 10.2 on account of that Eq. (10.19) assumes that the mispricing exponential growth/decline rates are normally distributed (as opposed to binary distributed as is the case in Fig. 10.2).

of the positive effect of mispricing (as Eq. (10.19)). Thus, consider again, investment in the stocks of Fig. 10.2, where at time 0, we invest *equal* amounts in each of the four stocks: Thus, $100 in half of an overvalued stock (priced at $200), $100 in two undervalued stocks (each priced at $50), and $100 in each of two fairly valued stocks (each priced at $100), with a total outlay of $400. At the end of the first period, two of our investments of $100 have doubled and two of our investments of $100 have halved in value, providing an outcome of $500, an increase by a factor 1.25, or 25%, again consistent with Eq. (10.19) (with $\varepsilon = 0.49$, as above).

In principle, therefore, we might recommend a strategy of equal-weighting as a means of outperforming a market-capital weighted index.[6] The problem with the strategy is that it obliges the investor to invest equally in the less liquid stocks of small firms. For an institutional fund manager, such stocks may be insufficiently liquid to allow either purchases or sales at the required quantity at the quoted price. Another issue is that a fund's mandate generally requires that the fund adhere to a representation of the market-capitalized equity market. In the following section, we therefore consider whether a general non-market-capital weighted portfolio that is designed to broadly represent the capitalized equity market is also capable of outperforming a market-capital weighted index.

---

[6]Why, then, you may ask, am I myself not already immensely rich on the proceeds? A good question, dear reader, a very good question. But if there is one piece of practical investment advice I now give to myself, it is, Do *not* sell out at the point that investments have gone badly against you. The market will come back! To hold on to your stocks in bad times can take courage, though. I know. Take heed of the quote from Adam Smith (a pseudonym) in *The Money Game* (1968):

> "When stocks start down, the tendency is to wait until they come back a little before lightening up. They head down further, and the idea that you have made a mistake, that you have been betrayed by your own judgment, can be so paralyzing that you wait a little longer. Finally faith evaporates entirely. If stocks were down 10 percent yesterday, they may be down 20 percent today. One day, when all news is bad, you have to get rid of the filthy things that have treated you so cruelly." (p. 79)

So be prepared. The above experience may yet descend on you! Better to sell when things are looking good. But this takes courage, also. The temptation is to respond to stocks and shares as we might respond to people. Thus, if the stock is "looking after us", it can be "relied on", and if the stock "let's us down", it "no longer can be trusted". But stocks are not people (the stocks do not even know that you own them)!

10.6. Exploiting Mispricing by Avoidance of Capital Weighting

For simplicity, we shall take it that the standard deviation of the mispricing exponential factor in Eq. (10.1), ε, is fixed across time and is the same for all assets. We identify the discrete return, R_t^*, from time t to time $t+1$ in the absence of mispricing, as

$$1 + R_t^* \equiv \frac{p_{t+1}^*}{p_t^*}, \tag{10.20}$$

so that Eq. (10.5) is written as:

$$p_{t+1} = p_t(1 + R^*)e^{(Z_{t+1}-Z_t)\varepsilon}. \tag{10.21}$$

For a portfolio of k assets, we may therefore express the market price of the portfolio at time $t+1$, P_{t+1}, in relation to its market price at time t, P_t, as

$$P_{t+1} = P_t \sum_{k=1}^{N} \omega_{k,t}\left(1 + R_{k,t}^*\right)e^{(Z_{t+1}-Z_t)\varepsilon}, \tag{10.22}$$

where $\omega_{k,t}$ represents the proportional allocation to stock k in the portfolio at time t, and $R_{k,t}^*$ represents the discrete return of asset k from time t to time $t+1$ in the absence of mispricing. In Eq. (10.22), on condition — but, note, only on condition — that the $\omega_{k,t}$ proportion allocations are independent of market prices, (i) $\omega_{k,t}(1 + R_{k,t}^*)$ and (ii) $e^{(Z_{t+1}-Z_t)\varepsilon}$ are independent of each other. In this case, we can take the expectation of the right-hand side of the equation as the product of the expectations for the factors individually. Thus, in regard to $E[e^{(Z_{t+1}-Z_t)\varepsilon}]$, we have Eq. (10.9):

$$VAR\left[(Z_{t+1} - Z_t)\varepsilon\right] = 2\varepsilon^2,$$

so that, following the argument as above:

$$E\left[e^{(Z_{t+1}-Z_t)\varepsilon}\right] = e^R, \tag{10.23}$$

where (Eq. (7.3)):

$$R = 0 + \frac{1}{2}(2\varepsilon^2) = \varepsilon^2, \tag{10.24}$$

so that

$$E\big[e^{(Z_{t+1}-Z_t)\varepsilon}\big] = e^{\varepsilon^2}, \tag{10.25}$$

and we arrive at (Eq. (6.11)):

$$E\big[e^{(Z_{t+1}-Z_t)\varepsilon}\big] \simeq 1 + \varepsilon^2, \tag{10.26}$$

consistent with Eq. (10.19), where we have ignored higher powers of ε^2. Thus, on taking expectations of Eq. (10.22):

$$E(P_{t+1}) \simeq P_t\big[1 + E\big(R^*_{p,t}\big)\big](1 + \varepsilon^2), \tag{10.27}$$

where $E(R^*_{P,t})$ is the expected return on the portfolio assuming no mispricing. Eq. (10.27) may be expressed

$$1 + E(R_{P,t}) \simeq \big[1 + E\big(R^*_{P,t}\big)\big](1 + \varepsilon^2), \tag{10.28}$$

where $E(P_{t+1})/P_t = 1 + E(R_{P,T})$ identifies the actual expected return on the portfolio, so that

$$E(R_{P,t}) \simeq E(R^*_{P,t}) + \varepsilon^2\big[1 + E\big(R^*_{P,t}\big)\big], \tag{10.29}$$

implying that the expected return on the portfolio $E(R_{P,t})$ exceeds the expected return assuming no mispricing, $E(R^*_{P,t})$, by the amount $\varepsilon^2[1 + E(R^*_{P,t})]$. Thus, we establish that by "immunizing" the portfolio from over-investing in overvalued stocks and under-investing in undervalued stocks, a non-market-capital weighted portfolio outperforms the market index.

10.7. Fundamental Indexation and the FF-3F Model: Models of Risk Assimilation or Stock Mispricing?

Section 10.6 has substantiated the claim of Arnott, Hsu, and Moore (2005) that the benefits of equal-weighting can be achieved by any allocation of assets that is uncorrelated with the market capitalized prices of the assets (such as allocation on the basis of the firm's book value, its dividend distribution, total earnings, etc.), which the authors refer to as a strategy of *fundamental indexation* (FI).

FI, as promoted by Robert Arnott and associates at *Research Affiliates*, represents a successful investment product. And FI appears to have worked well. Arnott, Hsu, and Moore (2005) report that over the 43-year period

1962–2004, a back-tested portfolio that weighted large firms in terms of fundamental attributes, such as revenue, earnings, dividends, and book value, outperformed capital-weighted indexation (CWI) portfolios, such as the S&P 500, by about two percentage points per year. Since 2005, a live FI portfolio has continued to outperform conventional capital-weighted indexes by the same margin.

Arnott (2005), in an editorial to *Financial Analysts Journal*, makes the point that the annualized standard deviation of stock returns that is not explained by general market movements is in the range of 30–40% (for some stocks it is much higher). If for 40% standard deviation, we attribute just one third to mispricing, which implies $\varepsilon = 0.13333$ and hence $\varepsilon^2 = 0.018$, we have the outcome that provided the mispricing of individual assets at the end of the year is independent of their individual mispricing at the commencement of the year, immunizing the portfolio against mispricing as above contributes an annualized 1.8% to portfolio performance (which accords with the reported findings of Arnott *et al.*, 2005). With $\varepsilon = 40\%$ per annum, we would have $\varepsilon^2 = 0.16$, implying a potential contribution from mispricing of as much as 16.0% per annum.[7]

A number of authors confirm that FI as proposed by Arnott *et al.* (2005) outperforms when benchmarked against the traditional capital asset pricing model (CAPM), but that FI does not outperform against the FF-3F model introduced in Chapter 3.[8] Additionally, it has been observed that FI portfolios tend to display a bias to high B/M and small firm stocks. Thus, it appears possible to interpret FI's reported performances as an application of the FF-3F model "value" (high B/M) and "small firm size" effects. Jun and Malkiel (2008) quote Fama and French as stating that FI is a "triumph of marketing, and not of new ideas", and consider that FI is "simply a 'repackaging' of ideas that have been in the academic literature for years". Perold (2007) and Kaplan (2008) both claim to have proved that market capital-weighting indexation does not lead to a "structural drag" as argued

---

[7]To ensure a similar outcome over each subsequent year, the portfolio must be rebalanced annually. Otherwise the benefits of the strategy become a once-off effect that is independent of repeated holding periods. The more frequent the rebalancing, the greater the probability that each mispricing cycle opportunity is exploited.

[8]For example, Jun and Malkiel (2007), Blitz and Swinkels (2008), McQuarrie (2008) and Malkiel and Jun (2009).

by Arnott *et al.* Perold states, "even though individual stocks may have random pricing errors ... capitalization weighting, in and of itself, does *not* create a performance drag [our italics]" (p. 36) and refers to such as Asness (2006), Bogle and Malkiel (2006) as having "explained eloquently how Arnott *et al.*'s fundamental 'indexing' is simply a particular packaging of quantitative value investing" (p. 35). Thus, for the critics of FI, there is nothing surprising about constructing an index that favors small-cap stocks or value stocks and then showing that such a model outperforms pure capital-weighted indexing.

Because FI outperforms against the CAPM expectations, but not against those of the FF-3F model, it does indeed appear that the outperformance of FI over capital-weighted portfolios is linked to the B/M and firm size effects of the FF-3F model. However, if it can be demonstrated that the outperformance of FI over capital-weighted portfolios is in fact the outcome of an exploitation of mispricing, we have as a counterargument to the claim that the benefits of FI can be explained by the FF-3F model, the intriguing possibility that mispricing as encapsulated by FI, represents an explanation of the explanatory variables in the Fama and French model.

Shi (2013) examines US stock prices (the Russell 1000) to establish whether FI outperformance can be attributed to an exploitation of stock mispricing, and to confirm the interdependence of FI outperformance with the Fama–French value (B/M) and small firm size factors. Thus, he considers that smaller firms are more likely to be mispriced due to lower levels of analyst coverage and lower liquidity, and that assuming that FI is due to a manipulation of stock mispricing, a strategy of FI portfolio formation should therefore be increasingly effective in outperforming a capital-weighted portfolio in the context of stocks of increasingly smaller firm size. Similarly, he argues that FI portfolio formation should be more effective in outperforming a capital-weighted portfolio in periods of high market volatility or crisis, than in more stable periods. The evidence supports the interpretation that FI outperforms market price indexes due to FI's ability to exploit stock mispricing.

Additionally, Shi, Dempsey and Irlicht (2014) control for the B/M ratio and small firm effects of the Fama and French model in stock selection by forming a matrix of 5×5 portfolios on the interaction of B/M and firm size. This is achieved by, firstly, categorizing the stocks into five groups based on the B/M ratio, and, secondly, categorizing each quintile into a further quintile based on stock size. Thus, for each month, 25 groups are created, with approximately 40 stocks in each group. We anticipate one of three general outcomes: (1) Because the outperformance of FI is essentially due to leaning toward higher B/M and lower capitalization stocks and *not* due to stock mispricing, there should be no outperformance of FI over CWI (capital-weighted indexation) when we control for the two effects. (2) Because the outperformance of FI is due to an exploitation of stock mispricing, but has no association with the B/M and small firm size factors, FI should more or less uniformly outperform CWI across the partitioned B/M and firm size portfolios. (3) Allowing that the outperformance of FI is due to its ability to exploit stock mispricing, and that portfolios with very high (low) B/M ratios represent stocks that are generally under (over) priced, FI will outperform CWI *more significantly* for portfolios of particularly high or low B/M (since stocks of these portfolios are more significantly mispriced; as well as for portfolios of small-cap stocks, which are also assumed to be subject to higher stock mispricing, although this effect may be muted in the present sample since none of the stocks lie outside the Russell 1000). Not only do the authors find that FI outperforms CWI in 20 out of the 25 portfolios, emphasizing the ability of FI portfolios to outperform controlling for B/M and firm size, but the outperformances of FI are much greater for *both* very high and very low B/M values, as well as for a combination of small firm size and low B/M. These are the portfolios whose stocks are assumed to be most mispriced.

Dempsey (2014) observes that although portfolios constructed on stocks of high (low) B/M and small (big) firm size, provide high (low) returns in the forward-looking monthly period as predicted by the FF-3F model, such portfolios are associated with low (high) returns in the preceding month. The tendency of stock performances to rebound between months has been documented by Debondt and Thaler (1985, 1987) and Jegadeesh (1990). Explanations have generally attributed the reversal pattern to either investor overreaction[9] or illiquidity.[10] These

---

[9]From such as Shiller (1984), Black (1986), and Subrahmayham (2005).

[10]From such as Jegadeesh and Titman (1995), Pastor and Stambaugh (2003), and Avramov, Chordia, and Goyal (2006).

Panel A: Book-to-market portfolios (low to high).

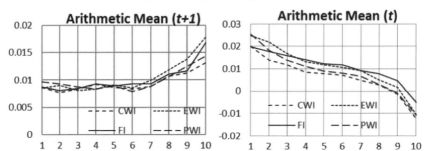

Panel B: Firm size portfolios (big to small).

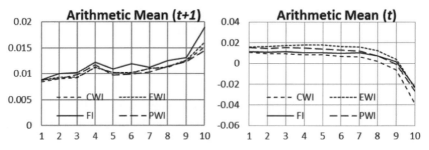

Figure 10.3. Prior and subsequent monthly performances for indexation strategies formed as a function of (i) firm B/M and (ii) firm capitalization.

In panel A, the dectile classifications on the x-axis are for portfolios with stocks of lowest B/M (portfolio 1) to stocks of highest B/M ratio (portfolio 10), and for panel B, the x-axis is for portfolios with stocks of largest firm capitalization (portfolio 1) to stocks of smallest firm capitalization (portfolio 10). The sample period is 1987–2010. Arithmetic Mean $(t+1)$ is the arithmetic mean return for the portfolio in the month following the formation of the portfolio; Arithmetic Mean (t) is the arithmetic mean return for the same portfolio in the month prior to portfolio formation.

interpretations imply a direct association with mispricing, in that over-reaction can be interpreted as mispricing, while illiquidity leads directly to mispricing.

The above outcome is highlighted in Fig. 10.3 for FI, CWI, price-weighted indexation (PWI) and equally weighted indexation (EWI) portfolios.[11] Thus, the left-hand graphs of panels A and B in Fig. 10.3

---

[11]The FI portfolios are constructed each month as a composite index on four fundamental variables: book value, cash flow, sales, and dividends, as recommended by Arnott *et al.*

display the return performances in month $t + 1$ for dectile portfolios at the end of the prior month t, formed on a ranking on stocks of low to high B/M values (panel A) and on stocks of large to small firm capitalization (panel B). The positive relation observed between portfolio performances in month $t + 1$ for portfolios of stocks of either high B/M or small firm capitalization formed at the end of month t is consistent with the FF-3F model. Adjacent in the panel, we display the return performances in month t as they relate to the identical dectile B/M portfolios (formed at the end of month t). Thus, in the graphs, Arithmetic Mean ($t + 1$) is the arithmetic mean return for the portfolio in the month *following* the formation of the portfolio, whereas Arithmetic Mean (t) is the arithmetic mean return for the identical portfolio in the month *preceding* the portfolio formation.[12]

The fact that stocks that underperform in a given month tend to be in portfolios of high B/M and small firm size at the end of the month can be interpreted as no more than the mathematical outcome of their relative decline. Consider, for example, that all stocks commence the month with identical book value and firm size. In this case, portfolios formed on stocks of high B/M and small firm size at the end of the month are more likely to capture those stocks that have under performed in that month. In which case, the structure of the right-hand graphs in Fig. 10.3 is what we expect. Nevertheless, the over (under) performances in month $t + 1$ of portfolios of stocks based on high (low) B/M or small (big) firm size in month t combined with their inverse performance relation in the preceding month suggests an interpretation of the B/M and firm size effects as the outcome of the tendency of stocks performances to rebound between months. Consistent with the findings of several authors above (footnotes 9 and 10), the pattern is interpreted as the outcome of stock mispricing.

(2005). Here, the EWI allocation is adopted as the most conceptually straightforward price-indifferent strategy, and PWI is interpreted as representing a milder version of CWI, for which mispricing of stock value is amplified by the number of stocks outstanding. Each month, the weight for each stock is calculated for each indexation strategy. The weights are then used to calculate the monthly return generated for each of the portfolios. Thanks Adam Randall and Paul Lajbcygier.
[12]The feature of reversals between the monthly-prior and monthly-following performances in the context of B/M and firm size has been verified for Chinese stocks by two of my former PhD Students, Dr Amanda Man Li and Dr Larry Li.

10.8. Time for Reflection: What Have We Learned?

We have extended the basic model of stock price growth and decline of Chapter 6 (Eq. (6.78)) to accommodate mispricing. We have observed that a manipulation of mispricing allows a non-capital-weighted portfolio to outperform a capital-weighted portfolio, consistent with the claims of Arnott *et al.* (2005). The observation that this outperformance appears to be captured by the FF-3F model is interpreted, not as the tilting in the outperforming portfolio to stocks of high B/M and small firms as risk factors, but rather as the outcome of a tilt to mispricing in the FF-3F B/M and firm size portfolios. Thus, controversially, rather than confirming that FI represents a repackaging of the FF-3F B/M and firm size factors, the weight of our evidence supports the interpretation that these factors are themselves the outcome of stock mispricing.

Chapter 11

Practitioner Client Portfolios, the Risk Premium, and Time Diversification

The demand for certainty is one which is natural to man, but is nevertheless an intellectual vice. So long as men are not trained to withhold judgment in the absence of evidence, they will be led astray by cocksure prophets, and it is likely that their leaders will be either ignorant fanatics or dishonest charlatans. To endure uncertainty is difficult, but so are most of the other virtues.

Bertrand Russell

The importance of money flows from it being a link between the present and the future. John Maynard Keynes

After a certain point, money is meaningless. It ceases to be the goal. The game is what counts. Aristotle Onassis

I spent a lot of money on booze, birds and fast cars. The rest I just squandered.

George Best

11.1. Introduction

Once we are at ease with a framework of perceptions, the framework inevitably encourages us to push the boundaries with further perceptions and insights and experiences. Even when subsequent investigations appear to contradict a model, the model nevertheless serves its purpose by highlighting such contradiction and stimulating the need for enhanced explanation.

This is the perspective we adopt in the present chapter, where we introduce three important observations by which the asset pricing model of Eqs. (9.12) and (9.13) (pp. 160–161, more generally, Eq. (9.32), p. 171) is challenged. They are:

(1) The observation that practitioners do not generally advise clients to invest in a specified "market portfolio" alongside a riskless asset

component (with the proportions depending on the investor's risk aversion) as dictated by the capital market line (CML) (Figs. 9.1 and 11.1a below).

(2) The observation that investor consumption patterns are missing from the model of Eqs. (9.32). Thus, the model fails to relate investment risk to investor consumption.

(3) The observation that, whereas practitioners advise clients that stock market investments are for the long haul, the optimal portfolio allocations determined from Eqs. (9.12) and (9.13) are independent of the investor's time horizon.

We take each observation in turn. Accordingly, the chapter is arranged as follows. Sections 11.2, 11.3, and 11.4 are given to a consideration of each of the above aspects of asset pricing — the CML, investor consumption, and time diversification, respectively — before a final section, Section 11.5, concludes with a discussion.

11.2. The Mutual Fund Separation Theorem

Canner, Mankiw, and Weil (1997) make the observation that the advice offered by the CML (represented by Figs. 9.1 and Fig. 11.1a) is straightforward — namely, that all investors should hold the same market portfolio of risky assets together with an individual allocation in the risk-free asset in accordance with their level of risk aversion, γ. The market portfolio is identified in Figs. 9.1 and 11.1a as the portfolio where the line from the risk-free asset is tangent to the frontier of portfolio possibilities. Nevertheless, Canner *et al.* report that financial advisors typically structure the investment portfolios of their clients with proportions of risky equity and bonds in response to the client's willingness to undertake market risk exposure — with little regard for inclusion of a risk-free asset. And, thus, it would appear, the model of Fig. 11.1a is actually ignored by practitioners.

A response can be made on two levels. On the first level, we might consider that the concept of a tangent CML from the risk-free asset to the efficient frontier of portfolios need not, on the face of things, be taken literally. The CML is generally depicted as in the left-hand side of Fig. 11.1, where the CML requires an *absence* of securities at low levels of standard

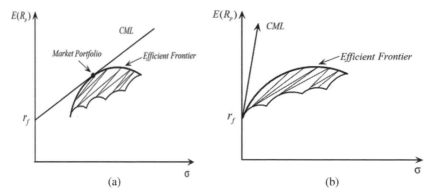

Figure 11.1. The CML with (a) an absence of low standard deviation (σ) assets and (b) with an available continuous standard deviation (σ) of assets.

deviation. Allowing a more realistic *continuum* of assets with low standard deviation, a theoretical outcome is as depicted in the right-hand side of Fig. 11.1, where the risk-free asset is located at the commencement of the efficient frontier. In this case, the concept of a tangent line from the risk-free asset to the efficient frontier is rendered impossible.

On the second level, working with the empirical evidence of *discrete* asset clusters (equity, and bonds, for example) in Fig. 9.1, we can respond as follows. The model produces a CML solution to the optimal portfolio problem, which is recognized as a somewhat stylized solution in relation to the input discrete asset clusters. Even conceding the existence of such a CML, however, we may note in relation to Fig. 9.1, that our market portfolio (M_0) comprises the contributions of *both* equity and bond assets. In the absence of being able to borrow at the risk-free deposit rate, investors who seek a greater return (who have lower risk-aversion, γ less than 2.65 in Fig. 9.1) are constrained to move along the efficient frontier from the market of equity and bond assets at M_0 towards the 100% equity cluster; which is to say, investors with decreasing risk aversion decrease the proportion of bond securities combined with the market equity portfolio — which is exactly what Canner *et al.* observe to be the case in practice. In the absence of the investor's ability to borrow at the risk-free deposit rate, the practitioners reported by Canner *et al.* are fundamentally in accord with the model framework of Fig. 9.1.

11.3. Consumption-Based Models

The model of Eqs. (9.12) and (9.13) (more generally, Eq. (9.32)) represents a static asset pricing model, in that utility in the model is identified with an immediate utility of wealth as opposed to the ultimate utility of *consumption* of such wealth. From an economist's perspective, it is utility derived from consumption that rationally dictates an agent's investment decisions.

A consumption-based asset pricing model is therefore, at least in principle, superior to the static one of Eq. (9.32). In a consumption-based model, market risk is identified — not as the risk of losing wealth as such — but as the risk of receiving negative shocks to consumption patterns. Consumption models aggregate investors into a single representative agent whose utility is determined as the aggregate level of consumption in the economy. Thus, in the model, market risk is the misalignment between society's aggregate consumption needs and market performance. The fundamental equation that expresses the relation between the price of an asset at time t, $\$p_t$, and its expected price, $\$p_{t+1}$ (inclusive of intervening dividends), at future time $t + 1$ is

$$\$p_t \frac{\Delta U(C_t)}{\Delta C_t} = \alpha E \left[\$p_{t+1} \frac{\Delta U(C_{t+1})}{\Delta C_{t+1}} \right], \qquad (11.1)$$

where $U(C_t)$ represents investor utility with consumption measured in dollars at time t and $\Delta U(C_t)/\Delta(C_t)$ is the sensitivity of this utility to a change in consumption. Thus, the left-hand side of the equation represents the investor's sensitivity to the loss of consumption utility from holding the stock rather than selling it and consuming the price at time t. Similarly, $E[\$p_{t+1}\Delta U(C_{t+1})/\Delta(C_{t+1})]$ represents the investor's sensitivity to the additional expected utility from selling the stock at subsequent time $t + 1$ and consuming the outcome price, $\$p_{t+1}$. Here, α denotes a subjective discount time factor that captures the preference for enjoying a given utility now rather than later.[1] At the outset of his text, *Asset Pricing*, John Cochrane (2005) introduces Eq. (11.1) as "*the* [Cochrane's italics] central asset pricing formula", and states that the organizing principle of the book is that everything can be traced back to this equation. By combining

---

[1] Equation (11.1) is Cochrane's (2005) first numbered Eq. (1.1) and also Mehra's (2003) Eq. (3).

Eq. (11.1) and utility functions of the class of Eq. (9.2):

$$U(W) = \frac{W^{1-\gamma}}{1-\gamma}.$$

Mehra and Prescott (1985) and Mehra (2003) deduce

$$E(R_E) - r_f = \gamma \sigma_{E,x}, \tag{11.2}$$

where $E(R_E) - r_f$ represents the expected return on equity, R_E, over and above a risk-free rate, r_f, and $\sigma_{E,x}$ is the covariance of the variation of equity returns, R_E, with the variation of investors' consumption, x.[2] Equation (11.2) represents a *consumption-based capital asset pricing model* (CCAPM). The equation captures the fact that the stronger the relation between investor consumption and equity performance, $\sigma_{E,x}$, the higher the equity risk premium.

We can see that the point of differentiation between Eq. (11.2) and Eq. (9.14):

$$E(R_E) - r_f = \gamma \sigma_{E,M},$$

is that in Eq. (9.14), consumption is implicitly identified with the wealth outcome of market investment, so that equity risk is measured as the covariance of equity returns with the market return, $\sigma_{E,M}$, (which is to say, the contribution of equity to the investor's total market risk) whereas Eq. (11.2) allows for an independent "variation of investor consumption", x.

Equation (11.2) can be expressed (with Eq. (6.72), p. 114) as

$$E(R_E) - r_f = \gamma CORR_{E,x} \sigma_E \sigma_x, \tag{11.3}$$

where $CORR_{E,x}$ is the correlation coefficient between the return on equity and investor consumption, and σ_E and σ_x are, respectively, the standard deviations of the return on equity and the rate of consumption.

Cochrane (2005) considers that, over the prior 50 years, real stock returns have averaged 9%, with a standard deviation, σ_E, of about 16%, while the real return on treasury bills was about 1%. Cochrane also estimates that, over the same period, aggregate non-durable and services consumption growth had a standard deviation, σ_x, of about 1%, and that

---

[2]Equation (11.2) is Mehra's (2003) Eq. (15).

equity returns have a rough correlation with consumption, $CORR_{E,x}$, of about 0.2. Inserting these values into Eq. (11.3) yields an unacceptable risk aversion coefficient, γ, of 250.[3] The intuition is that any risk not strongly correlated with consumption should not require a high risk premium. And historically, changes in stock prices do not appear to have significantly impacted changes in consumption.[4]

---

[3]Alternatively, Siegel (2005) determines that even if investors have a more reasonable risk aversion in the region $\gamma = 2$ or 3, the equity risk premium would be of the order of only 0.3–0.4%. Adding to the difficulties of the model, high risk aversion drives the risk-free rate above plausible levels (Weil, 1989). Many explanations have been advanced to solve the equity risk-premium puzzle via imposing modifications on the Mehra and Prescott (1985) analysis. Siegel (2005) reports that in the past 20 years, more than 320 articles have been published with the term *equity premium* in the title. Explanations revolve around changing the representative agent's utility specification (for example, Gordon and St-Amour, 2004); time-varying risk aversion (for example, Epstein and Zin, 1991; Constantinides, 1990); market frictions (such as transaction costs and limits on borrowing or short sales: for example, Campbell and Mankiw, 1990; Mankiw and Zeldes, 1991; Basak and Cuoco, 1998; Alvarez and Jermann, 2000; Constantinides, Donaldson and Mehra, 2002); incomplete markets (for example, Constantinides and Duffie; 1996; Kocherlakota and Pistaferri, 2009); general utility functions allowing for psychological preferences derived from habit formation and the insights of prospect theory (for example, Campbell and Cochrane, 1999; Tversky and Kahneman, 1992); and theory that allows for departure from rational expectations (for example, Rietz (1988) explores the role in markets of possible but highly unlikely negative outcomes, and Abel (2002) explores the effect of pessimism).

[4]It is almost as though Cochrane and Mehra and Prescott are saying that if the representative economic agent were not so highly risk-averse to owning stocks ($\gamma = 250$), casinos would have sprung up offering our representative economic agent the opportunity to bet on future stock price movements (just as it is possible for a person to place a bet on a race or game taking place that afternoon or sometime in the future). Recognizing the high return on stocks in relation to risk, and wishing to make payoffs exciting, the casino should be able to offer, say, call options on the stocks at a price above their fair Black–Scholes price (see Chapter 12), and the representative economic agent would still find the prices attractive. The casino could then cover its own exposure by continually holding the underlying stocks and put options so as to delta hedge its exposure both to stock upside and downside outcomes. Because it offers the call options at a price above their fair value, the casino makes a risk-free profit. And the punters win most of the time — and on average! What could be better? Of course, many people *do* bet on stocks essentially in this way on-line from their trading platform. However, the fact that the casinos are empty of people betting on stocks — but are full of people betting on games offering explicit negative NPV investments — hardly argues for the conclusion that our representative economic agent is highly risk-averse.

Little advancement has been made on the above impasse between the theoretical models and empirical observations. Savov (2011) argues that a new measure of consumption, namely municipal solid waste (as measured by the US Environmental Protection Agency), or simply garbage, is more volatile and more correlated with stocks than the traditional measure of consumption expenditure. Thereby, Savov is able to reconcile both the equity premium and the risk-free rate with $\gamma = 26$. Nevertheless, such a risk coefficient is unacceptable. To see this, consider that whereas a log-wealth utility investor (with $\gamma = 1$) would be indifferent between an investment that offered either a doubling of investment wealth or a halving of it with equal probability, an investor with $\gamma = 26$ would require a 99.999997% probability of doubling investment wealth as opposed to a halving of it.[5] We are left to conclude that the representative agent of the CCAPM falls short of reality and is not actually representative of institutional investors.

Individuals, and investment institutions on behalf of individuals, clearly do not make investments to ensure their *immediate* consumption patterns, or those of their clients.[6] Rather, they invest in equities, bonds, and cash to ensure that consumption patterns are maintained in the event of *once-off* demands for highly significant expenditures (provision for their children's schooling, life insurance, or retirement needs, or provisions in their wills, for example). In this case, *at the point of liquidation* of their investments, in seeking to preserve consumption patterns, individuals are actually *extremely*

---

[5]To see this, consider that given an investment opportunity that either doubles or halves one's wealth with equal probability, an investor with $\gamma = 26$ would require a probability, p, of doubling determined by (with Eq. (8.8), p. 139 and Eq. (9.2), above):

$$p\frac{(2X)^{-25}}{25} + (1-p)\frac{\left(\frac{1}{2}X\right)^{-25}}{25} = \frac{X^{-25}}{25}.$$

which implies a probability of doubling, $p = 99.999997\%$.

[6]My colleague John at BP Oil Company at work on the afternoon every Friday checked his share portfolio before going down to the BP bar for a couple of pints before going home. He explained to me that if his portfolio had done well, he would reward himself with two pints to celebrate his good fortune, and if they not had done so well, he would award himself two pints in self-commiseration. The consumption of our representative economic agent John was *unaffected* by day-to-day share price movements. So why did John have them in the first place? Well, I believe it was a combination of making provision for eventualities such as retirement, school fees, even "unknown eventualities".

dependent on the historical performance of their investments. Investors' retirement needs, for example, have often prospered by the stock markets, but they have also left investors bereft as pension schemes folded during the global financial crisis either directly or indirectly as an outcome of the market demise. For the fortunate, consumption has continued unchecked during the stock market's decline, while for the unfortunate, consumption must remain suppressed even as stock markets recover. The observation that individual consumption patterns (as they equate with the wrappings or leftovers encountered in household garbage) do not move in lockstep with stock price movements, is of no concern to the individual investor who is investing for payouts to sustain household consumption patterns at the point of retirement. The observation is simply irrelevant.

Rather than a concern for the covariance of equity returns with background consumption patterns, the representative long-term investor equates the risk (of ultimate consumption) with the risk of the equity itself as it contributes to the total risk of the overall market of the investor's risky investments, which is $\sigma_{E,M}$. In this case, we recover Eq. (9.14). Which is to say, the static equations of the Eq. (9.32) model of Chapter 9 are preserved.

11.4. Time Diversification

A student in a lecture once volunteered a question along the lines of: If you are telling us it is possible to diversify the non-market risks of assets by holding many assets, then, it must be possible to diversify the exposure to ups-and-downs of market risk across time by investing over many time periods? The other members of the class who were not sleeping offered a vague nodding of heads in agreement.[7] In other words, they were saying that they might choose to invest \$X in the market with the intention of leaving it there for some number of years, but would not wish to invest that amount for, say, a month or so — which accords with the professional advice that is often provided: "Stocks are for the long haul".

Nevertheless, provided the model inputs remain unchanged, an investor's optimal portfolio solution as Eq. (9.33) (p. 172) is *time invariant*. This is because, as described in Chapter 9.2, the outcome portfolio solution is actually an estimate of utility optimization as Eq. (9.7) (p. 159), which

---

[7]It is possible that they were vaguely nodding because they were sleeping.

is time invariant (Section 9.5). This is the position that is emphasized by Paul Samuelson.[8] Samuelson has argued repeatedly that the investment horizon has no effect on the preferred riskiness of a portfolio: "Then it is an exact theorem that *The Investment Horizon Can Have No Effect on Your Portfolio Proportions*" [Samuelson's emphasis and capitals] (1994); and again, "A rising mean does *not* overcome the increase in dispersion" (also, Samuelson, 1963, 1969, 1989, 1994; Merton and Samuelson, 1974).

As well as arguing mathematically, Samuelson argues more picturesquely by considering an investor who intends to invest for, say, ten years, but is adamant that he would not allow himself to invest for a time period as short as, say, one month. In this case, one month prior to the end of the ten-year period, the investor will face a one-month investment period and will withdraw his funds. But, then, knowing that this is his intention, he must recognize at the commencement of the preceding month that he is now about to encounter the final month of his investment period — which, again, if he is adamant, he will refuse. So, he must agree that he must withdraw his funds two months prior to the termination of the originally planned ten-year investment period. By induction, he must follow the logic back to a decision not to invest at all; refusing to invest for one month has precluded investing for ten years. A case of a long march begins with a single step.[9]

---

[8]Paul Samuelson was the first Nobel Memorial prize winner in Economic Science and is regarded as one of the greats of finance and economics. His textbook *Foundations of Economic Analysis*, first published in 1948, remains a best-selling economics textbook. It shows how economic behavior can be understood as maximizing or minimizing subject to a constraint. His quote on investing: *"Investing should be more like watching paint dry, or watching grass grow. If you want excitement, take $800 and go to Las Vegas"* (which I actually intend to do when my poker skills have improved significantly).

[9]I similar-ish dilemma can occur playing Texas Hold'em poker. A set of three of a kind (three 5's, three 6's, etc.) is a powerful hand in hold'em and will often win. If my first two cards are a pair (two 5's, say), the probability that I will make a set if I hold to a showdown is approximately 20% or 1 in 5 — remember that I have the flop (3 cards), the turn (1 card), and the river (1 card) ahead on which to make another "5". However, the poker books argue that if I don't make my "5" on the flop or the turn card, the odds of making it on the final river card (4%) will typically not justify paying to stay in. By the same argument working backwards (I don't know if Samuelson ever played poker), the books argue that if I haven't already made my set on the flop, it is typically not worth staying in to see the turn (with similar odds of only 4%). So, allowing that it is unlikely that I will be able to see the turn

Two possible approaches present themselves to explaining the conundrum. One is to recognize that human beings are capable — indeed, often need to be capable — of handling ambiguity.[10] Natural selection has ultimately favored the genes of those who suppress risks to seek long-term accomplishments — from such as those who commit to marriage and raise a family to those who leave all behind as emigrants to face unknown risks and adversaries abroad — with "faith in the future". Having said that, we are also designed to be particularly sensitive and alert to very immediate risks. We react in a split second when swerving a car or jamming the breaks to avoid an obstacle — or even "leap out of our skin" if someone so much as surprises us by tapping our shoulder from behind. Thus, while acts of self-preservation in response to immediate risk are acceptable (turning and running from the approaching dinosaur), we consider that we should not allow ourselves to be continuously distracted by a sense of risk exposure from achieving our life's worth — "the coward dies many times before his death".[11] Aligned with this perspective, Hudson, Keasey, Littler, and Dempsey (1999) consider that by investing for many periods, investors are transforming what they regard as gross "uncertainty" into what more closely resembles "risk" and a higher level of quantification assurance.

---

or the river card without paying, I am likely to fold unless I hit my set on the flop ("no set, no bet" is a dictum of the game), for which the probability is 12.5% or 1 in 8. Thus, my probability of achieving a set with my initial pair is not 20% but only 12.5%. You may wish to counsel me here by email. I need the winnings. Another casino scenario that has led to argument with friends relates to playing Blackjack. If played optimally (without card counting), the odds are only very slightly in favor of the casino. So allowing for volatility of outcomes, I must (so the argument goes) find myself ahead at *some* point, and at that point, I can withdraw (exercising the valuable option I hold of being able to choose when to abandon the game). Furthermore (and here the argument is more obviously fallacious), I can return indefinitely to the casino for repeated winning encounters.

[10] We return to this concept in relation to ethics in Chapter 15.

[11] An over-adherence to backward induction is likely to prove depressing! Apparently, people who are overly realistic about themselves and their prospects tend to be the more depressed ("If I knew exactly what was going to happen to my day, I wouldn't get out of bed"). We require, apparently, at least a little uncertainty to "keep us going". Thus, while taking out insurance (risk aversion), we buy lottery tickets (risk seeking). Happy people, it seems, are more likely to be "uncertain" about where exactly they are heading. This possibly helps explain why a majority have a preference for free market economies — even those who do not appear to particularly prosper by them — rather than centrally planned ones.

A second approach to the issue of time diversification is to allow that market prices can be subject to periods of speculative growth and decline, albeit with ultimate correction. The assumption of mispricing has led us to consider that when an asset with price p_t at time t is made subject to normally distributed growth rates over N subsequent periods, the outcome price p_{t+N} at time $t + N$ is determined from Eq. (10.12):

$$p_{t+N} = p_t e^{N\mu + Z\sqrt{N\sigma^2 + 2\varepsilon^2}},$$

where ε is the standard deviation of the mispricing growth/decline exponential rates that impact the asset's fundamental valuation (in Eq. (10.1), p. 176) and μ and σ, respectively, are the fundamental mean or drift growth rate and the standard deviation of the normally distributed growth about such rate per time period. Equation (10.12) compares with Eq. (6.78), which assumes no such mispricing:

$$p_{t+N} = p_t e^{N\mu + Z\sqrt{N}\sigma}.$$

Thus, whereas with no mispricing, we have the utility per period for a portfolio from Eq. (9.10):

$$U_P = R_P - \frac{1}{2}\gamma\sigma_P^2,$$

with mispricing, we have utility per period as

$$U_P = R_P - \frac{1}{2}\gamma\left(\sigma_P^2 + \frac{2\varepsilon^2}{N}\right), \tag{11.4}$$

which is to say, the utility per period *increases* with the duration of an investment over N periods. Consistently, in terms of the portfolio allocation model of Eq. (9.32), with a longer investment horizon, the input standard deviation as $\sqrt{\left(\sigma_P^2 + \frac{2\varepsilon^2}{N}\right)}$ decreases (larger N) and the optimal risk-free asset allocation thereby decreases. Allowing self-correcting mispricing, we thereby arrive at a mathematical refutation of Samuelson's position. As for Samuelson's backward induction argument from the "last day's investment decision", it need hardly apply. There are too many life uncertainties. The investor no doubt adopts an attitude of "crossing that bridge" when s/he comes to it (they may decide to leave their wealth invested indefinitely for their children, they may have had a midlife crisis and have decided to spend their investment wealth in a mad spree, if indeed they can be certain that will be still alive at the end of their initially intended investment horizon).

11.5.   Time to Reflect: What Have We Learned?

When a model does not fit with reality, our first response must be to re-examine the underlying assumptions in the model. Following such a procedure, even when the observations appear not to align naturally with the model, the model is exhibiting its usefulness.

Thus, Canner *et al.*'s critique has obliged us to consider that the asset pricing model of Eqs. (9.12) and (9.13) (generalized as Eq. (9.32)) has been derived in relation to *discrete* asset clusters (as equity and bonds, for example). Nevertheless, the model is consistent with practitioner recommendations of selections between portfolios of equity and bonds in accordance with risk-return preferences, as reported by Canner *et al.*

The asset pricing model of Eqs. (9.12) and (9.13) provides a realistic model of the dynamic of market growth as it sustains investor long-term consumption needs (by providing provision for school fees, health insurance, and retirement needs, for example). From the perspective of the model, the aggregate of investors' consumption at any time in relation to the stock market's performance at that time, as identified by the "consumption capital asset pricing model", is a red herring.

The insistence of Paul Samuelson, *The Investment Horizon Can Have No Effect on Your Portfolio Proportions*, is also judged to be misplaced. Recognition of self-correcting price movements allows that investors rationally decline the market short-term, but choose to invest in the market for the longer term.

Chapter 12

Option Pricing: The Black–Scholes Model

A mathematician, like a painter or poet, is a maker of patterns. If his patterns are more permanent than theirs, it is because they are made with ideas.

G. H. Hardy

Derivatives are financial weapons of mass destruction

Warren Buffett

Everything that is really great and inspiring is created by the individual who can labor in freedom.

Albert Einstein

Hell, there are no rules here — we're trying to accomplish something.

Thomas A. Edison

12.1. Introduction

Options represent a bet on an "underlying" asset or instrument (a share, a bond, foreign exchange, etc.) such that the outcome wealth on the option position is determined, not by the absolute price value of the underlying, but by the *change* in the price value of the underlying from a pre-determined price. Options thereby provide a means of *leveraging* a *speculative* position on an underlying asset or instrument. On the other hand, if an investor holds the underlying, an option can be used to *hedge* (reduce the risk) exposure to the underlying by engaging in an option that benefits when the underlying deteriorates in value. Leading up to the global financial crisis, the use and application of option positions proliferated in complexity and design (options on defaults, for example). Nevertheless, the fundamental building blocks of complex options remain the "Call" and "Put" options that were originally traded in financial markets.

The holder of a *Call* option holds the "option" — but not the "obligation" — to *buy* a designated asset (the "underlying" asset to the option) at or before "expiration" of the option (at the end of a time period, T), at a price (the "exercise" or "strike" price, $X) agreed on at the time of the option's purchase. For example, I might hold an option that allows me to purchase a barrel of oil for $96 at expiration of the option at, say, the end of the month. If the price of the barrel of oil at the end of the month is greater than the exercise price $96, the option is "in the money" and the value of the option at the end of the month is simply the difference between the price of the barrel of oil at the end of the month and the exercise price, $96. If the price of the barrel of oil at the end of the month is less than $96, the option is "out of the money", and the option is of no value.

An option, of course, must be purchased at a price (the option "premium"). And, hence, someone must have originally sold the option (we say "written" the option). The option is termed "European" if the option can be "exercised" only at the end of the time period, T (at "expiration" of the option), whereas the option is termed "American" if it can be exercised at any time in the intervening period. The holder of a *Put* option similarly holds the option, but not the obligation, to *sell* the underlying asset at the exercise or strike price, $X.

Options are a "zero-sum" game in that the gains to a holder of the option at expiry are forthcoming at the expense of the original seller or "writer" of the option. Unlike the writer of an option, the holder of the option cannot be made liable for any additional payment after purchase of the option. The holder of the option will "exercise" the option if it is to h/h (or the institution's) advantage to do so. Otherwise s/he (or the institution) will choose to simply walk away from the option. On the other hand, the maximum gain to the option writer is the purchase price received (the option premium).

Although, as indicated above, the value of an option at expiration is entirely straightforward, the value of the option in advance of expiration presents a challenge. In this, the final chapter of this section, we derive the Black–Scholes (1973) formulae for the fair price for a "European" Call (C) and for a Put (P) option on an underlying asset.[1] This chapter is a capstone chapter in that, while not contributing any original

---

[1] Both Myron Scholes, and Robert Merton — who was quick to recognise the work of Black and Scholes and reinterpret their result in the context of his own continuous time differential equations — received the Nobel Prize in Economics for their work in 1997. Fischer Black was duly mentioned in the citation, but strictly ineligible by the rules as he was deceased.

material of substance, the derivation of the Black–Scholes model serves to demonstrate consistency with the model-building of previous chapters. Thus, we demonstrate that the Black–Scholes formula follows naturally from the building blocks of normally distributed exponential growth rates for the underlying asset, combined with the realization that such growth can be modeled as successive binomial outcomes over successive short intervals (as in Chapters 6 and 7). Specifically, we find ourselves having resource to the structural equation of a normal distribution (Eq. (6.50), p. 103) and the insight that exponential growth rates about zero produce a positive return (Eq. (7.3), p. 126). Finally, we shall argue that the volatility "smiles/smirks" departures from the Black–Scholes model are in accordance with the model building of Chapter 9.

To see why the Black–Scholes closed solution to the problem of valuing an option represents a highlight of academic thinking, consider the following. Commencing from first principles, we can state that the value of an option at expiration is either zero (if the option is not exercised) or the difference between the option exercise price and the underlying asset price (if the option is exercised). The required equation to value the fair price of a European Call option is, in principle, then determined as

Price of a Call option

$$= [\text{probability that the option is in the money}]$$
$$\times [\text{expected value of the option if it is in fact in the money}] \times e^{-r^*},$$
$$(12.1)$$

where r^* is the appropriate discount factor. It therefore appears that to compute the value of an option, we need to know investors' forecast for the price range of the underlying asset at expiration, and, in addition, the appropriate discount factor (r^*) with which to discount expectations for the value of the option.

In short, even if we simplify the problem by constraining that the underlying asset does not pay a dividend in the interval between now and the option's expiration, and that the option is "European", the obstacles to a successful solving of Eq. (12.1) appear insurmountable. Indeed in spite of the application of some good minds, a solution to Eq. (12.1) had proved elusive until Black and Scholes.

In the following section, Section 12.2, we demonstrate the principle of risk neutrality as it applies to the valuation of an option, before in the following section, Section 12.3, we derive the Black–Scholes model. In Section 12.4, we consider the application of the Black–Scholes model to a dividend-paying index of stocks, and in Section 12.5, we consider the limitations of the model. Section 12.6 concludes with a brief discussion.

12.2. The Principle of Risk Neutrality

The solution of Black and Scholes is founded on two essential assumptions: (1) The growth of the underlying asset is subject to continuously compounding growth and decline rates that are normally distributed about a mean or drift rate, μ, with standard deviation, σ, and (2) the principle of *risk neutrality* — which states that due to the fact that an option can be applied to hedge the risk of the underlying asset, the price of the option can be determined in relation to a hedged position, which is to say in relation to the risk-free rate.

To fix ideas in relation to the principle of risk neutrality, consider the following. A small oil exploration company is searching with a seismic survey for oil on a prospect. The company's stock price currently stands at $20. At the end of the month, the company will either have found evidence of oil, in which case the company's stock price will rise to $S_{up} = \$40$. Otherwise, the company will abandon the survey and the stock price will decline to $S_{down} = \$10$, as in Fig. 12.1.

Now suppose additionally that European Call and Put options exist on the above stock at the current time zero, both with exercise price $25 and with expiration at the end of the month. Thus, if the stock price is $40 at expiration, at this time, the value of the Call option $C_{up} = \$40 - \$25 = \$15$ (and the value of the put option $P_{up} = $ zero), and if the stock price is $10 at expiration, the value of the Put option $P_{down} = \$25 - \$10 = \$15$ (and the value of the call option $C_{down} = $ zero), as indicated in Fig. 12.2.

$$S_0 = \$20 \begin{cases} S_{up} = \$40 \\ S_{down} = \$10 \end{cases}$$

Figure 12.1. Binomial growth example.

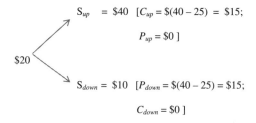

S_{up} = $40 $[C_{up} = \$(40-25) = \$15;$

$P_{up} = \$0\,]$

$20

S_{down} = $10 $[P_{down} = \$(40-25) = \$15;$

$C_{down} = \$0\,]$

Figure 12.2. Outcomes for Call and Put options with binomial outcomes.

To complete the scenario, we assume that the risk-free interest rate is 1% per month. However, although we have attributed outcome prices to the two possible outcomes as in the figures, note that we have not placed any estimates on their probability of occurrence.[2]

The question is: Can we determine a current fair price for the Call and Put options without placing some kind of estimates of probability on the possible outcomes for the underlying stock price?

Surprisingly, the answer is: Yes. A solution is possible as the outcome of a *riskless*, which is to say, a *fully hedged* portfolio. Such a portfolio is constructed by combining Δ (yet to be determined) stocks with a "short" position on one Call (meaning that we sell ("write") one Call option), as follows. At time zero, letting S_0 equal the price of the stock (which we know) and C the present price of the Call (which we do not know), the cost of the above portfolio at time zero is $\$(\Delta S_0 - C)$. The delta ($\Delta$) amount of stocks for the hedge is determined by noting that if the stock goes up in value, the portfolio at expiration is worth (Fig. 12.2):

$$\Delta S_0 - C = \Delta 40 - 15,$$

whereas if the stock goes down in value, the portfolio at expiration is worth

$$\Delta S_0 - C = \Delta 10 - 0.$$

Equating the two outcomes: $\Delta 40 - 15 = \Delta 10 - 0$, and solving gives us $\Delta = \frac{1}{2}$. Thus, we observe that the outcome wealth generated by the

---

[2]On the other hand, and we refer to this point later on, the *market* — by attributing a price of $20 to the underlying stock price at the present time — has implicitly imposed some notion of probability on the two possible outcomes.

portfolio is:

$$\Delta S_{up} - C_{up} = \frac{1}{2} \times 40 - 15 = \$5, \text{ if the stock price goes up}$$

and

$$\Delta S_{down} - C_{down} = \frac{1}{2} \times 10 - 0 = \$5, \text{ if the stock price goes down.}$$

The present value of \$5 must therefore equal the cost of purchasing the portfolio, which recall was: $\Delta S_0 - C$ (with $S_0 = \$20$ and $\Delta = \frac{1}{2}$). Thus, we have

$$\frac{1}{2}20 - C = 5e^{-0.01}.$$

Which yields $C = \underline{\$5.05}$.

To determine the present price of a Put, we use the put-call parity relation[3]:

$$S_0 + P - C = Xe^{-r_f}, \tag{12.2}$$

where r_f is the risk-free rate over the time T to expiration, which with

$$S_0 = \$20, \quad C = \$5.05, \quad X = \$25, \quad r_f = 0.01, \text{ yields} \quad P = \underline{\$9.80}.$$

We have actually deduced the fair price of an option without needing to know either (1) the probabilities to attach to the possible outcome prices for the underlying asset at expiration; which is to say, we do not need to know investors' "expected" (Eq. (6.61), p. 107) return for the underlying asset, or (2) the "price of risk" (e^{-r^*} in Eq. (12.1)) that is appropriate for an option.

---

[3]The put-call relation follows by considering that when I hold an asset with a Put option on the asset and a short position on a Call option on the asset, both with expiration time T, my position is fully hedged. This is because if the asset is priced above the exercise price X at time T, the holder of the Call will "call" the asset from me at price \$X, and if the asset price falls below \$X, I will use the Put option at time T to "put" the asset at price \$X. Thus, with either eventuality, I am left with \$X. The present fair price for an asset with a long Put option and a short position on a Call option on the asset (which is to say, $S_0 + P - C$) is therefore determined as the present price of the certain outcome, \$X, which is Xe^{-r_f}. Hence, the put-call relation: $S_0 + P - C = Xe^{-r_f}$.

To see what is at play here, suppose that initial reports from the seismic survey considered above have provided vague encouragement for a successful outcome. We therefore might anticipate some upward movement in the price of the Call option, but, note, a rational upward change in the price of the option must somehow align with an upward change in the underlying stock price. If investors do not see fit to change the price of the underlying stock (from $20), they should not see fit to change the price of the option (from $5.05). Suppose, however, that reports from the survey indicate a near certainty of success! How is our option price affected? The answer is that we simply take the new stock price (much closer now to $40, no doubt) and substitute this price in the above calculation repeated to determine the new option price.

The point is, we do not need to know the new probabilities of possible outcomes — all we need to know is the new stock price! The insight of Black and Scholes was to recognize that the inherent risk-return dynamic of the situation is captured in the underlying stock price to the extent that the option is able to lever off the stock price so as to determine its own price.

Almost incredibly, because the expected growth rate for the underlying stock in Fig. 12.1 does not enter the calculations, we are perfectly at liberty to assign to it *any* value. Taking the argument to a logical conclusion, in calculating the fair price of an option, we are free to assume that the expected growth rate for the underlying asset is the risk-free rate, r_f, and, consequently, that the risk-free rate, r_f, represents investors' price of risk, and hence the appropriate discount factor (r^*) in Eq. (12.1). This is the Black and Scholes assumption of *risk neutrality*.

To see the validity of this assumption, let us impose the probability, p, of an up-movement (and hence of a down-movement, $1 - p$) in Fig. 12.1, so that the expected growth rate for the asset is the risk-free rate. In other words, we choose p in Fig. 12.1 so that

$$S_0 e^{r_f} = p S_{\text{up}} + (1 - p) S_{\text{down}}, \qquad (12.3)$$

where r_f is the risk-free rate for the period to option expiration. We can see that the probability of the up-movement, p, is determined with Eq. (12.3) as

$$p = \frac{e^{r_f} - d}{u - d}, \qquad (12.4)$$

where $u =$ the up-movement tick $= S_{up}/S_0 = 40/20 = 2$, and $d =$ the down-movement tick $= S_{down}/S_0 = 10/20 = \frac{1}{2}$. Substituting $u = 2$, $d = \frac{1}{2}$, and $r_f = 0.01$ in Eq. (12.4), we have

$$p = \frac{e^{0.01} - 0.5}{2 - 0.5},$$

$$= 0.34.$$

We therefore have the present price of the Call, C, as

$$C = [pC_{up} + (1 - p)C_{down}]e^{-r_f}, \tag{12.5}$$

which, with $p = 0.34$, $C_{up} = 15$, $(1 - p) = 0.66$, $C_{down} = 0$, $r_f = 0.01$, yields $C = \$5.05$, as above. In other words, the assumption of risk neutrality is consistent with the above outcome derived from a fully hedged portfolio. In the same manner, we can determine the price of the Put:

$$P = [pP_{up} + (1 - p)P_{down}]e^{-r_f}, \tag{12.6}$$

with $p = 0.34$, and with $P_{up} = \$0$, and $P_{down} = \$15$. That is,

$$P = [0 + 0.66(15)]e^{-0.01} = \$9.80,$$

also as the above outcome.

12.3. Derivation of the Black–Scholes Formula

We can rewrite Eq. (12.1) for the price of a Call, C, quite generally as

$$C = \big[\textit{the probability-weighted summation over all in-the-money outcome}$$

$$\textit{prices} - \textit{the probability-weighted cost of purchase of the asset}\big]e^{-r^*}. \tag{12.7}$$

The second right-hand side term, *the probability-weighted cost of purchase of the asset*, is the exercise price, X, multiplied by the probability that the Call option is in the money. We therefore proceed to determine:

(i) The probability that the Call is in the money,
(ii) The probability-weighted summation over all in-the-money outcome prices, followed by,
(iii) A closed expression for the price of a Call option as Eq. (12.7).

In regards to (i) and (ii), we shall assume as Black and Scholes, that the outcome continuously compounding growth rates for the underlying asset are normally distributed. In regards to (iii), we shall assume that the principle of risk neutrality as demonstrated above for a single binomial branch is applicable to a normal distribution. The justification is that a normal distribution of return outcomes can be represented as the repetition of a succession of such branches (Chapter 6.12).

12.3.1 *The Probability That the Call is in the Money*

The probability, p, that the Call option is in the money is the probability that the price of the underlying stock at expiration time, T, exceeds the exercise price, X. We can express this as the probability that

$$S_0 e^y > X, \tag{12.8}$$

where S_0 is the current stock price and y is the stock's outcome exponential growth rate for the period to expiration; which is to say (with Eq. (6.15), p. 82), the probability that the Call option is in the money, is the probability that

$$y > \ln\left(\frac{X}{S_0}\right). \tag{12.9}$$

The probability that $y > \ln(X/S_0)$ is the probability that

$$z \equiv (y - \mu)/\sigma > \left[\ln\left(\frac{X}{S_0}\right) - \mu\right]\Big/ \sigma, \tag{12.10}$$

where the stock is assumed to have a mean exponential growth rate, μ, with standard deviation, σ,[4] and $z = (y - \mu)/\sigma$ is therefore normally distributed with mean $= 0$ and standard deviation $= 1$ (Chapter 6.6). With Eq. (12.10), the minimum value of $z = (y - \mu)/\sigma$ that allows the Call option to be in the money is

$$z^* = \left[\ln\left(\frac{X}{S_0}\right) - \mu\right]\Big/ \sigma. \tag{12.11}$$

---

[4]To be precise, the growth rates here are for the specific time period up to the option's expiration; thus, if the time to expiration is, say, one *week*, the growth rates μ (and y) are the growth rates *per week*.

The probability that z is *less* than z^* is obtained from Table 6.1 as $N(z^*)$. By symmetry of the unit normal distribution, the probability that the outcome z is *greater* than z^* (which is what we require) is equal to the probability that the outcome is less than minus $-z^*$. Thus, the probability, p, that the option is in the money is expressed:

$$P(S_T > X) = N\left\{-\left[\ln\left(\frac{X}{S_0}\right) - \mu\right]\Big/\sigma\right\} \qquad (12.12)$$

which (with Eq. (6.4), p. 75, and Eq. (6.18), p. 83) can be expressed:

$$P(S_T > X) = N\left\{\left[\ln\left(\frac{S_0}{X}\right) + \mu\right]\Big/\sigma\right\} \qquad (12.13)$$

12.3.2   The Probability-Weighted Summation Over All In-the-money Outcome Prices

We can write the summation over all in-the-money outcome prices weighted by their probability of occurrence as

$$\sum_{z=z^*}^{\infty} S_0 e^{\mu+\sigma Z}, \qquad (12.14)$$

where as above, μ and σ, respectively, are the mean exponential growth rate and standard deviation for the stock for the period to expiration, and Z is the distribution of z values on the range $-\infty$ to $+\infty$ that are probability-weighted as the unit normal distribution in Fig. 6.3; and the summation sign, Σ, implies a summation over the range from z^* (the minimum return z^* that is required to take the option into the money) from Eq. (12.11):

$$z^* = \left[\ln\left(\frac{X}{S_0}\right) - \mu\right]\Big/\sigma,$$

to $+\infty$. More explicitly, we have the probability distribution for the outcomes, z, in expression (12.14) as the unit normal distribution function of Eq. (6.50) (p. 103). Thus, we can write expression (12.14) as

$$\sum_{z=z^*}^{\infty} S_0 e^{\mu+\sigma z} \frac{1}{\sqrt{2\pi}} e^{-\frac{1}{2}z^2} \Delta z, \qquad (12.15)$$

where consistent with Fig. 6.3, $\frac{1}{\sqrt{2\pi}}e^{-1/2z^2}\Delta z$ is the probability that z lies in the small interval Δz surrounding z. By summing progressively over successive intervals of Δz for z greater than z^* in expression (12.15), we thereby arrive at the expected outcome for the underlying stock price S_T allowing $S_T > X$ at expiration. The problem is to evaluate expression (12.15).

To make progress, we observe that we have (Chapter 6.6):

$$\sum_{z=-\infty}^{\infty} \frac{1}{\sqrt{2\pi}}e^{-\frac{1}{2}z^2}\Delta z = 1. \tag{12.16}$$

And for any z^*:

$$\sum_{z=z^*}^{\infty} \frac{1}{\sqrt{2\pi}}e^{-\frac{1}{2}z^2}\Delta z = 1 - N(z^*), \tag{12.17}$$

with $N(z^*)$ determined from Table 6.1 as the area under the unit normal curve to the left of z^*.

A direct application of Eq. (12.17) to solving expression (12.15), is, however, obstructed by the occurrence of the $e^{\mu+\sigma z}$ term (since it relates to z) in expression (12.15). We can, however, get around the problem in two stages. First, we write expression (12.15) as

$$S_0 e^{\mu+\frac{1}{2}\sigma^2}\sum_{z=z^*}^{\infty} \frac{1}{\sqrt{2\pi}}e^{-\frac{1}{2}(\sigma-z)^2}\Delta z, \tag{12.18}$$

which brings the variable z into a single representation as $e^{-\frac{1}{2}(\sigma-z)^2}$, and then by substituting

$$w = \sigma - z, \tag{12.19}$$

we can express expression (12.18) as

$$-S_0 e^{\mu+\frac{1}{2}\sigma^2}\sum_{z=z^*}^{\infty} \frac{1}{\sqrt{2\pi}}e^{-\frac{1}{2}w^2}\Delta w. \tag{12.20}$$

As z increases with intervals Δz from the value in Eq. (12.11):

$$z^* = \left[\ln\left(\frac{X}{S_0}\right) - \mu\right]\bigg/\sigma,$$

to infinity, w in expression (12.20) (with Eq. (12.19)) decreases with intervals of Δw measured negatively from

$$w^* = \sigma - \left[\ln\left(\frac{X}{S_0}\right) - \mu\right]\bigg/\sigma, \qquad (12.21)$$

to minus infinity. Thus, by making successive increments of Δw measured positively from minus infinity to $w^* = \sigma - [\ln(X/S_0) - \mu]/\sigma$, we can write expression (12.20) as

$$S_0 e^{\mu + \frac{1}{2}\sigma^2} \sum_{w=-\infty}^{w^*} \frac{1}{\sqrt{2\pi}} e^{-\frac{1}{2}w^2} \Delta w. \qquad (12.22)$$

The above summation identifies the area under the unit normal curve to the left of w^*, which we express as $N(w^*)$. We may therefore rewrite expression (12.22) for the required probability-weighted summation over all in-the-money outcome prices as

$$S_0 e^{\mu + \frac{1}{2}\sigma^2} N(w^*). \qquad (12.23)$$

12.3.3 *A Closed Expression for the Price of a Call Option*

We are now in a position to apply Eq. (12.7):

$C = \big[$*the probability-weighted summation over all in-the-money outcome*

  prices $-$ *the probability-weighted cost of purchase of the asset*$\big]e^{-r^*}.$

The *probability-weighted summation over all in-the-money outcome prices* has been determined as expression (12.23):

$$S_0 e^{\mu + \frac{1}{2}\sigma^2} N(w^*).$$

The *probability-weighted cost of purchase of the asset* is equal to the exercise price, X, multiplied by the *probability that the Call is in the money*, which has been determined as Eq. (12.12):

$$P(S_T > X) = N\left\{-\left[\ln\left(\frac{X}{S_0}\right) - \mu\right]\bigg/\sigma\right\},$$

which with Eq. (12.21), can be expressed:

$$P(S_T > X) = N[w^* - \sigma]. \tag{12.24}$$

We therefore have Eq. (12.7) as

$$C = \left[S_0 e^{\mu + \frac{1}{2}\sigma^2} N(w^*) - X \cdot N(w^* - \sigma) \right] e^{-r^*}. \tag{12.25}$$

The above provides a closed expression for the value of the Call option that is the outcome of statistical algebra. The practicality, however, is that in Eq. (12.25), we know neither the exponential growth rate, μ, of the underlying (which also occurs in the expression for w^* in Eq. (12.21)) nor the appropriate discount rate, r^*.

At this point, we need to recall the insight of risk neutrality that allows us to assume that investors are risk-neutral and that the underlying asset grows at the risk-free rate, r_f, over the time to expiration of the option. Thus, we have Eq. (7.3):

$$R = \mu + \frac{1}{2}\sigma^2,$$

with $R = r_f$; and hence

$$\mu = r_f - \frac{1}{2}\sigma^2. \tag{12.26}$$

With Eq. (12.26), we are able to express

$$e^{\mu + \frac{1}{2}\sigma^2} = e^{r_f}, \tag{12.27}$$

and (Eq. (12.21)):

$$w^* = \left\{ \left[\ln\left(\frac{S_0}{X}\right) + r_f + \frac{1}{2}\sigma^2 \right] \Big/ \sigma \right\}. \tag{12.28}$$

And we have directly (the principle of risk neutrality):

$$e^{-r^*} = e^{-r_f}. \tag{12.29}$$

Substituting Eqs. (12.27) and (12.29) into Eq. (12.25), we have the price of a Call option C as

$$C = S_0 N(w^*) - X e^{-r_f} N(w^* - \sigma). \tag{12.30}$$

For simplicity, we have taken it that the risk-free rate, r_f, and standard deviation, σ, are measured over the time to expiration, T, of the option. In general, r_f and σ are quoted on an annual basis, in which case, r_f and σ must be replaced by $r_f T$ and $\sigma\sqrt{T}$, respectively, where T is the time in years to expiration of the option. Thus, finally, we can write

$$C = S_0 N(w^*) - Xe^{-r_f T} N(w^* - \sigma\sqrt{T}). \tag{12.31}$$

A similar argument for the fair price, P, of a Put leads to

$$P = Xe^{-r_f T} N(\sigma\sqrt{T} - w^*) - S_0 N(-w^*), \tag{12.32}$$

where

$$w^* = \left[\ln\left(\frac{S_0}{X}\right) + \left(r_f + \frac{1}{2}\sigma^2\right) T \right] \bigg/ \sigma\sqrt{T}. \tag{12.33}$$

Equations (12.31)–(12.33) are the Black–Scholes model for the fair price of a Call and a Put option on an underlying asset with price, S_0.

12.4. Options on the Index with Dividends

An option on an index has the additional complication that the index generates a more or less continuous dividend stream. Suppose, for example, an index whose underlying stocks are judged to maintain a dividend yield of, say, $d\%$, per annum. On reviewing the previous arguments for the derivation of the basic model, we can see readily that the only adjustment that needs to be made is that the riskless return to an investor holding the stock must be identified as

$$r_f = \mu + \frac{1}{2}\sigma^2 + d, \tag{12.34}$$

so that $\mu + \frac{1}{2}\sigma^2$ is replaced by $r_f - d$, in the expression for the option price, C (Eq. (12.25)), and μ is replaced by $r_f - 1/2\sigma^2 - d$, in the expression for w^* (Eq. (12.21)). We thereby determine

$$C = S_0 e^{-dT} N(w^*) - Xe^{-r_f T} N(w^* - \sigma\sqrt{T}), \tag{12.35}$$

$$P = Xe^{-r_f T} N(\sigma\sqrt{T} - w^*) - S_0 e^{-dT} N(-w^*), \tag{12.36}$$

where

$$w^* = \left[\ln\left(\frac{S_0}{X}\right) + \left(r_f - d + \frac{1}{2}\sigma^2\right)T \right] \Big/ \sigma\sqrt{T}. \qquad (12.37)$$

12.5. Testing the Black–Scholes Model

The inputs in the basic Black–Scholes model (Eqs. (12.31)–(12.33)) are five: the current price of the underlying asset (S_0), the exercise price (X), the time to expiration of the option (T), the risk-free rate (r_f), and the volatility (σ) of growth outcomes for the underlying asset. Of these, the first three can be precisely identified, and the risk-free rate can be approximated with some confidence, so that only the volatility is likely to be materially imprecise. The outcome is that we can make the Black–Scholes model fit the observed option price by choosing the "implied" volatility of the underlying asset. Nevertheless, the implied underlying volatility should remain consistent for options with different exercise prices (X) on the *same* underlying stock (S_0) and with the *same* expiry date (T). Neither do we expect to see a systematic dependence of the implied underlying volatility on the option's time to expiration.

In practice, a volatility surface as the three-dimensional (3D) graph of implied volatility against exercise price and time to expiration is not flat. The typical shape of the implied volatility curve for a given expiration depends on the underlying asset. Equities tend to have skewed curves: Compared to at-the-money, implied volatility is substantially higher for low strikes (in-the-money Calls), and slightly lower for high strikes (out-of-the-money Calls) (a "smirk"). Currencies tend to have more symmetrical curves, with implied volatility lowest at-the-money (a "smile"). Commodities often have the reverse behavior to equities, with higher implied volatility for higher strikes. The explanations are not clear-cut, but it appears that a key component of the explanation is that price movements — rather than being independent across time as required to generate a normal distribution — are capable of self-fuelling decreases leading to fatter tails for the downside distribution (price increases that are self-sustaining tend to be more gradual, as observed in Section 9.9). Furthermore, because volatility tends to increase (decrease) with downward (upside) price movements, the anticipation of downside (upside) price movements implies an anticipation of increased (decreased) volatility.

The above explanations can be reconciled in terms of the model development of Chapter 9. We stated (Section 9.7) that the standard deviation of equity stocks as measured under conditions of market stability (17.5% annualized in the example of Chapter 9.6) may need to be augmented to capture the possibility of self-sustaining market increases or decreases (leading to a proposed standard deviation closer to 30% annualized). Investors who are trading options that are at- or near-the-money, are, in effect, betting on stock movements *relative to the exercise price* over the time period of the option. Such investors, *in periods of relative market calm*, will generally tend to suppress the possibility of stock price self-sustaining increases/decreases occurring abruptly within the limited time period of the option; in effect, they tend to assume a standard deviation that captures market conditions as projected to occur within the time frame of the option (17.5% annualized, for example, in the above case). In contrast, for deep in-the-money Call options, the buyer (seller) of a Call option is effectively buying (selling) the stock. For such options, the total price to be paid by the buyer of the option — the option price (C) in combination with Xe^{-r_fT} (the discounted exercise price $X paid at expiration) — must be the price of the stock, S_0; yielding, $C = S_0 - Xe^{-r_fT}$ (left-hand side of Fig. 12.3). For such deep-in-the-money Calls, the outcome value of the call tends to symmetry about the underlying outcome price: each dollar gained (lost) by the underlying is a dollar gained (lost) to the option. Nevertheless, with increasing deep in-the-moneyness, the possibility of "losing everything" (the Call is out-of-the

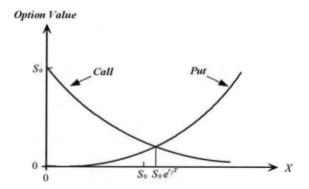

Figure 12.3. Call and Put prices as a function of exercise price.

money at expiration) is increasingly reduced. Thus, with increasingly deep-in-the-money Calls, which implies deep out-of-the-money Puts, there is increasingly less opportunity for "action" surrounding either option that differs from buying/selling the underlying share. We might hypothesize that the clientele for such options should tend to those investors who are sensitive to the possibility of more extreme stock price movements as captured by the higher volatility (30%) reflecting the probability-weighted outcomes due to self-sustaining price increases/decreases, but who do not wish to be exposed to the possibility of losing heavily in proportion to the outlay of purchasing the option that may occur with at- or near-the-money options. In which case, during periods of market stability, deep in-the-money Call options are priced on a higher volatility than are options close to the exercise price. Investors, of course, quickly become sensitized to the possibility of market self-sustained increases or decreases in periods of market "nervousness" (captured by the VIX market indicator that captures changes in the implied volatilities of options).

It follows, also, that in periods of market calm, options of longer duration will generally have a higher implied volatility. This is because with longer time to option maturity, there exists a higher probability of a sudden increase in the underlying asset volatility.

12.6. Time for Reflection: What Have We Learned?

The original derivation by Black and Scholes (1973) for the price of a Call option, C, in relation to the underlying stock price, S, relies on the solution to a differential equation in continuous time as

$$\frac{\partial C}{\partial t} + \frac{1}{2}\sigma^2 S^2 \frac{\partial^2 C}{\partial S^2} + r_f S \frac{\partial C}{\partial S} - r_f C = 0. \qquad (12.38)$$

Robert Merton (1973, 1990) has extended the interpretation and application of the model with added mathematical sophistication that requires a grasp of Ito's lemma and stochastic calculus in infinitesimal time.[5] This chapter has

---

[5]If you have an inclination to follow Myron Scholes and Robert Merton by solving their stochastic differential equations in infinitesimal time, Good Luck! Just don't let either Myron or Robert hear you mention Long Term Capital Management. My actual experience with infinitesimal time relates to when I was taking driving lessons in Australia. My instructor told me that at a STOP sign, I must actually stop, and not just slow down to an "almost" stop.

demonstrated the Black–Scholes formula as following algebraically from the building blocks of continuous growth rates that were demonstrated in Chapters 6 and 7.

Understanding the volatility smiles and smirks has led to a great deal of research both by academics and practitioners, seeking to understand more precisely how options should be priced. Not surprisingly, the mathematics gets tough with often only incremental benefits to a deeper theoretical understanding. We note, however, that in seeking to understand deviations of observations from the simple model predictions, a recognition that large market movements in stock prices are more frequent than predicted by a normal distribution, is again a part of the explanation.

Otherwise, when I came to take the test, the driving examiner would fail me for breaking the law. When I asked him how long I must stop for, he told me there was no minimum time. I didn't need to stay there for any *finite* amount of time, just an *infinitesimally short* period of time. So, what *is* an infinitesimally short period of time? (You might, consider, for example, that the unit of measurement remains important, so that an *infinitesimally short* period of time measured in years is an infinitesimally small number that is nevertheless 365 times smaller than the infinitesimally small number measured in days for the *same infinitesimally short* period of time. Check out Eq. (6.23) (p. 93), and also Eq. (6.38) (p. 98), which illustrate the point.) Unlike Black, Scholes, Merton, and my driving instructor, I sometimes struggle with the concept.

PART D

Corporate Financial Decision Making

Chapter 13

Valuation of the Firm's Cash Flows

The mathematician's patterns, like the painter's or the poet's must be beautiful; the ideas like the colours or the words, must fit together in a harmonious way. Beauty is the first test: there is no permanent place in the world for ugly mathematics.

G. H. Hardy

Nowadays people know the price of everything and the value of nothing.

Oscar Wilde

Price is what you pay. Value is what you get.

Warren Buffett

You see that building? I bought that building ten years ago. My first real estate deal. Sold it two years later, made an $800,000 profit. It was better than sex. At the time I thought that was all the money in the world. Now it's a day's pay.

Gordon Gekko

13.1. Introduction[1]

The evaluation of future cash flows lies at the very heart of investment decision making. The discounting of future cash flows is particularly important in situations when a firm's valuation is a basis for negotiation between two parties, for example, in cases of contested merger and acquisitions, the privatization of state enterprises when such calculations are applied to determine the fair offer price to the public, or in the case of regulated industries, where the valuation of future cash flows determines

---

[1] This chapter develops ideas that were first presented in the *Journal of Business Finance and Accounting* (1996, 1998, 2001), also, *Journal of Banking and Finance* (2001), *Accounting and Business Research* (1998b), *Accounting and Finance* (Dempsey and Partington, 2008) and *The Journal of Applied Research in Accounting and Finance* (Dempsey, McKenzie and Partington, 2010), and *European Financial Management* (2013). I am indeed grateful and indebted to the editors and reviewers of these journals for supporting and publishing this work.

the fair price at which the regulated commodity (electricity, water, etc.) must be priced to the public. In such cases, billions of dollars turn on how projected cash flows are discounted.

Given the above observations, the degree of confusion and ambiguity that continues to reside in the academic literature in the area of discounting methodology is embarrassing. Confusion prevails even when the models are simplified to the point of ignoring the reality of individual tax liabilities as they impact on "money in the pocket" outcomes of investments.[2]

In response, under general conditions where investors have individual tax liabilities separately on income from equity income, income from bonds, and on capital gains, we demonstrate that the four popular methods of discounting cash flows are algebraically equivalent; which is to say, all four methods are "saying the same thing". To demonstrate this consistency, we advance two propositions, each of which represents an expression of mathematical consistency.

Accordingly, the rest of the paper is organized as follows. In the following section, Section 13.2, we summarize the four most common methods of discounting along with issues that have frustrated attempts at coherence. In Section 13.3, we present our two guiding propositions. In Section 13.4, we proceed to clarify the discounting methods in the context of personal taxes. In Section 13.5, we apply the various methods of valuation to a worked example and thereby demonstrate the equivalence of the four methods. Section 13.6 briefly reviews the likely appropriate

---

[2]Even allowing the assumption that the implications of investors' individual tax liabilities on income/capital gains can be ignored, the question of whether the methods of discounting are consistent with one another continues to be debated with contradictory outcomes. For example, Fernandez (2004) proposes that the present value of tax savings is not their discounted value. This is countered by Cooper and Nyborg (2006), who show that Fernandez's result is the outcome of combining equations that hold under the assumption that debt exposure is fixed with expressions that hold when debt leverage is fixed (and debt exposure is variable). Again, Inselbag and Kaauford (1997) demonstrate that the adjusted present value (*APV*) and free cash flow (*FCF*) methods are consistent under either view of the riskiness of the tax deductibility of interest payments, whereas Massari, Roncaglio and Zanetti (2008) insist that the two methods are generally inconsistent, and that the differences in outcome are non-trivial. In turn, Dempsey (2013) confirms that the error in Massari *et al.* is similar to that in Fernandez (2004). Oded and Michel (2007) provide additional examples of internal inconsistencies in textbooks with respect to the application of discounting methods.

method of choice for the evaluator. In Section 13.7, we demonstrate consistency between the capital asset pricing model (CAPM) and the principle of additivity of risk-return relations as encapsulated in Modigliani and Miller's Proposition 2, and in Section 13.8, we demonstrate that the consistency invoked by the proposition is violated by the Fama and French three-factor (FF-3F) model. Section 13.9 discusses the introduced "capitalization" factors and their simplification of the cost of capital expressions. Section 13.10 argues that the chapter's proposed capitalization approach is required if gross errors in, for example, the assessment of the market's valuation of imputation tax credits, are to be avoided. Section 13.11 briefly summarizes and concludes the chapter.

13.2. Complicating Issues in Discounting

In one sense, a degree of confusion in discounting is understandable. There are four popular methods of discounting, each of which takes a somewhat different perspective:

(1) *The cash flow to equity (CFE) approach*,
    which determines the market value of the firm's shares, V_E, as the discounted value of future cash flows to the firm's equity holders.
(2) *The APV approach*,
    which discounts the firm's operating free cash flow, *FCF*, available to shareholders at the unlevered cost of equity, K_U, assuming that the firm has *no debt*, so as to determine the value of the otherwise-equivalent unlevered cash flow (V_U). The present value of the tax savings (*PVTS*) due to the tax deductibility (at the corporate tax rate, T_c) of the interest payments on the firm's debt, V_D (as discussed in Chapter 5), is calculated separately, and added to V_U to determine the value of the firm, V_{firm} (as market equity + market debt, $V_E + V_D$), as the present value of the levered cash flow.
(3) *The capital cash flow (CCF) approach*,
    which estimates the value of the cash flow to the firm, V_{firm}, directly as the present value of the levered *CCF* by combining the operating cash flows available to the holders of equity and debt and discounting this total cash flow using a weighted average of the shareholders' and bondholders' costs of capital (K_{AV}).

(4) *The operating free cash flow* approach,

which is the industry favored approach, which estimates the value of the cash flow to the firm, V_{firm}, directly by discounting the operating *FCF* available to the firm's shareholders assuming that the firm has no debt by a weighted average cost of capital (*WACC*) that is designed to capture the fact that the firm's interest payments are tax-deductible at the corporate tax rate (T_c). Thus, unlike the above *APV* method, which captures the value of the firm's tax deductibility of interest payments as a separate component of value, the *FCF* approach captures the tax deductibility in the discount rate.

In addition to the above, we have the complication that the appropriate rate at which to discount the tax deductibility of the firm's interest payments is somewhat subjective (Chapter 5). Whereas Modigliani and Miller (1963) regard the interest rate on the debt as the appropriate rate with which to discount the tax savings from the self-same debt, a more common position holds that because the tax savings are correlated with the firm's unlevered cash flow (the argument is that the firm's propensity to take on debt — which ultimately determines the tax deductibility of the firm's interest payments — likely varies with the value of the firm's unlevered cash flow), the firm's unlevered cost of equity represents a more appropriate discount rate.

And finally, as a complicating issue, investors encounter personal taxes on their income from dividends, income from bonds, and on capital gains. Thus, for shares, tax rates are structured differently depending on whether the benefits of firm ownership are received as dividends or as capital gains, which may differ again for income from bonds. Added to which, different classes of investors (individuals, mutual funds, pension funds, insurance funds) have differing tax liabilities even when they receive income by the same means.[3] As a final complication, under an imputation tax system, such as in Australia, shareholders (as owners of the company) are imputed

---

[3]Prior to Dempsey (2001), Taggart (1991) is one of the very few authors to address the issue of consistency of discounting methods in the presence of personal taxes. Taggart's paper models personal taxes by assuming a "representative" investor whose personal taxes differ between equity and bonds, but which do not differentiate between dividends as income and capital gains.

to have made the corporate tax payments, which, accordingly, are offset against their personal tax liabilities. In this case, taxes at the corporate and individual level are inextricably linked.

13.3. Towards Coherence in Discounting

We require two propositions to achieve consistency between the four discounting methods, which we present in the following two sub-sections.

13.3.1 *A Discount Model for Cash Flows Subject to Taxes (Proposition 1)*

We have Eq. (6.6):

$$PV = \frac{\$X_1}{(1+i)} + \frac{\$X_2}{(1+i)^2} + \frac{\$X_3}{(1+i)^3} + \cdots + \frac{\$X_N}{(1+i)^N},$$

which identifies the present value (*PV*) of future amounts $\$X_1, \$X_2,$ $\$X_3, \ldots, \$X_N$, at the end of $1, 2, 3, \ldots, N$ periods, respectively, using a discount rate, i, per period. Consistent with Eq. (6.6), the market value of the firm's equity, V_E, as a discounting of the firm's future dividends is generally expressed:

$$V_E = \frac{\$dividend_1}{(1+k)} + \frac{\$dividend_2}{(1+k)^2} + \frac{\$dividend_3}{(1+k)^3} + \cdots, \qquad (13.1)$$

where *dividend*$_1$, *dividend*$_2$ ... are investors' expected future dividends for the firm in each future period, and k can be interpreted either as the firm's cost of equity per period or, reciprocally, interpreted as shareholders' required expectation of return, $E(R)$, per period (in principle, computed from the CAPM, Eq. (2.1)).

A difficulty with Eq. (13.1) is that allowing for a tax effect on shareholders' returns, we cannot expect that $1 of dividends in the numerator terms on the right-hand side of the equation necessarily equates with $1 of equity value (the V_E term on the left-hand side of the equation). The linear transformation from cash dividends to equity value must therefore be carried out by the discount factor, k. However, k does not act in a linear manner on the numerator, but rather as $(1+k)^i$, where i denotes the ith dividend in Eq. (13.1). The k denominator must therefore be disqualified

Stock Markets, Investments and Corporate Behavior

as a means of converting cash dividends (the right-hand side of Eq. (13.1))
to a market valuation (the left-hand side of Eq. (13.1)).

Following the principle of *dimensional consistency*, we therefore
choose to identify the present market value of the firm's equity, V_E, as
the discounted valuation of the *market* values of the firm's distribution to
shareholders as

$$V_E = \sum_{i=1}^{N} \frac{market\ value\ of\ distributions\ to\ sharehodlers_i}{(1 + K_E)^i}, \qquad (13.2)$$

where K_E is the discount rate, which we identify as investors' required
capital growth rate for the firm inclusive of the firm's cash distributions.[4] It
is therefore the required growth rate *between* the firm's cash disbursements,
which is to say between the ex-dividend day and the subsequent (with-)cum-
dividend day. Thus, in the case of a firm whose distributions to shareholders
are as dividends, K_E is identified as

$$K_E = g + d \cdot q_E, \qquad (13.3)$$

where g represents shareholders' expectation for the firm's capital growth
rate (net of the firm's dividend payments); d represents shareholders'
expectation for the firm's dividend yield, and q_E identifies the market value
of \$1 of the firm's distributions as dividends. These components of capital
appreciation are represented in Fig. 13.1.

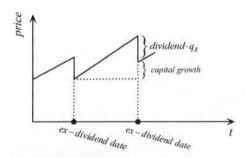

Figure 13.1. The components of a stock's capital appreciation.

---

[4]The discerning reader will again have observed that we have continued our switchover
from the notation $E(R_E)$ to K_E (as in Chapter 5). The former notation emphasizes the
discount factor as investors' required expectation of return, the latter, as here, emphasizes
the discount factor as the reciprocal firm's cost of capital.

We thereby arrive at

Proposition 1: The firm's equity (V_E) as the discounted value of the firm's distributions to shareholders can be expressed as:

$$V_E = \sum_{i=1}^{N} \frac{\text{distribution to shareholders}_i \cdot q_E}{(1 + K_E)^i}, \qquad (13.4)$$

where q_E is the market value of \$1 of the firm's distributions to shareholders.

Equation (13.4) allows that the complications of taxes are subsumed in the market valuation of the firm's distributions. The advantage is that we do not need to be concerned with the value of a dollar as a function of its distribution to each of its possible recipients: We need know only the *market* value of the firm's distributed dollar. In effect, we designate the market (and not individual shareholders) as the arbiter of value. The symbol q_E may be regarded in analogy with Tobin's q, which is the ratio of the market value of a firm's assets to the cash value of the assets.

13.3.2 *The Cost of Equity and Leverage (Proposition 2)*

Although it is not a restrictive assumption (see footnote 9), we shall for simplicity allow that the firm's bonds are held in perpetuity. As we observed in Chapter 5, the interest payments on the firm's bonds are tax-deductible at the corporate rate. A question that emerges is whether the consequent tax savings to the firm should be discounted at the rate of interest on the debt, i_D (as Modigliani and Miller, 1963) or at the unlevered cost of equity, K_U (on the basis that the variability of the tax benefits is as the firm's debt capacity, which, in turn, is as the unlevered cash flow).[5]

Provided consistency is maintained, the valuator is allowed to choose either of the above (or, indeed, any other) discount rate. Thus, without specification at this stage, we allow that the tax deductibility of interest payments creates an additional "corporate tax shield" value for the firm, whose market value we denote as present value of tax savings (*PVTS*) as yet to be determined.

In principle, the additional cash flow tax savings due to the firm's debt can be sold off at a price equal to their market *PVTS* valuation. It follows

---

[5]For example, Cooper and Nyborg (2007).

that the weighted average of the market costs of debt (K_D) and equity (K_E) capital, K_{AV} as Eq. (5.2)[6]:

$$K_{AV} \equiv \frac{V_D}{V_D + V_E} K_D + \frac{V_E}{V_D + V_E} K_E,$$

is determined as a weighted average of what the firm's overall cost of capital would have been in the case that the firm had no debt (unlevered), K_U, and the cost of capital for the *PVTS* (tax shield) component of the firm's equity, which we shall call K_{TS}. We are therefore able to write

$$\begin{aligned} K_{AV} &\equiv \frac{V_D}{V_D + V_E} K_D + \frac{V_E}{V_D + V_E} K_E \\ &= \frac{V_D + V_E - PVTS}{V_D + V_E} K_U + \frac{PVTS}{V_D + V_E} K_{TS}. \end{aligned} \quad (13.5)$$

Rearrangement of Eq. (13.5) leads to:

Proposition 2: A levered firm's cost of equity (K_E) relates to that firm's unlevered cost of equity (K_U) and the firm's cost of debt (K_D) as

$$K_E = \left[1 + \frac{V_D - PVTS}{V_E} \right] K_U - \frac{V_D}{V_E} K_D + \frac{PVTS}{V_E} K_{TS}, \quad (13.6)$$

where V_D is the market value of the firm's debt, V_E is the market value of the firm's equity, and K_{TS} is the cost of capital applied to the present value of the firm's tax shield savings (PVTS) due to corporate debt.

Allowing for personal taxes, the above proposition 2 formally replaces Modigliani and Miller's proposition 2 (Eq. (5.6)) assuming no taxes (personal or corporate):

$$K_E = K_U + \frac{V_D}{V_E}(K_U - K_D).$$

---

[6]Defining the firm's leverage ratio, L, as

$$L \equiv \frac{V_D}{V_D + V_E},$$

we may choose to express $V_D/(V_D + V_E)$, $V_E/(V_D + V_E)$ and V_D/V_E, respectively, in the equations as, L, $1 - L$, and $L/(1 - L)$.

In the special case that investors do not have personal taxes, the expected corporate tax saving, TS, at the end of each period, due to the firm's debt, V_D, held through that period, may be expressed as the difference between the firm's pre-corporate-tax cash distributions to debt holders and the value of that cash flow if it were to be distributed to shareholders after passing through the corporate tax rate, T_c, as[7]

$$TS = V_D i_D [1 - (1 - T_c)],$$

which allowing personal taxes, has a market value determined as

$$TS = V_D i_D [q_D - (1 - T_c) q_E],$$ (13.7)

where, as above, q_E is the market valuation of \$1 of the firm's distributions to the firm's equity holders and q_D is the market valuation of \$1 of the firm's distributions to the firm's bond holders. We may express Eq. (13.7) as

$$TS = V_D K_D \alpha,$$ (13.8)

where

$$K_D = i_D q_D$$ (13.9)

and

$$\alpha = 1 - (1 - T_c) \frac{q_E}{q_D}.$$ (13.10)

If, as Modigliani and Miller (1963), we allow that the TS of Eq. (13.8) is in perpetuity with $K_{TS} = K_D$, we have (with Eq. (6.9), p. 77):

$$PVTS = \frac{V_D K_D \alpha}{K_{TS}} = \frac{V_D K_D \alpha}{K_D} = V_D \alpha,$$ (13.11)

which when substituted in Eq. (13.5) with $K_{TS} = K_D$ provides

$$K_{AV} = K_U - \frac{V_D}{V_D + V_E} \alpha (K_U - K_D),$$ (13.12)

---

[7] Strictly, the interest rate, i_D, is the "expected" interest rate allowing for the possibility of default on the firm's debt, V_D. Note, also, that because we are assuming that the firm's debt is in perpetuity, the interest payment on the firm's debt can be expressed as either the firm's actual nominal debt (D) multiplied by the firm's required interest rate payment on the debt (i), or, equivalently, as the market value of the debt (V_D) multiplied by the market required interest rate (i_D).

while substituting in our proposition 2 as Eq. (13.6) provides

$$K_E = K_U + \frac{V_D}{V_E}(K_U - K_D)(1 - \alpha). \qquad (13.13)$$

As a second case, if we set K_{TS} = the unlevered cost of equity (K_U) the *PVTS* terms in Eq. (13.5) cancel and we have the firm's weighted average cost of capital, K_{AV}, as

$$K_{AV} \equiv \frac{V_D}{V_D + V_E}K_D + \frac{V_E}{V_D + V_E}K_E = K_U \qquad (13.14)$$

and Eq. (13.6) becomes

$$K_E = K_U + \frac{V_D}{V_E}(K_U - K_D). \qquad (13.15)$$

Equations (13.14) and (13.15), respectively, reproduce Eqs. (5.5) and (5.6), which assume no corporate or individual taxes. In other words, the assumption $K_{TS} = K_U$ allows that the form of Modigliani and Miller's proposition 2 remains unchanged when we allow for corporate and individual taxes.

Before proceeding to a demonstration of the consistency of the four discounting methods in Section 13.5, we clarify the adjustment of cash flows in relation to their market valuation.

13.4. The Market Valuation of the Firm's Component Cash Flows

13.4.1 *Free Cash Flow*

In the absence of personal taxes, the firm's "free cash flow", *FCF* (which, by definition, assumes no debt), is expressed

$$FCF \equiv EBIT(1 - T_c) - NINV,$$

where $EBIT$ = earnings before interest and tax, and $NINV$ = capital expenditure + increases to net working capital − depreciation and amortization. With personal taxes for investors, the firm's *FCF* is capitalized by the markets as

$$FCF = [EBIT(1 - T_c) - NINV]q_E, \qquad (13.16)$$

where we allow that the market capitalizes cash flows available to shareholders at a single rate, q_E.

13.4.2 *Cash Flow to Equity and to Debt (CFD)*

Although we are allowed to choose our assumptions, we are required to be consistent. For example, if we allow that the firm's equity, V_E, grows by an amount, say, g percent in a time period while the firm's market debt, V_D, is maintained fixed, we must adjust the firm's leverage and, hence, the firm's cost of equity accordingly in the subsequent time period. To avoid such complexities, we shall allow that that the firm maintains a target leverage, which requires that with a constant growth rate in equity, g, the firm increases the capitalized value of its debt by the same percentage, g, which is to say, the amount $V_D g$. The outcome is that the firm's leverage, L, and, thereby, its cost of equity, K_E, remain unchanged. However, we must note that the debt finance, $V_D g$, raised in each period so as to maintain a fixed leverage, contributes to the firm's cash flow to equity (*CFE*) in that period.[8] In this case, the market capitalized value of the firm's cash flow available to equity (*CFE*) at the end of the period is determined as

$$CFE = [(EBIT - V_D i_D)(1 - T_c) - NINV]q_E + V_D g. \qquad (13.17)$$

Consistently, the issue of debt, $V_D g$, represents a reciprocal negative cash flow to debt (*CFD*) at the end of the period, which therefore has the capital value:

$$CFD = V_D i_D q_D - V_D g$$
$$= V_D (K_D - g). \qquad (13.18)$$

13.4.3 *Capital Cash Flow*

The *CCF* is the sum of the *CFE* and the *CFD*. Thus, combining Eqs. (13.17) and (13.18), the $V_D g$ term cancels and we write

$$CCF = [(EBIT - V_D i_D)(1 - T_c) - NINV]q_E + V_D K_D. \qquad (13.19)$$

---

[8]Otherwise, we would find ourselves subtracting the repayments of the firm's debt from the firm without crediting the firm with the debt in the first place.

13.5. The Discounting Methods

The terminology and the four methods are summarized in Table 13.1. The methodology as it derives from propositions 1 and 2 allows for a general uneven cash flow (to simplify calculations, we assume a growing perpetuity in our worked example). Additionally, the propositions allow for an arbitrary discount rate for the tax deductibility of interest payments due to debt ($K_{TS} = 9.5\%$ in our worked example). We proceed to demonstrate the four methods by a worked example as follows.[9]

Consider a firm that is projected to grow at a constant rate of 4.5% per annum indefinitely, while maintaining its current capital structure. Thus, its earnings before interest and tax (*EBIT*) are expected to grow at this rate, with a commensurate growth rate in its market equity and debt valuation. We take the firm's unlevered cost of equity (K_U) as 12.5%. We further suppose that the firm's expected *EBIT* at the end of the first year is $3.0 million, and that the firm's current market debt, V_D, stands at $5.0 million with a market interest rate, i_D, equal to 5.0%. The firm's net investment (*NINV* = Capital Expenditure + Increases to Net Working Capital − Depreciation and Amortization) to sustain growth opportunities at the end of the first year is $875,000, which also grows indefinitely at 4.5% per annum. The corporate tax rate, T_c, is 30%. We consider that the appropriate discount factor, K_{TS}, for the expected corporate tax savings due

---

[9]The example here is simplified as the aim is to highlight the consistency of the methods. Ruback (2002) presents a more realistic example (incorporating uneven cash flows, depreciation, payback of debt, investments, and other expenses) to confirm the equivalence of just two of the methods — the *CCF* and *WACC* methods (in the absence of personal taxes). His example provides a realistic template example with which to verify the consistency of the four methods presented here in the context of personal taxes. I did send this contribution off to a journal together with the spreadsheet calculations and algebraic proofs of the equivalence of the four methods and received back from the sub-editor the reply that the paper did not say anything particularly interesting that went beyond my previous work and would not be of general interest to the journal's readership. I think I was being told that, my contribution was boring. I have taken the hint and not included any of this in the present text. I have, however, retained the paper — just in case anyone really would like to see how all the methodologies work more fully. If you ask me nicely, I can even send you the excel spreadsheet.

Table 13.1. Summary of discounting methods.

Abbreviations	Valuation formula

Market valuations

Input:

V_D = market debt value.

$$(1)\ APV:\ V_{firm} = \frac{FCF_1}{K_U - g} + PVTS;$$

$$PVTS = \frac{TS_1}{K_{TS} - g}$$

Outputs:

$PVTS$ = market value of corporate tax savings due to debt.

V_E = market equity value.

$V_{firm} = V_D + V_E$

$$(2)\ FCF:\ V_{firm} = \frac{FCF_1}{WACC - g}$$

$$(3)\ CFE:\ V_E = \frac{CFE_1}{K_E - g}$$

$$(4)\ CCF:\ V_{firm} = \frac{CCF_1}{K_{AV} - g}$$

Cash flow abbreviations

$EBIT$ = earnings before interest and tax.

T_c = corporate tax rate.

g = per period growth rate.

$NINV$ = capital expenditure *plus* increases to net working capital *minus* depreciation and amortization.

q_E = market value of $1 income from equity.

q_D = market value of $1 income from bonds.

$\alpha = 1 - (1 - T_c)q_E/q_D$.

Cash flows

Capitalized corporate tax saving due to debt

$TS = V_D K_D \alpha$

Capitalized FCF

$= [EBIT(1 - T_c) - NINV]q_E$

Capitalized CFE

$= [(EBIT - V_D i_D)(1 - T_c) - NINV]q_E + V_D g$

Capitalized CFD

$= V_D(K_D - g)$

Capitalized CCF

$= CFD + CFE = [(EBIT - V_D i_D)(1 - T_c) - NINV]q_E + V_D K_D$

Independent discount factors

i_D = interest rate on debt.

K_D = capitalized interest rate on debt $= i_D q_D$.

K_U = unlevered cost of equity.

K_{TS} = rate used to discount the corporate tax savings TS due to debt.

Dependent discount factors

K_E = levered cost of equity

$$= \left[1 + \frac{V_D - PVTS}{V_E}\right] K_U - \frac{V_D}{V_E} K_D$$

$$+ \frac{PVTS}{V_E} K_{TS} \text{ where } PVTS = \frac{TS_1}{K_{TS} - g}$$

$$WACC = L K_D(1 - \alpha) + (1 - L)K_E$$
$$K_{AV} = L K_D + (1 - L)K_E$$

to debt is 9.5% (an arbitrary number). In addition, we assume that the firm's distributions to shareholders and bond holders are priced in the market at, respectively, 80 cents ($q_E = 0.80$) and 75 cents ($q_D = 0.75$) per dollar of distribution.

We have the capitalized cost of the firm's debt (Eq. (13.9)):

$$K_D = i_D q_D$$

$$= 0.05(0.75) = 0.0375.$$

And (Eq. (13.10)):

$$\alpha = 1 - (1 - T_c)\frac{q_E}{q_D}$$

$$= 1 - (1 - 0.3)\frac{0.80}{0.75} = 0.2533$$

Thus, at the end of the first year, we have the market value of the tax savings due to debt (TS_1) as (Eq. (13.8)):

$$TS_1 = V_D K_D \alpha$$

$$= \$5.0(0.0375)(0.2533) = \$47,500,$$

where the subscript *1* denotes that the cash flow is at the end of the first period.

The *PVTS* due to debt, *PVTS*, is then calculated as (Eq. (6.8), p. 77):

$$PVTS = \frac{TS_1}{K_{TS} - g}$$

$$= \frac{\$47,500 \text{ million}}{0.095 - 0.045} = \$0.950 \text{ million.} \qquad (13.20)$$

The valuations for the firm are then calculated by the four discounting methods as follows.

(i) The *APV* approach.

The *APV* method first discounts the *FCF*s by the unlevered cost of equity (K_U) and then adjusts with the *PVTS*. Thus, the firm's present valuation $V_{firm}(= V_D + V_E)$ is calculated as

$$V_{firm} = \frac{FCF_1}{K_U - g} + PVTS, \qquad (13.21)$$

where (Eq. (13.16)):

$$FCF_1 = [EBIT(1 - T_c) - NINV]q_E$$
$$= \$(3.0 \times 0.7 - 0.875)(0.8) = \underline{\$0.980 \text{ million}}$$

and hence

$$V_{firm} = \frac{\$0.980 \text{ million}}{0.125 - 0.045} + \$0.950 = \underline{\$13.2000 \text{ million}}.$$

The market equity valuation for the firm, V_E, is derived by subtracting the value of the initial debt (\$5 million) to give \$8.2000 million.

And, hence, the firm's leverage ratio, $L = V_D/(V_D + V_E) = \$5/\$13.2000 = 37.88\%$.

(ii) The *CFE* approach.

The *CFE* method discounts the market value of the firm's cash flows to equity by the cost of equity (K_E) to determine the firm's market equity value, V_E, which with constant growth, g, is determined as

$$V_E = \frac{CFE_1}{K_E - g}, \qquad (13.22)$$

where (Eq. (13.17)):

$$CFE_1 = [(EBIT - V_D i_D)(1 - T_c) - NINV]q_E + V_D g,$$

which at the end of the first period

$$= \${[(3.0 - 5.0 \times 0.05)0.7 - 0.875]0.8 + 5.0 \times 0.045\} \text{ million}$$
$$= \$1.065 \text{ million}.$$

Following Eq. (13.6):

$$K_E = \left[1 + \frac{V_D - PVTS}{V_E}\right] K_U - \frac{V_D}{V_E} K_D + \frac{PVTS}{V_E} K_{TS},$$

K_E is determined as[10]

$$K_E = \left[1 + \frac{(5.0 - 0.950)}{8.2000}\right]0.125 - \frac{5.0}{8.2000}0.05(0.75)$$

$$+ \frac{0.950}{8.2000}0.095$$

$$= 17.49\%,$$

so that

$$V_E = \frac{\$1.065 \text{ million}}{0.1749 - 0.045} = \$8.2000 \text{ million}.$$

Thus, we have

$$V_{firm} = V_E + V_D = \$8.2000 + \$5.0 = \underline{\$13.2000 \text{ million}}.$$

as for the *APV* approach.

(iii) The *CCF* approach.

The *CCF* method discounts the levered capital (*CFE* + cash flow to debt) at the rate $K_{AV} \equiv LK_D + (1 - L)K_E$ to determine the value of the firm ($V_{firm} = V_D + V_E$):

$$V_{firm} = \frac{CCF_1}{K_{AV} - g}, \tag{13.23}$$

where (Eq. (13.19)):

$$CCF_1 = [(EBIT - V_D i_D)(1 - T_c) - NINV]q_E + V_D K_D$$

$$= \${[[(3.0 - 5.0 \times 0.05)0.7 - 0.875)]0.8$$

$$+ 5.0(0.05)(0.75)\} \text{ million}$$

$$= \$1.0275 \text{ million}.$$

---

[10]The discerning reader should note the use of the valuation of equity ($8.2000 million) calculated from the previous *APV* method. Thus, we cannot strictly apply MM's proposition 2 as Eq. (13.6) so as to determine K_E unless we know V_E, which is the objective of the valuation exercise in the first place. The textbooks rarely, if ever, remark on this inherent circularity when applying MM's proposition 2 to determine a levered discount rate. Nevertheless, the substitution is justified here in that the purpose of the exercise is to demonstrate the algebraic *consistency* of the four discounting methods.

We also have (Eq. (5.2)):

$$K_{AV} \equiv LK_D + (1 - L)K_E$$

$$= 0.3788(0.05)(0.75) + (1 - 0.3788)0.1749 = 12.284\%^{11}.$$

We then have

$$V_{firm} = \frac{\$1.0275 \text{ million}}{0.12284 - 0.045} = \underline{\$13.2000 \text{ million}},$$

as for the other two methods.

(iv) The *FCF* approach.

In the absence of personal taxes, the *FCF* method discounts the firm's *FCF* to the firm (which assumes no debt), *FCF*, by the weighted average cost of capital or *WACC* defined as

$$WACC \equiv \frac{V_D}{V_D + V_E}i_D(1 - T_c) + \frac{V_E}{V_D + V_E}k, \qquad (13.24)$$

where k is as in Eq. (13.1). Allowing personal taxes, i_D, k, and T_c, respectively, are replaced by their capitalized equivalents K_D, K_E, and α. Equation (13.24) is then recast as[12]:

$$WACC \equiv \frac{V_D}{V_D + V_E}K_D(1 - \alpha) + \frac{V_E}{V_D + V_E}K_E. \qquad (13.25)$$

The *WACC* expression requires K_E, which was calculated above (with proposition 2 as Eq. (13.6)) = 17.49%. With this value, we calculate

---

[11]As a point of interest, in the case that we had chosen $K_{TS} = K_U(= 12.5\%$ in the problem description above), we would at this point have determined $K_{AV} = 12.5\%$, consistent with Eq. (13.14): $K_{AV} = K_U$ (when $K_{TS} = K_U$).

[12]Ultimately, the justification for Eq. (13.25) (and Eq. (13.24)) is that its application leads to the correct valuation, as testified by the other methods. Algebraically, we can see that this is the case as follows. Allow $V_0 = V_{firm}$ at initial time $t = 0$ to represent the market value of the firm as the market value of the expected cash flows to the firm, and V_1 to represent, at the end-of-period-1, the market value of the expected cash flows to the firm forward from

the *WACC* as Eq. (13.25) as

$$= 0.3788(0.0375)(1 - 0.2533) + (1 - 0.3788)(0.1749) = 11.924\%.$$

The *FCF* method:

$$V_{firm} = \frac{FCF_1}{WACC - g}, \qquad (13.26)$$

then provides (with $FCF_1 = \$0.98$ million, above):

$$V_{firm} = \frac{\$0.98 \text{ million}}{0.11924 - 0.045} = \underline{\$13.2000 \text{ million}},$$

which is the valuation obtained using the other methods.

---

this time; that is, *net* of the end-of-period-1 CCF_1 contribution: $[(EBIT_1 - V_0 Li_D)(1 - T_c) - NINV_1]q_E + V_0 LK_D$ (Eq. (13.19)) to the firm's value.

The market value of the firm at the end-of-period-1 *inclusive* of the above CCF_1 contribution can therefore be expressed as:

$$[(EBIT_1 - V_0 Li_D)(1 - T_c) - NINV_1]q_E + V_0 LK_D + V_1,$$

which can equivalently be expressed as:

$$(1 - L)V_0(1 + K_E) + LV_0(1 + K_D).$$

Equating the two expressions, we arrive at

$$V_0 = \frac{FCF_1 + V_1}{1 + WACC},$$

with $FCF_1 = [EBIT(1 - T_c) - NINV]q_E$ (Eq. (13.16)) and *WACC* as Eq. (13.25).
One period forward, we similarly can write:

$$V_1 = \frac{FCF_2 + V_2}{1 + WACC},$$

and so on. So that we can write

$$V_0 = \sum_{t=1}^{N} \frac{FCF_t}{(1 + WACC)^t},$$

which is the *FCF* approach.

13.6. Choice of Discount Method

Because the discounting methods are algebraically equivalent, the evaluator is free to choose the method that is best suited to the purpose at hand. We review the methods briefly as follows.

The *APV* method captures the implications of debt separately in the *APV* term. This may be an important consideration for an evaluator who wishes to separately assess the contribution of debt financing to valuation.

Discounting the *FCF*s by the *WACC* is probably the most popular method among practitioners. This method has the advantage of allowing a particular cash flow's feasibility to be assessed without needing to directly identify the interest repayments in the calculation of the cash flow. We may observe, however, that an exact determination of the *WACC* is likely to be elusive since the leverage ratio $V_D/(V_D + V_E) = L$ in the *WACC* (Eq. (13.25)) requires that we know the debt and equity valuations assigned to the cash flow, the determination of which is the *objective* of the discounting exercise in the first place. In practice, the circularity is circumvented by allowing that the cash flows are subject to a fixed "target leverage", L, which is then applied in the calculations.[13]

The *CFE* method identifies the cash flow that can, in principle, be distributed to shareholders. Hence (apart from timing differences), this method is equivalent to the discounting of dividends model advocated in the textbooks. Because firms are typically concerned with maximizing shareholder wealth, a direct assessment of the firm's equity value (V_E) appears appropriate. This method does, however, have the disadvantage that the discounting cost of equity (K_E) — as can be seen in Eqs. (13.13) and (13.15) — is sensitive to the level of leverage, V_D/V_E, in the cash flow. Again, we may observe that we cannot strictly apply our proposition 2 in a straightforward manner as Eqs. (13.13) and (13.15) unless we know V_E, which is the objective of the valuation exercise in the first place. Again, the

---

[13]A more sophisticated approach is to compute the *WACC* and the value of the cash flows simultaneously, for which, common numerical methods are available. However, when the firm wishes to *rank* project proposals of a similar nature and capital structure, the *WACC* value is typically assigned across such projects by the firm at some common rate.

problem is circumvented in practice by assuming a target leverage ratio, $L = V_D/(V_D + V_E)$.

Finally, in regard to the *CCF* method, we have observed that provided we allow $K_{TS} = K_U$, the firm's average cost of capital K_{AV}, remains as the unlevered cost, K_U (Eq. (13.14)). For this reason, in the case of known but changing debt levels, the *CCF* method is likely to be the most practical method (Ruback, 2002).

13.7. Consistency of the CAPM with the Principle of Additivity of Investors' Risk-Return Exposures (as Proposition 2, Eq. (13.6))

The CAPM is consistent with our proposition 2 (Eq. (13.6)) (and thereby MM's proposition 2). To see that this is so, consider that by the same argument as Eq. (13.5):

$$
\begin{aligned}
K_{AV} &\equiv \frac{V_D}{V_D + V_E} K_D + \frac{V_E}{V_D + V_E} K_E \\
&= \frac{V_D + V_E - PVTS}{V_D + V_E} K_U + \frac{PVTS}{V_D + V_E} K_{TS},
\end{aligned}
$$

we may allow that the firm's exposure to the market (measured by beta, β) is distributed between equity and debt holders as:

$$
\begin{aligned}
\beta_{AV} &\equiv \frac{V_D}{V_D + V_E} \beta_D + \frac{V_E}{V_D + V_E} \beta_E \\
&= \frac{V_D + V_E - PVTS}{V_D + V_E} \beta_U + \frac{PVTS}{V_D + V_E} \beta_{TS},
\end{aligned} \tag{13.27}
$$

where β_D and β_E are the betas for the debt and equity of the levered firm, respectively, and β_U is the beta of the unlevered firm, with β_{TS} the appropriate beta for the *PVTS* component of the firm's equity. Equation (13.5) was rearranged to give our proposition 2 from Eq. (13.6):

$$
K_E = \left[1 + \frac{V_D - PVTS}{V_E} \right] K_U - \frac{V_D}{V_E} K_D + \frac{PVTS}{V_E} K_{TS}.
$$

Similarly, Eq. (13.27) is rearranged to give

$$\beta_E = \left[1 + \frac{V_D - PVTS}{V_E}\right]\beta_U - \frac{V_D}{V_E}\beta_D + \frac{PVTS}{V_E}\beta_{TS}. \qquad (13.28)$$

The CAPM is consistent with Eq. (13.6) — and hence with MM's proposition 2 as a special case — provided the implied relation between levered and unlevered betas remains as Eq. (13.28) when we substitute the CAPM expressions for K_E, K_U, and K_D (Eq. (2.1)):

$$K_E = r_f + \beta_E(K_M - r_f), \qquad (13.29)$$

$$K_U = r_f + \beta_U(K_M - r_f), \qquad (13.30)$$

$$K_D = r_f + \beta_D(K_M - r_f), \qquad (13.31)$$

in Eq. (13.6). Such substitution (recognizing $K_{TS} = r_f + \beta_{TS}(K_M - r_f)$) immediately determines the condition for consistency of the CAPM with Eq. (13.6) as Eq. (13.28).

13.8. In-consistency of the FF-3F Model with the Principle of Additivity of Investors' Risk-Return Exposures as MM's Proposition 2 (and Proposition 2, Eq. (13.6))

The issue of whether the FF-3F model is consistent with the MM propositions has received surprisingly little attention. Yet, unless the FF-3F model is consistent with the principle of addition of investor risk-return exposures as captured in MM's proposition 2, it is at odds with the theoretical foundation of additive consistency for the risk-return relations.

The conditions under which the FF-3F model is consistent with MM's proposition 2 as Eq. (13.15)[14]:

$$K_E = K_U + \frac{V_D}{V_E}(K_U - K_D),$$

are determined — as was the case for the CAPM in the previous subsection — by substituting the FF-3F model expressions for K_E, K_U, and

---

[14]Equation (13.15) is our proposition 2 (Eq. (13.6)) allowing $K_{TS} = K_U$.

K_D (Eqs. (3.1), p. 33):

$$K_E - r_f = b_E(K_M - r_f) + s_E K_{SMB} + h_E K_{HML}, \qquad (13.32)$$

$$K_U - r_f = b_U(K_M - r_f) + s_U K_{SMB} + h_U K_{HML}, \qquad (13.33)$$

$$K_D - r_f = b_D(K_M - r_f) + s_D K_{SMB} + h_D K_{HML}, \qquad (13.34)$$

(where b_U, s_U and h_U are the loadings on the factors for the unlevered firm, and b_D, s_D and h_D are the loadings on the factors for the firm's risky debt) in the MM proposition Eq. (13.15).

We therefore deduce the conditions for consistency with MM's Proposition 2 as

$$b_E = b_U + \frac{V_D}{V_E}[b_U - b_D], \qquad (13.35)$$

$$s_E = s_U + \frac{V_D}{V_E}[s_U - s_D], \qquad (13.36)$$

$$h_E = h_U + \frac{V_D}{V_E}[h_U - h_D]. \qquad (13.37)$$

Alternatively, the conditions for consistency with our Proposition 2 (Eq. (13.6)) allowing $K_{TS} = K_D$, as Eq. (13.13):

$$K_E = K_U + \frac{V_D}{V_E}(K_U - K_D)(1 - \alpha),$$

are determined by substituting Eqs. (13.32)–(13.34) into Eq. (13.13), which delivers

$$b_E = b_U + \frac{V_D}{V_E}[b_U - b_D](1 - \alpha), \qquad (13.38)$$

$$s_E = s_U + \frac{V_D}{V_E}[s_U - s_D](1 - \alpha), \qquad (13.39)$$

$$h_E = h_U + \frac{V_D}{V_E}[h_U - h_D](1 - \alpha). \qquad (13.40)$$

Equations (13.35) (derived assuming $K_{TS} = K_U$) and (13.38) (derived assuming $K_{TS} = K_D$ with $PVTS = V_D\alpha$) are consistent (on substituting the relations $\beta_{TS} = \beta_U$ or $\beta_{TS} = \beta_D$ with $PVTS = V_D\alpha$ in Eq. (13.28)) with the required relation between levered and unlevered betas as Eq. (13.28), consistent with the principle that the firm's total market risk exposure either remains unaltered (in the case of Eq. (13.35)) or is impacted rationally as an outcome of the corporate tax deductibility of the firm's debt (in the case of Eq. (13.38)).

However, the leverage relations for the sensitivities on the additional risk factors, s_j and h_j, as either Eqs. (13.36) and (13.37) or Eqs. (13.39) and (13.40), contradict Fama and French's own interpretation of the FF-3F model. For example, Fama and French (1997) consider that the loading factors s_E and h_E for equity for each industry over time are related to firm size (*ME*) and to firm book-to-market equity (*BE/ME*) as

$$s_E = s_1 - s_2 \ln(ME), \tag{13.41}$$

$$h_E = h_1 + h_2 \ln\left(\frac{BE}{ME}\right), \tag{13.42}$$

where the values of s_1, s_2, h_1, and h_2 are estimated from industry-specific regressions.

The above form of the loadings is as we might expect: Smaller firms and firms with higher book-to-market ratios have higher loading sensitivities on the respective premiums. However, it is clear that s_E and h_E as Eqs. (13.41) and (13.42) will generally not comply with leverage as either set of equations, Eqs. (13.36) and (13.37) or Eqs. (13.39) and (13.40). Indeed, substantial violations of economic rationality can be implied under conditions of leverage when Eqs. (13.41) and (13.42) are taken at face value for the individual firm. For example, the equation can be made to predict that the cost of equity declines with leverage (Lally, 2004).

Working backwards from Eqs. (13.41) and (13.42), compatibility of the FF-3F model with our Proposition 2 (and thereby MM's Proposition 2) requires that the adjustment to the s_E and h_E factor sensitivities with leverage are as

$$s_E = (s_1 - s_2 \ln(ME_U)) + (s_1 - s_2 \ln(ME_U) - s_D)\frac{V_D}{V_E}(1 - \alpha), \tag{13.43}$$

$$h_E = \left(h_1 + h_2 \ln\left(\frac{BE_U}{ME_U}\right)\right)$$
$$+ \left(h_1 + h_2 \ln\left(\frac{BE_U}{ME_U}\right) - h_D\right)\frac{V_D}{V_E}(1 - \alpha), \tag{13.44}$$

(without the inclusion of $(1 - \alpha)$ in the case $K_{TS} = K_U$), where ME_U and BE_U/ME_U refer to the unlevered firm. However, Eqs. (13.43) and (13.44) are without a plausible justification, in addition to contradicting the application of Eqs. (13.41) and (13.42) as intended by Fama and French.

We conclude that as a model of risk-return, the FF-3F model as a claim to embracing the CAPM and the MM propositions of consistency is self-contradicting.

13.9. The Capitalization Factors, q_E and q_D

As a practical issue, when applying the above methods of discounting, we need estimates of the capitalization factor, q_E, as the market value of \$1 of the firm's distribution to shareholders, and, similarly, the capitalization factor, q_D, or market value of \$1 of payments to the firm's bond holders. There has been considerable debate about how the capitalization of the firm's distributions to shareholders (q_E) differs from one. Theoretically, following Elton and Gruber (1970) and Auerbach (1979), q_E is identified as:

$$q_E = \frac{(1 - t_d)}{(1 - t_g)}, \qquad (13.45)$$

where t_d and t_g represent investors' effective marginal tax rate on, respectively, dividends and capital gains (as effective rates, t_g includes the effect of, for example, offsets against losses and delay in the payment of capital gains, and t_d includes, for example, the effect of tax credits under an imputation tax system). By analogy, the market value of \$1 of the firm's interest payments is determined as:

$$q_D = \frac{(1 - t_i)}{(1 - t_g)}, \qquad (13.46)$$

where t_i represents investors' marginal tax rate on interest payments from bonds. Equations (13.45) and (13.46) may be understood as the capitalization rate consistent with rational equilibrium across investor returns as income and as capital growth.[15]

---

[15]To see this, consider that equilibrium around the time the firm pays a dividend (*DIV*) requires that investors are indifferent between buying and selling the share as cum-dividend or ex-dividend. Since an investor's after-personal tax return if receiving the dividend is $DIV(1 - t_d)$, but the after-personal tax return from realizing the capitalized

Equations (13.45) and (13.46) ensure that the cost of equity equations developed with the capitalization factors q_E and q_D remain consistent with expressions developed by assuming "representative" shareholder taxes, t_d, t_g and t_i. For example, when we substitute for q_E and q_D with Eq. (13.45) and (13.46) in the *WACC* expression as Eq. (13.25) (with Eqs. (13.9) and (13.10)), we reproduce the expression of Clubb and Doran (1992) (see Dempsey, 2001a), which confirms that the two analytical approaches, the after-personal tax cost of capital analysis followed by Clubb and Doran, and the analysis at the level of the markets as followed here, are consistent.

The above capitalization approach, however, leads to expressions that are much more compact. So, for example, Lally and van Zilj (2003) develop their expression for the CAPM under an imputation tax regime as

$$r_j = r_f + \beta_j(r_m - r_f) + \Delta_j, \tag{13.47}$$

with

$$\Delta_j = T_1[-r_f(-\beta_j) + (d_j - d_m\beta_j)]$$
$$+ T_2\left[d_jU\left(\frac{IC_j}{DIV_j}\right) - d_mU\left(\frac{IC_m}{DIV_m}\right)\beta_j\right], \tag{13.48}$$

where r_j represents the expected return on company j inclusive of imputation tax credits (r_m similarly for the market portfolio), r_f represents the risk-free rate, d_j represents the company's dividend yield (d_m similarly for the market portfolio), U represents the market wide utilization rate for the imputation credits (IC_j) attached to the cash dividend, DIV_j, for company j (IC_m, DIV_m similarly for the market portfolio), and T_1, T_2 both represent weighted averages over $[(t_i - t_g)/(1 - t_g)]$, where t_i, t_g, represent shareholders' marginal tax rate liabilities on interest and capital gains. Dempsey and Partington (2008) show that the above Eqs. (13.47) and (13.48) can be represented equally algebraically as

$$K_j = r_f q_D + \beta_j(K_M - r_f q_D), \tag{13.49}$$

---

value of the dividend as a capital gain is $DIVq_E(1 - t_g)$, equilibrium requires that $DIVq_E(1 - t_g) = DIV(1 - t_d)$. Solving for q_E gives Eq. (13.45) (with a similar argument to support Eq. (13.46)).

where K_j (and similarly K_M for the market portfolio) is defined as Eq. (13.3), and r_f is the interest rate on risk-free bonds that retain their par value.

Ex-dividend studies estimate q_E as the "drop-off" ratio of the ex-dividend change in share price to the dividend paid. However, the interpretation of ex-dividend studies is problematic in regard to the issue of whether prices about the ex-dividend date are set by short-term dividend arbitrageurs or long-term investors. Nevertheless, Graham, Michaely, and Roberts (2003) conclude that the drop-off ratio is consistent with the relative pricing of dividends and capital gains on the ex-dividend day. As summarized by these authors, a good deal of evidence suggests that the dividend drop-off ratio has been consistently below one. However, there are exceptions to this view. For example, Boyd and Jaganathan (1994) suggest that a value of one is a good approximation for the dividend drop-off ratio.

Several studies have sought to examine the effective personal tax rate on dividend disbursements under an imputation tax system (in Australia and the UK, predominantly).[16] However, due to the one-day gap between observation of cum-dividend and ex-dividend prices, measurements of q_E are extremely noisy. Walker and Partington (1999) study cum-dividend trading in the ex-dividend period in Australia and obtain measures of q_E that are consistently greater than one for fully franked dividends. Another approach which seeks to avoid traditional measurement problems, takes advantage of rights issues where the newly issued shares do not qualify for the forthcoming dividend. Such studies have been conducted for Australia (Chu and Partington, 2008) and for the UK (Armitage, Hodgkinson and Partington, 2006), and show that dividends which benefit from imputation tend to have a q_E greater than one.

---

[16]The imputation tax system recognizes that the firm's tax paid at the corporate level represents a payment by the firm's shareholders (who own the firm), which is therefore credited ("imputed") as a pre-payment of their tax liabilities on dividends received. The logic applied is that (with a corporate tax rate equal to, say, 30%), each 70 cents of cash dividends received by the shareholder equates with $1.0 of the firm's earnings before corporate tax. Thus, if the shareholder has a marginal tax liability of, say, t_{inc} on income received as dividends, the shareholder on receiving a 70 cents dividend is credited with allowing to retain $1.0(1 − t_{inc})$. The outcome is that the shareholder's effective tax rate t_{eff} on each $1 of cash dividend received is computed as $(1 − t_{eff}) = (1 − t_{inc})/0.7$; which is to say, $t_{eff} = 1 − (1 − t_{inc})/0.7$.

13.10. Valuation of Imputation Tax Credits

Since the introduction of the Australian imputation tax system, there have been problems in the measurement of the market value of imputation tax credits with internal inconsistencies and implementation errors in the outcome approaches (Dempsey and Partington, 2008). Differential tax rates for dividends and capital gains have led to debates about which version of the CAPM to use and how to encapsulate the implications of such tax rates.

A traditional non-capitalized approach to evaluating the value of imputation tax credits will generally lead to error. To see this, consider the following regression equation as appears in the literature:

$$V_E = \sum_{i=1}^{N} \frac{dividend_i}{(1+k)^i} + \sum_{i=1}^{N} \frac{imputation\ tax\ credits_i}{(1+k)^i}, \quad (13.50)$$

made subject to historical data, whereby the value of imputation tax credits is identified by evaluating the statistical significance of the right-hand side summation of the imputation tax credits in explaining the equity value of the firm, V_E. The result that the right-hand side summation of the tax credits has little explanatory power comes as no surprise on account of that the left-hand side summation of the *dividend_i* terms is already implicitly *marked to market* on a dollar for dollar basis (implicitly, as the expression attributes $q_E = 1$), which, to a first approximation, is the outcome we might anticipate allowing that investors have fully valued the imputation tax credits. In this case, the right-hand side *additional* summation over *imputation tax credits_i* effects is *redundant* in attempting to determine the impact of the imputation tax credits on the dependent equity variable, V_E (the argument that imputation tax credits are *not* valued in the market implies a *negative* dependence on the right-hand side of Eq. (13.50), so as to counteract the implicit valuation of the imputation tax credits in the *dividend_i* terms).[17]

---

[17]It is hardly surprising that the use of "non-capitalized" regressions to identify the market valuation of the tax credits has led to the conclusion that the market places zero value on the credits. Examples of such lines of research are Siau, Sault, and Warren (2013), Feuerherdt, Gray, and Hall (2010), Gray and Hall (2006), and Cannavan, Finn, and Gray (2004). Their findings are contradicted by Truong and Partington (2008) and Fenech, Skully and Xuguang (2014).

Similarly, if applying models such as the Black–Scholes model as Eqs. (12.32)–(12.34) to determine the market value of dividends or imputation tax credits from an index:

$$C = S_o e^{-dT} N(\omega) - X e^{-r_f T} N(\omega - \sigma\sqrt{T}),$$

$$P = X e^{-r_f T} N(\sigma\sqrt{T} - \omega) - S_o e^{-dT} N(-\omega),$$

with

$$\omega = \left[\ln\left(\frac{S_o}{X}\right) + \left(r_f - d + \frac{1}{2}\sigma^2\right) T \right] \Big/ \sigma\sqrt{T},$$

where d is the index dividend yield, it must be recognized that the formulism is implicitly capitalizing the dividends on a dollar for dollar basis. The formulism must accordingly be adapted as

$$C = S_o e^{-DT} N(\omega) - X e^{-RT} N(\omega - \sigma\sqrt{T}), \tag{13.51}$$

$$P = X e^{-RT} N(\sigma\sqrt{T} - \omega) - S_o e^{-DT} N(-\omega), \tag{13.52}$$

with

$$\omega = \left[\ln\left(\frac{S_o}{X}\right) + \left(R - D + \frac{1}{2}\sigma^2\right) T \right] \Big/ \sigma\sqrt{T}, \tag{13.53}$$

where

$$D = d \cdot q_E, \tag{13.54}$$

$$R = r_f\, q_D. \tag{13.55}$$

13.11. Time for Reflection: What Have We Learned?

Responsible and sound decision making is underpinned by a robust evaluation of future cash flows. Nevertheless, the diversity of discounting methods and assumptions, combined with a fragmented treatment in the literature, leads to confusion as to the correct application of the methods to discounting cash flows in both the textbooks and the literature. This is unfortunate. The objective of the present chapter has been to present the models coherently and unambiguously allowing a general environment of personal taxes. This has been achieved by invoking two propositions. As an outcome, the four methods of discounting considered here have been shown to be algebraically equivalent.

The CAPM and the propositions of Modigliani and Miller represent principles of rationality at a fundamental level. The FF-3F model violates the principle embodied in the Modigliani and Miller propositions. For this reason, although the FF-3F model may claim to encapsulate historical findings that apply on the average over many stocks, it remains unacceptable as a coherent theoretical model of asset pricing.

Ignoring the concept of the "q" capitalization of dividends introduced in the chapter generally leads to error in estimating the contribution of dividends to the value of the firm. This is because ignoring the concept implicitly models the dividends as marked to market on a dollar for dollar basis.

Chapter 14

Corporate Finance in a Strategic/Behavioral Context

Acquisitiveness, although it is the main-spring of the capitalist system, is by no means the most powerful of the motives that survive the conquest of hunger. Rivalry is a much stronger motive.

Bertrand Russell

In the business world, the rearview mirror is always clearer than the windshield.

Warren Buffett

The world as we have created it is a process of our thinking. It cannot be changed without changing our thinking.

Albert Einstein

They're analysts, they don't know pre-ferred stock from livestock, alright? When it hits south, we raise the sperm count on the deal.

Gordon Gekko

14.1. Introduction[1]

The Modigliani and Miller (MM) propositions provide a principle that appears entirely reasonable: Just as the size of the cake is not affected by how it is divided, so the value of the firm is independent of its ownership structure between equity and debt holders. Nevertheless, as we have seen (Chapter 5), the propositions of themselves lead to unacceptable predictions: the statement that both the firm's level of debt leverage and its dividend policy are irrelevant (while allowing for taxes, the statement that firms should strive for 100% debt, and pay no dividends). Reflecting such outcomes, we consider that the propositions are fundamentally disengaged

---

[1]This chapter encapsulates ideas that have appeared in *Abacus* (Dempsey, 2014), *Critical Perspectives on Accounting* (Dempsey, 1996) and *Accounting, Accountability and Performance* (Dempsey, 2003) journals. I am grateful to the editors and reviewers of these journals for supporting and publishing this work notwithstanding its unorthodoxy. More journals such as these would be welcomed.

from the reality of business. More specifically, we consider that they fail to engage with the humanity of business, as well as, more broadly, with the concept of corporate strategic management and the notion of an ethical content to business. We observe that these notions are explored in what is commonly referred to as the "management" and "organizational behavior" literatures. Accordingly, we must advocate that corporate finance theory look outward to such disciplines if it is to claim real-world relevance.

The chapter is arranged as follows. In Section 14.2, we review selected highlights from a traditional *Management* literature over many years, before, in Section 14.3, we consider how the particular concerns of corporate financial management might be integrated into a more realistic context. Section 14.4 concludes with a discussion.

14.2. Corporate Finance and the Management Literature

Since early years, writers in management theory have emphasized a world in which managers face overwhelming *complexity*. Decision problems are potentially "messy" (Ackoff, 1970), "ill-structured" (Mintzberg, Raisinghani, and Theoret, 1976; Mitroff and Emshoff, 1979), with "wicked problems of organized complexity" (Mason and Mitroff, 1981, p. 12; Duhaime and Thomas, 1983). The outcome is that problems of investment and financing as encountered by the firm are characterized by challenges of complexity, interconnectedness, uncertainty, ambiguity, conflict, and societal constraints.

Consequently, management authors have stressed that organizations experience tremendous *difficulty* in responding to change[2] and that structural and political factors create additional inertia.[3] Dent (1990) considers that this may be explained by the fact that organizations have been *selected* more or less *deterministically* to their distinct niches in the first place, on the basis that their particular capabilities are valued.

From this perspective, we must be careful even as to the extent to which an organization has volition in its choices (Astley and Van de Ven, 1983). Certainly the capabilities of firms are defined by sunk costs,

---

[2] Starbuck and Hedberg (1977), Pettigrew (1985).

[3] Mintzberg (1978), Miller and Friesen (1980, 1984), Pettigrew (1985).

irreversible investments, and the characteristics of its personnel built up in the past, so that the organization's strategies are determined by where it has been in the past and by what it has done. Investment decisions that are directed at realigning a firm's competitive posture in terms of new competitive strengths and distinctive competences are the exception (Pfeffer and Salancik, 1978).

From early years, management authors have sought to clarify how, within a paradigm of overarching strategy, a firm's everyday tactical and implementing activities take place over a range of departments, with engineering, marketing, and production departments responsible for crucial investment decisions.[4] Investment decision making is ultimately a *process* of investigation, which occurs at many points in the organization, and which is spread out over time, from "triggering" and "recognition" of a problem through to a fuller "definition" of an investment proposal, as it is eased through the system to formal appraisal and ultimate acceptance by higher management.[5] The process is typically seen to involve readily available information, precedent, general strategic considerations, and environment factors, together with the qualitative judgments of technical, production, and marketing staffs, against which a manager's belief about future profitability might depend rather simply on optimism and confidence in the economy.

Reputation based on past performance and lobbying and exhortations have a part to play as commitment and trust relationships are engendered. Personal and political reasons (prestige, personal/departmental ambition, empire building) also underlie a project idea's initial proposal. Negative reactions are part of the appraisal process. For this reason, a new project idea may require a sponsor with reputation who is prepared to back the project and be identified with it.[6] The bottom-up development of division plans and top-down strategic management come together in the approval of plans and budgets. At this stage, ultimate endorsement of an investment proposal is likely viewed as an endorsement of the proposer(s) or as a reflection

---

[4]Petty, Scott and Bird (1975), Ross (1986), Mukherjee and Henderson (1987).

[5]Bower (1972), Hopwood (1974), King (1975), Petty *et al.* (1975), Ross (1986), Mukherjee and Henderson (1987), Butler, Davies, Pike and Sharp (1993).

[6]Bower (1972, p. 77), Hopwood (1974, p. 134), King (1975).

on the track record, prestige, and/or political influence of the proposer(s).[7] Dempsey (1996a) considers the role that managerial credibility has to play in capital investment appraisal by quoting one financial director:

> "If you get a project and do it well, then you go onto the next one. And then you'll be given more opportunity. If you don't, then you're going to be on the wayside. People are pretty careful. It happens on a human level almost more than on a numbers level. The whole process of who gets selected to do what comes out of people having watched what various people are doing" (p. 629).

Financial criteria such as net present value (NPV), payback, internal rate of return (IRR), and accounting rate of return (ARR), might constitute a framework on which to formalize investment decisions, but the techniques alone are unable to determine the decision outcomes in an adequate manner.[8] It is generally impossible to meaningfully assess either projected cash flows or the appropriate discount rate for the kind of investment decisions that actually impact significantly on the firm. Financial figures are called for when the project has the backing of a sponsor with "reputation", and when they are called for, the numbers are likely to be sufficiently exposed to manipulation that they merely reflect the aspirations and commitments of the project sponsors (Mukherjee and Henderson, 1987).

From this perspective, middle managers at tactical and routine levels in the firm may more correctly be viewed as implementers rather than as investment decision makers. We might even think of managers as acting out the paradigm of the firm. In this view, a manager's job is to sense what constitutes a satisfactory level of performance, whose ideas are worth listening to, and what events are significant predictors of future opportunities and calamities. A successful decision maker depends more on an ability to anticipate problems along with an ability to recognize a range of alternative courses of action than on an ability to carefully choose between them. Hence, perhaps, the managerial response to academic enquiry into their decision making quoted by Dempsey (1996a): "It's a

---

[7] Ross (1986), Mukherjee and Henderson (1987).
[8] Bower (1970, p. 45), Hopwood (1974, p. 135).

matter of applying judgment and common sense. You guys overcomplicate these matters — it's like I know when the house needs painting!" (p. 629)

Carr, Tomkins, and Bayliss (1994) report that German managers view their US and UK counterparts as spending too much time attempting to manipulate financial markets rather than their product base. The German managers believe that a thorough knowledge of the business and the perceived direction of markets, technologies, and competition are more important than financial maneuverings and do not believe that the insights of business can be captured in NPV calculations. They consider that the sure grasp of a business can take a lifetime to acquire and that this does not happen for MBA executives who had been parachuted into the industry. Carr *et al.* (1994) quote one chief executive as follows:

> "Finance is not enough; it must be paired with intuition and intimacy with products, markets and customers. US and UK managers sit too much in their offices over their figures... When I talked of intuition it was not just out of the blue. Intuition is the very last thing when you know everything. You have to have every kind of information about your competitors, but the rest is intuition" (p. 107).

The authors also cite another executive as stating, "When it is a success you get a big explosion, and I believed in that explosion" (p. 113).

14.3.　Towards a Corporate Management Context for Corporate Finance

Economic decisions at all levels are made by individuals based on partial knowledge of current conditions coupled with a best guess as to what may happen. Following the global financial crisis, we now countenance the fact that, fundamentally, things can go wrong. The firm typically faces a complexity of possibilities about which it "simply does not know", and for which there exists the possibility of surprise.

Nevertheless, the MM propositions hold that corporate finance can be grounded on fundamental laws of cause and effect. Thus, risk and uncertainty are encapsulated in a single NPV calculation and a positive NPV calculation implies an increase in share value. A firm's projects can be lined up with given cash flows and shareholder wealth maximized by choosing the projects with the highest NPVs. But this reasoning is far too simplistic. Real decisions are never made in this manner. Not only are the future cash flows likely to be fungible, but the cost of capital is too nebulous and elusive a parameter to play a key role in financial policy, at least on an everyday or recurring budgeting level (Durand, 1989).

Having removed the invisible hand of a cost of financial capital as that which works to coordinate the provision and utilization of investment finance in well-functioning markets, we are obliged to postulate alternative mechanisms of coordination. Dempsey (1996) recognizes that NPV calculations cannot realistically capture the subjective and strategic dimensions of the investment decision and argues that corporate financial activity is more appropriately recognized and understood within a framework of:

(i) *Reputations* based on past performance.
(ii) Commitment and *trust* relationships.

Thus, in response to the need to integrate the firm's strategic dimensions with the reality of ambiguity and genuine uncertainty, the organizational structure of the firm recognizes "reputations based on past performance" and allows for "commitment and trust relations" to ensure that financing decisions and arrangements are supported by a cross-referencing of personnel who have excelled in the past. In this way, decisions are evaluated within the organization's framework of reputations and trust relationships that ensures that the decisions are overseen by the collective experiences of respected personnel. An evaluation of future cash flows indeed lies at the heart of financial decision making, but not in the mechanistic manner advocated by the finance textbooks.

Thus, important investment decisions are made and carried through by personnel who have built their reputations based on past performance, and have built their status and influence on commitment and trust relationships within and outside the firm (Dempsey, 1996). A project does not simply look after itself. Bonds of commitment to the project's success are required in order to bring the project to a successful outcome. These ideas are supported by such as Mukherji and Nagarajan (1996), who extend the concept of trust to investment decision making, and Chami and Fullenkamp (2003), who relate trust to efficiency within the firm; while Tinsley, O'Connor, and Sullivan (2002) explore how reputation extends the potential for negotiation and action in investment decision making. In the context of mergers and acquisitions, Robert Bruner (2004, 2005) reports that business transactions require *trust* and that firms attain sustainability built on *reputation*. Reputation is significant in shaping the expectations of counterparties, while implicit trust and reputation translate into more effective and economically attractive business transactions as the firm's clients respond to the firm's reputation and integrity. Bonds of trust and reputation actually pay.

14.4. Time for Reflection: What Have We Learned?

Even in business schools, investment decision making within corporations is still taught as the application of cost of capital discounted cash flows. The NPV/cost of capital framework posits a world where all possible outcomes and risk can be quantified and thereby allowed for. In such a world, investment decisions are reduced to a quantifiable NPV calculation and it is simply assumed that a firm's strategy is absorbed by the calculations. As such, the reality of investment decision making within firms is grossly misrepresented. Investment decision making is a far more complex issue. The assessment of uncertain cash flows must be tempered by the collective "experience" of those with "reputations based on past performance"; while ultimate success for the firm's projects requires "commitment and trust relationships" with those individuals inside and outside the firm who are integral to the firm's endeavors. Nevertheless, the simplistic models remain seductive to business schools that wish to project to students the notion that they are receiving clear and unambiguous knowledge — along with a tool kit for ensuring the correctness of the firm's investment decisions. The graduate MBA student has been equipped to parachute into a firm and rescue it!

But all this is illusion. Indeed, a little knowledge can be dangerous. What is required is *wisdom*, a concept that is more difficult to impart to young people with little or no experience of the real world. One reason is that students are uneasy in the face of ambiguity. Rather than open-endedness, they prefer precise solutions and the traditional finance textbook approach panders to this preference.

With mature MBA students, who together possess an assortment of business experiences, the ability to disseminate real-life experiences to the class while maintaining a structure to the lecture (within the lecture's time-frame) will always be challenging. So, again, the easy way out is to follow the textbook, trusting that the (expensive) textbook, by virtue of being a textbook, has authority in the eyes of the class. At the outset, at least, it does. And good lecturers — with sufficient anecdotes and observation of relevant news events — are able to impart real-world wisdom and knowledge. Over-reliance on the textbook, however, will nearly always result in students coming to feel that they are being sold short and that their corporate finance course experience has been reduced to that of being prepared for the final exam questions, with only little expectation of the usefulness of their course thereafter.

Chapter 15

Ethics

The first step in the evolution of ethics is a sense of solidarity with other human beings.

Albert Schweitzer

If we care about universal principles such as freedom, democracy and the rule of law, we cannot leave them to the care of market forces; we must establish some other institutions to safeguard them.

George Soros

The rich are always going to say that, you know, just give us more money and we'll go out and spend more and then it will all trickle down to the rest of you. But that has not worked the last 10 years, and I hope the American public is catching on.

Warren Buffett

If you need a friend, get a dog.

Gordon Gekko

15.1. Introduction[1]

A motivation for considering ethics is the need to discover the kind of professional person one is *called on* to be in the workplace. A more fundamental motivation considered here, is the need to decide the kind of person we might *wish* to be in the workplace. Everyone has to be "someone".

Quite fundamental questions for discussion, such as:

- Is ethics about respecting the norms of society, or is it about adhering to a morality that transcends the norms of society?
- Is ethics about obeying the law — or even the spirit of the law — or is it about elevating our activities above the mentality of the law?
- Does ethics of its nature support good business, or must good business ethics expect to pay a price for its good ethics?

---

[1]This chapter encapsulates ideas that have appeared in *Critical Perspectives on Accounting* (Dempsey, 2000). I am indeed grateful to the editors and reviewers of this journal for supporting and publishing this work notwithstanding its unorthodoxy.

while occasionally leading to invigorating discussion, typically do not lead to a structure of well thought-out arguments from a firm foundation. A short lecture course on ethics will often avoid the prospects of ambiguity and lack of closure by restricting the debate to a discussion of industry codes of practice. The Chartered Financial Analyst (CFA) Institute's Code of Ethics and Standards of Professional Conduct, exhorts that its practitioners should:

- Act with integrity, competence, diligence respect, and in an ethical manner with the public, clients, prospective clients.
- Place the integrity of the investment profession and the interests of clients above their own personal interests.
- Use reasonable care and exercise independent professional judgment when conducting investment analysis.
- Practice and encourage others to practice in a professional and ethical manner that will reflect credit on themselves and the profession.
- Promote the integrity of, and uphold the rules governing capital markets.

The above are perfectly reasonable exhortations. So there is little likelihood of disagreement (and equally of any invigorating discussion). But what do the codes mean beyond "Do not lie, do not cheat or deceive"? Unless they are unpackaged, they have the appearance of platitudes, or motherhood statements.

In this chapter, we argue that it is in the nature of ethics that they act to restrain excesses, while acting to sanction norms *as they currently exist*. For this reason, the employee individual is in fact called on to be ethical on the institution's, as opposed to the individual's own terms. Indeed, a criterion of employment suitability in the first place is likely to be that the individual is not at variance with the implications of the profit motive as they broadly direct market activity.

Consistently, the debate that has been captured within the domain of institutionalized ethics has been restricted to a *reflexive* one, concerned with the micro-behavior of actors who operate in terms of one another *within* the system; the outcome of which is that the debate represents a consolidating agenda, rather than a revolutionary one.

In developing these arguments, we progress from a consideration of the nature of conceptual frameworks generally to a consideration of ethical frameworks, and, in particular, corporate and financial ethics. We consider that the development of society's ethical content can be understood in terms of the development of its institutions; and, aligning with Foucault's analysis, we consider the outcome that our institutions progress from being the "object" of our knowledge base as we attempt to understand them, to becoming ultimately "subject" to our understanding of them. What this means is that our corporate institutions are no longer driven by individuals as such, but by the knowledge base in terms of profit and loss that we have created about them, which sets the parameters within which professional ethical behavior has adapted.

If we accept the above constraints, we might ask: Is it possible for a person to be truly ethical? It is possible that the answer is: No! We are obliged to live in the world as we find it. The probability is that, at the very least, a compromise must be made with the organization that has employed us as to how we behave. But that's life. Indeed, we might consider that determining how we wish to stand in the world as we find it, represents one of the most significant challenges on life's adventure. Perhaps, the least fulfilling response is to hold too enthusiastically to the sentiment: "I work to live; I do not live to work". After all, the most part of our lives is actually played out in the workplace.

The chapter is arranged as follows. In Section 15.2, we consider the nature of ethics, which progresses in Section 15.3 to a consideration of the institutionalization of ethics, followed in Section 15.4 by a consideration of specifically corporate ethics. Section 15.5 considers ethics on an individual level, before Section 15.6 concludes with a discussion.

15.2. The Nature of Ethics

The fundamental concepts of ethics are represented by the words "good" and "ought" or even "duty". With "good", a distinction can be made between good as a means and good as an end. Socrates seems to have held that the first and main function of ethics was to define ethical terms, and that we could not really be virtuous unless we knew the definitions of the virtues. But if the words of ethics are not to be defined circularly in terms of each other, they must be defined relative to non-ethical concepts, in which case ethics ultimately becomes a compartment of that science to which the non-ethical concepts belong. Thus, if "good" is "what is conducive to a stable society", ethics is a branch of sociology; whereas if "good" is "what God wills", it is a part of theology. Ethics is concerned with the transcendental concept of "goodness" (which comes close to a theological concept of a Greater Good) and to the concept of "duty" (which comes close to a sociological concept of assigned responsibilities within society). But ethics at the same time is neither of these departments. And, so, we arrive at ethics as lying somewhere between the two. And, accordingly, ethics has its own particular purpose.

Dobson (1993) attempted to introduce the concept of ethical awareness to finance. He considers that a true role for ethics in the corporate community requires that its members aspire to an "internal good" or "ethical ideal". He adds: "It is what classical philosophers describe as 'virtue', the internal good toward which all human endeavor should strive"; with the outcome that: "A *truly* ethical individual, pursuing internal goods, would never sacrifice honesty for material gain, but would only too readily sacrifice material gain for honesty". Dobson quotes the evolutionary economist Robert Frank (1988): "Satisfaction from doing the right thing must not be premised on the fact that material gain may follow; rather it must be *intrinsic* to the act itself". As for how such aspirations are to take place in society, Bowie (1991) is quoted: "Looking out for oneself is a natural, powerful motive that needs little, if any, social reinforcement. . . Altruistic motives, even if they too are natural, are not as powerful: they need to be socially reinforced and nurtured".

It seems to me that the above authors are asserting a claim for an absolute or self-evident ethics. But this is untenable. By definition, their ethical stance is exactly that — *their* ethical stance. One person may proclaim an ethic of respect and piety (Confucius), while another adheres to a code of risk-taking and ingenuity — and even arguments for war-making (Nietzsche). I may, of course, find that another person's ethical code is unacceptable or repugnant — and may be prepared to take up arms to confront that ethical code. In this case, the term "unethical" denotes my confrontation with that ethical code. Nevertheless, I cannot be "unethical" any more than I can be "inhuman". To talk as Dobson of an ethical code being unethical is, in the end, simply to communicate that he finds that the code is incompatible with his own. Ultimately, there can be no grounding for considering that one's own ethic is absolute. Perhaps, I actually *object* to being "socially reinforced and nurtured". Does Dobson regard me as unethical?

My own understanding of the purpose or need for ethics is as follows. We may assume that while natural selection has favored individuals who have learned to be "self-seeking" (egotistic), it has also favored societies whose members have learned to be cooperative (altruistic). The outcome of the natural selection process is that as individuals, we possess an *instinct* to care for ourselves, and a *conscience* to care for others. Our conscience has the potential to inflict a sense of *guilt* at self-benefiting actions that are detrimental to the broader society; or, more positively, has the potential to provide a sense of *self-satisfaction* on the self-knowledge that one has sacrificed oneself materially for the greater good.

When an individual's cooperation is visible within the society, the individual can be rewarded by society, so that the conflict between the demands from the self and the society is resolved. In this case, egotism (selfishness) and altruism (selflessness) may be one and the same. However, when altruism is not public, there exists within the individual the potential for conflict between the developed urges to egotism and altruism.

I believe that the purpose or need for ethics is to make coherent sense of these impulsive urges. That is, ethics represents the attempt to resolve the conflict between selfishness and selflessness; between our material desires and our conscience. It attempts to make sense of our relationships by harmonizing our need to live with others as well as with our self.

To the end of resolving the conflict between selfish instinct and conscience, we are, as human beings, capable of accommodating a sense of ambiguity — a kind of intellectual self-deception — that is to our advantage. When we witness this in others, we are likely to call it hypocrisy. That is, rather than maximizing my overall wellbeing by attaining some conscious compromise between my instincts of ego and altruism, I maximize overall wellbeing by avoiding a confrontation with the dilemma that could be expected to precipitate any real action. I learn to engage in subterfuges so that "now" is never the appropriate time to act. So, my checkbook is unfortunately not close to hand, and "later" becomes the appropriate time. I learn to see ritual concern (donating a dollar) as material. And so on. Such self-delusions — intellectually putting our heads in the sand, so to speak — appear to be an essential apparatus of the manner in which we negotiate our ethical dilemmas.[2]

Nevertheless, the ethics of society must ultimately work to coordinate and achieve the cooperation of the society. To this end, society's ethics requires itself to be recognized and understood and agreed upon by a consensus of that society. Without such a consensus of recognition and understanding, intelligent correspondence is not possible; and without agreement, there is conflict rather than cooperation around the ethical dictates. In this way, the society's ethics represents a part of the self-functioning apparatus of the society, serving the dual purpose of harmonizing the activities of its individual members while sanctioning acceptability for its institutions. Like the Christian ethic of John Conrad's parsonage in *Lord Jim*, ethics must be fashioned to be "made for the righteousness of people in cottages without disturbing the ease of mind of those whom an unerring Providence enables to live in mansions".

15.3. The Institutionalization of Ethics

The French philosopher Michael Foucault (1977), in his study of the emergence of the institutional asylum (*Madness and Civilization*), observed

---

[2]The passage from George Orwell — *Inside the Whale and Other Essays* — addresses this kind of ambiguity and self-delusional escape from ethical conflict for the ruling classes at that time as Orwell saw it:

> "For long past there had been in England an entirely functionless class, living on money that was invested they hardly knew where, the *idle rich*, the people whose photographs you can look at in the *Tattler* and the *Bystander*, always supposing that you want to. The existence of these people was by any standard unjustifiable. They were simply parasites, less useful to society than his fleas are to a dog. . . But the British ruling class obviously could not admit to themselves that their usefulness was at an end. Had they done that they would have had to abdicate. For it was not possible for them to turn themselves into mere bandits, like the American millionaires, consciously clinging to unjust privileges and beating down opposition by bribery and tear-gas bombs. After all, they belonged to a class with a certain tradition, they had been to public schools where the duty of dying for your country, if necessary, is laid down as the first and greatest of the commandments. They had to *feel* themselves true patriots, even while they plundered their countrymen. Clearly there was only one escape for them — into stupidity. They could keep society in its existing shape only by being *unable* to grasp that any improvement was possible. Difficult though this was, they achieved it, largely by fixing their eyes on the past and refusing to notice the changes that were going on round them" [Orwell's emphases] (p. 80).

the phenomenon that there came a point when the asylum moved from being the *object* of the developing knowledge system — still effectively governed by the doctor in his own right — to becoming *subjected* to the power and control that emanated from such knowledge; that is to say, *governed by the knowledge base rather than by the individuals in their own right*. At this point, the asylum "institution" had been created.

The original owner capitalists of commercial institutions naturally sought to understand their acquisitions — which they invested in for profit — in terms of their profitability. Their knowledge base has developed to the sophistication of the balance sheet and profit and loss statements and other corporate statements and our understanding of capital markets in which ownership of these institutions is traded. The institutionalized knowledge base is underpinned by the belief that the firm exists to maximize profits and that a non-profitable company "dies".

The instinct to survive and prosper is thereby transmitted to the commercial company as an entity in its own right in our recognition of its inalienable right to seek profits. In a Foucaultian sense, these institutions and those that work within them have now moved from being the object of knowledge — as managers are allowed/encouraged to explore alternative approaches to conducting their business — to being subject to this knowledge and — as Foucault saw it — its attendant power. In this view, we are no longer governed by individuals in their own right, but by the knowledge base of accounts and capital markets.

In this perspective, as individuals, we are abstracted into a kind of element within the organization, which applies equally whether we are the controller or the controlled. The managers of firms and their investor shareholders are actually *incapable* of providing jobs in depressed areas at the expense of profits, or of not actually contributing to the increasing degradation and deformation of life and the exploitation of workers abroad. Denhardt (1981) observes:

> "We originally sought to construct social institutions that would reflect our beliefs and our values; now there is a danger that our values reflect our institutions; that is, organizations structure our lives to the point that we become locked in their grasp. We end up doing certain things not because we choose to do them, but because that's how things are done in the world of organizations" (p. 322).

Within the context of the firm, our individuality exists as a legally defined contract and is constrained by ethical codes that serve the company's profit line. For Lovell (1995), although the ascription "professional" may carry with it notions of freedom and independence, in a Rousseauian sense, maybe it is merely a different set of chains. Echoing Seedhouse (1988), we are "dwarfed" by our institutions. In the end, as workers, we are paid to obey. For many of us, as we attempt to resolve the tension between the ethical codes induced by our "institutional" and "society" existences, the outcome is a sort of schizophrenia between our attitudes at work and away from work.

The "mad" of Foucault's asylums distinguished themselves by their "disruption of the rhythms of collective life and their inability to work". Foucault observed that through the Middle Ages and the Renaissance period, the mad had actually enjoyed a degree of freedom of expression, when their condition had been associated with a particular form of knowledge and expression. It was only during the Classical period, that those with an "inability to work" would lose their claim as of right to being a member of the community. Their "madness" was placed on the other side of bars "under the eyes of reason that no longer felt any relation to it and that would not compromise itself by too close a resemblance" (*Madness and Civilization*, Foucault, p. 70), as their confinement in the vacated leprosarium became symbolic with their disease.

As the Frankenstein creation, we might acknowledge that our institutions are "out of control", or, rather, that their knowledge base is "in control". Our attitudes to those with an "inability to work" are inevitably molded by, if not made subordinate to, the institutionalized knowledge base of profit and loss, so that those who cannot contribute to the profit and loss statements and the balance sheet must continue to be confined and shamed. We might conclude that our institutions have become as successful mutations that have learned to optimize their position in the environment. As the self-learning robots of science fiction, they have learned to head off threats to their survival — survival that is viewed as threatened by constraints on their functioning to deliver profits to the financial markets. They can even appear to be our masters, to which we are beholden.[3]

---

[3] At one time, the community's place of worship was the tallest building in society. It would have been presumptuous to build higher. Then, the town's civic buildings dominated. Now,

15.4. Corporate Ethics

In a survey of 500 managers by Digital Equipment Company, "short-term profit" actually came at the bottom of the list of priorities. Their agenda is "the wholesome development of their staff, the community and the environment". Nevertheless, and consistent with Orwell's depiction of the British ruling class,[2] the tough decisions relating to the conflict between capitalism's growth and the broader issues for mankind are never presented as a matter of choice. They are unavoidable and hence not an issue of ethics.

Thus, the pursuit of profit is presented as a response to the pressures of the market place: Not to pursue maximum profits at every opportunity would not only be an act of irresponsibility to the firm's shareholders, but would act to undermine the company's survival, and hence, in the long run, to undermine all the company's stakeholders. Globalization, productivity enhancing technological change, down-sizing and re-engineering are inevitable.

Prior to the global financial crisis, discourse of business ethics by business executives and political leaders was invariably aimed at representing a positive affirmation of the processes of the system, rather than any genuine criticism of its activities. Neimark (1995) suggests that the periodic identification and punishment of individuals and corporations whose actions edged past the boundaries of acceptable business conduct, actually allowed the official discourse of business ethics to reassure that the system was working and that honesty balances rapaciousness: "It is a distraction and a means of defeating the cynicism and dissonance created by the growing tension between capitalism's growth and the broader visions we have for society". Lovell (1995) agrees, concluding that while ethical codes are part of the moral atmosphere, in many respects they are a defensive strategy, necessary to assuage public fears. Thus, the official discourse acts to deflect attention from the culpability of capitalism itself and to deflect attention from contradictions and tensions that would otherwise translate into social conflict. In this context, Mitchell, Puxty, and Sikka (1994) consider that ethical statements have actually acted to protect the

---

it is the buildings of financial institutions that dominate the skyline, lit up at night as one with the stars and humbling all below.

accounting professions from sustained scrutiny. They are a smokescreen for the pursuit and protection of sectional interests, while the mere existence of disciplinary procedures is used to reassure the public.

Nevertheless, we may observe that ethical systems at least function as a *constraint* on behavior. Neimark observes that the requirement for consensus for a working ideology ensures that while the ideology might serve partisan interests by legitimating and maintaining a prevailing social order, the need to make the ideology appear plausible and universal implies that the ideology must act at least to a degree as a constraint on the excesses of individual sections in the society. The ideology of corporate social responsibility, for example, creates the expectation that corporate behavior will bear at least *some* relationship to its claims — by not polluting the environment, by not discriminating in hiring, promotion and other personnel activities, by considering the impact of plant relocations on local communities, by treating employees as "valued" resources, and so on. In finance, the notion of corporate social responsibility acts at least as a constraint on the behavior of its participants, with regard to such as insider-trading, as well as sustaining the obligation of the professional member to uphold and foster the "reputation" of the corporate community.

15.5. Ethics and the Individual

Bruner (2004, 2005) considers the commitment to advance "reputation" and "trust" as essentially *identifying* the ethical dimension of business, and that *un*ethical practices so defined cannot provide a foundation for sustainable enterprise. The legacy of the firm's *reputation* is the foundation of the firm's sustainability, and *trust rewards* when a bond with clients and customers is built by trustworthy behavior. The global financial crisis can be understood as these relationships gone awry, as individuals sacrificed their reputations and that of the firm, along with trust relationships with their clients, because they were seduced by short-term bonuses linked to deal making. Bruner (2004) quotes Warren Buffet: "We can afford to lose a lot of money. But we cannot afford to lose one shred of our reputation" (p. 18).

In Chapter 14, we proposed a framework of (i) reputations based on past performance, and (ii) commitment and trust relationships, for recognizing and understanding corporate financial behavior. From Bruner's perspective, such concepts constitute a framework of ethical responsibility at the level of the firm and of the individual. In this case, an ethical framework of behavior is no longer an "add-on" to be applied to exceptional circumstances of cheating or deception, but, rather, is identified directly with a framework within which we can begin to understand the functioning of a firm. Ethical behavior is "bound up", so to speak, in the personal codes of behavior of the firm's employees and the organization's practices at the broadest level. And, thus, we may conclude, individuals are called on to assert themselves and their codes of relationships in the workplace. It is in this context that we recognize the codes of behavior espoused by the CFA Institute in the Introduction to this chapter.

15.6. Time for Reflection: What Have We Learned?

We have argued that the development of ethical frameworks may be interpreted in terms of a process of natural selection with regard to the mutual interdependence of the individual and the community; the outcome of which is that the ethics of a community work to coordinate the activities of its members. In this case, we should not expect that corporate and financial ethics look outwardly "to do good", but rather that they act reflexively to *consolidate* and *sanction* internal activity. In addition, we must expect that the individual employee is called on to be ethical on the profit-motivated terms of the institution, rather than on the individual's own terms.

Our institutions are subject to the knowledge base that has been built around them. Thus, their development takes place consistent with the development of how collectively we come to define our expectations for their function. It is in this contained context, that a person must identify themselves.

The young person in their early career (after many frustrating months and more of applications and rejections) is sufficiently humbled at the point of finally gaining entry into the workplace, that the call to "wear the suit" — to be transformed into another person in the workplace — is overwhelming, intoxicating, and exciting. But to what extent must the individual in the workplace be prepared to disconnect from who they are when they "lose the suit"?

In response, we have argued that the dynamic of professional financial activity cannot be divorced from the individual reputations for competence linked to trustworthiness of its members. In this perspective, the individual person in the workplace is *not* called on to subordinate their personality to mere activity, but, rather, to assert their reputations for competence linked to trustworthiness. Their attitudes to life are allowed to – indeed should — permeate their dealings with clients, subordinates, and superiors — as they transmit "their message" as to what it is to be human in the workplace.

In which case, we may venture that individuals — albeit at the margin — do make a difference, as changes in attitudes are precipitated, as society reassesses itself from the bottom-up and moves forward.

FINAL CHAPTER

Chapter 16

Academic Finance: Responsible Enquiry or Stamp Collecting?

All science is either physics or stamp-collecting.

Lord Rutherford

Nothing truly valuable arises from ambition or from a mere sense of duty; it stems rather from love and devotion towards men and towards objective things.

Albert Einstein

Words ought to be a little wild, for they are the assaults of thoughts on the unthinking

John Maynard Keynes

Father McKenzie writing the words of a sermon that no one will hear.

Lennon and McCartney

16.1. Summary of the Text

In this, the final chapter, we summarize the theory development of the text (Section 16.1), before Section 16.2 considers the importance of academic finance. Section 16.3 closes the text.

We have critiqued the capital asset pricing model (CAPM) of Jack Treynor, William Sharpe, John Lintner and Jan Mossin (Chapter 2) and the Modigliani and Miller (MM) propositions of Franco Modigliani and Merton Miller (Chapter 5) as adequate foundation paradigms on which to build insight and understanding of financial markets and corporate finance. We do not deny the *principles* (i) that expected returns for risk exposure remain in proportion to risk exposure (the CAPM) and (ii) that the distribution of the firm's claims on its profitability — between equity and debt holders and the tax authorities — should not affect the total value of their combined claims (the MM propositions). Nevertheless, the paradigms have had a distinct entrapment effect in shutting out recognition of first-order effects: decision

275

making under uncertainty, the economic cycles within which the firm operates, the dynamics of financial leverage, the psychology of markets, broader principles of management, the firm as a social construct, and ethical behavior as defining human enterprise.

We have argued that the three-factor model of Eugene Fama and Kenneth French (FF-3F model) is conceptually unconvincing as an encapsulation of risk (Chapter 3), as are additional "factor model" extensions of the CAPM aimed at aligning the model more closely with historical data (Chapter 4). We have preferred to identify the additional FF-3F model factors of book-to-market and small firm size effects, not with risk, but, rather, with the mispricing of stocks (Chapter 10). Ultimately, the FF-3F model has been rejected on its own terms as failing to adhere to the principles of the CAPM and the MM propositions (Chapter 13).

Commencing from a fundamental model of growth allowing continuously compounding growth rates that are normally distributed (Chapter 6), we have observed that random variations in such rates do not cancel with one another as Harry Markowitz's theory supposes (Chapter 7). Rather, they contribute *positively* to the portfolio's performance. Combined with the notion of a log-wealth utility, the model implies that risk creates its own reward (Chapter 8). This insight suggests that markets have an inherent resilience to downward shocks and depressed prices: Markets do inevitably recover. By providing a less volatile component of returns, the firm's dividends support a greater allocation to risky assets in an investor's portfolio than would otherwise be the case (Chapter 8).

Historical stock market performances imply that either (1) investors have a level of risk aversion greater than that of a log-wealth utility function or (2) investors perceive market risk exposure greater than that which is implied by the standard deviation of stock returns in times of market stability. Recognizing that market volatility is not fixed, and that prices are liable to deteriorate in a self-referencing manner, allows for the latter interpretation (otherwise, a Pratt's measure of relative risk aversion γ somewhat less than three is implied, Chapter 9). The "consumption capital asset pricing model" (CCAPM) proposed by John Cochrane as the foundation of asset pricing — whereby stock market risk is perceived as the threat to *concurrent* consumption — implies unacceptably high measures of γ, and is rejected in favor of the model developed in Chapter 9, which is supported as conceptually acceptable as well as implying acceptable measures of risk aversion (Chapter 11). Allowing for mispricing of assets with self-correction (Chapter 10), we argue that an investor may rationally choose "stocks for the long haul" (Chapter 11). The model thereby refutes Paul Samuelson's claim that a rational investor's decision to invest in the risky stock market cannot be influenced by the duration of the investment. The assumptions underlying the model of Chapter 9 lead naturally to an exposition of the option pricing model of Fischer Black and Myron Scholes (Chapter 12).

We have developed a consistent framework of valuation models allowing for personal taxes (Chapter 13). We progress to recognize that the concept of a cost of capital with net present value (NPV) calculations represents only a contributing apparatus for investment decision making. The phenomenon of management shared responsibility with strategic content leads us to consider (i) reputations based on past performance, and (ii) commitment and trust relationships, as dimensions for recognizing and understanding corporate investment behavior (Chapter 14), with the outcome that the concept of ethical behavior constitutes a significant contribution to an understanding of firm behavior (Chapter 15).

16.2. Finance Theory as Performative

The philosopher Michel Foucault has proposed that our institutions progress from being the "object" of our knowledge base as we attempt to understand them, to becoming ultimately "subject" to our understanding of them — so that, ultimately, we allow ourselves to be governed by the knowledge base of our institutions rather than by individuals in their own right. Once imposed, a knowledge base derives almost tangible *power* — as the knowledge base asserts itself as the gatekeeper to subsequent attempts to supervise or regulate — as power resides in the knowledge base *through* which we encounter our institutions. Despite (or, more likely, because of) its removal from a commonplace understanding, academia is capable of exerting a hold on our perceptions as to how the world works, so that its theories are influential in determining how corporate and financial institutions are understood and thereby governed. Keasey and Hudson (2007) observe what they refer to as the *performative* aspect of academic financial economics in its legitimation of external reality — meaning that academic finance affects, rather than merely describes, financial markets.[1] Cai, Clasher, and Keasey (2013) expand on the notion that the ideas promoted by academia duly permeate the industry and *do* make a difference. Academic model building has the power to promote good outcomes as well as to commit harm when it promotes bad ideas.

Academic finance has succeeded in *imposing* the belief that markets are efficient, the markets know best, and that regulations restrict their efficient behavior. Leading up the global financial crisis, the belief lent support to the spread of ever-increasing complex financial instruments — the derivatives, securitizations, collateralized debt obligations, and credit default swap instruments — that developed without regulatory oversight, while the purchasers of the instruments succumbed to the hype of the bank's promoters who claimed that they were contributing to the building of sophisticated interdependences that allowed investors to transfer risk, when they were in reality creating the house of cards that duly tumbled for everyone.[2]

The belief in markets has worked to side-line government and regulators from imposing themselves on market operations — to warn against excesses, to dictate stronger balance sheets for banks, or to curtail executive pay. The denial of market failure also played a part in discouraging central banks from attempting to curtail asset price bubbles before they might lead to departures of prices from a reasonable assessment of fundamental values.

Prior to the global financial crisis, a belief in markets had encouraged the accounting profession to see markets as the arbiter of value on the firm's balance sheet. With stock prices rising, "mark-to-market" valuations or *fair value accounting* (FVA) encouraged banks to increase their financial

---

[1]They quote MacKenzie and Millo (2003), who show how the academic modeling of derivatives eventually legitimated derivatives and the means by which they are valued and traded. Similarly, Moosa (2013) relates how the perceived status of the "gurus" to the finance industry succeeded in promoting the belief in markets as efficient and capable of pricing the most complex products of financial engineering through arbitrage.

[2]Ball (2009) argues that attempting to lay the blame for the global financial crisis at the door of a simple proposition — the "efficient market hypothesis" — is naïve. True, but the point made here is that theories are capable of "taking hold" and thereafter punching above their intellectual weight in referencing what is considered to be responsible behavior by participants, as well as what is considered to be appropriate interference by those with responsibility as regulators.

leverage on their balance sheets.[3] In reverse, at the outset of the financial crisis, a "mark-to-market" downgrading of their valuations required banks to contract their balance sheets, which provoked contagion in financial markets as banks sold assets at a price below their fundamental value, and the price of the forced sales became relevant to other institutions, which were required by FVA to mark their assets to market, in a rapidly developed downward spiral. The levels of debt of banks and their inherent exposure to illiquid assets when the bubbles burst were such as to cause the banks to lose confidence even in each other.[4] Bear Stearns and Lehman were brought down by a bank run — the only difference was that this time, the run was led by institutions rather than by small depositors.

Accredited theories have succeeded in transmitting the firm as a financial entity, transmuting it as an efficient investment counter, rather than an organization with an assortment of broader responsibilities. The outcome is that managers are encouraged by institutionalized bonuses and stock options to treat the firm as such — an investment counter — looking to talk up the firm to the markets, rather than focusing on the long-term direction and financial health of the company with a sense of its broader obligations — while providing information publically about the firm and thereafter leaving it to the stock markets to get on with *their* job of placing a value on the firm's shares.

Managers at both Lehman Brothers and Bear Stearns were compensated with stock holding aimed at aligning pay to incentives. Nevertheless, they ran their companies into receivership.[5] Academia has often chosen

---

[3]This was linked to the fact that the substantial bonuses for a bank's senior staff were typically linked to the short-term returns to the bank's equity. For the Royal Bank of Scotland (RBS) — the biggest bank in the world prior to the crisis — and Citi bank — at the time the biggest bank in the US, the leverage ratios were in the region of 50. In effect, they were capable of absorbing only $2 in losses on each $100 of assets.

[4]Regulatory authorities failed to foresee that a significant proportion of the bank's assets must be capable of quickly being wound down in the case that its financial viability is threatened, as well as failing to foresee that, ultimately, provision must be made for a large international bank to go bankrupt without bringing down the whole system (Dempsey and Jones, 2015).

[5]Even after having been rescued by government bailouts, investment bankers have continued to pay themselves extravagant bonuses from, in effect, public taxes as subsidies, leading to the observation that banks are allowed "to capitalize their profits and socialize their losses".

to champion explicitly the wisdom of executive remuneration packages.[6] Executives and their remuneration consultants defend their remuneration increases with the argument that the remunerations are "set by efficient

---

Bonuses may be the worst thing that has happened to industry. The natural response to a bonus is, after all, to play to win the bonus — not because one is greedy necessarily — but as a natural response to a challenge: Successfully obtaining a bonus equates with success; failure to do so is identified with, just that, failure. Thus, the bonus encourages managers to aim for a short-term objective independent of any consideration of the long-term impact on the firm. Better, in my view, to reward managers with a salary and allow them to get on with managing the firm to the best of their ability, motivated (like the rest of us) by the incentive of enhancing their reputation. Or are we to understand that the firm's executives are alone amongst its employees in requiring such short-term inducements as share options and bonus targets before they can be expected to align themselves with the firm's success?

[6]An influential paper by Jensen and Zimmerman (1985) concluded that (1) executive compensation is *positively* related to share price performance, as well as arguing that (2) the adoption of new short- and long-term executive compensation plans and golden parachutes is associated with *positive* share price reactions. Jensen and Murphy (1990) went so far as to argue that US CEOs have *insufficient* incentives to increase shareholder wealth, while Conyon and Murphy (2000) argued that incentives among British CEOs "pale compared to their American counterparts" and recommend that UK remunerations be re-examined to avoid the potential damaging effect to British companies if their managers seek to go abroad. The issue, they argue, is that of selecting the correct performance measure, as well as educating shareholders to understand the relation between executive pay and firm performance (Murphy, 1985). Also in UK studies, Main, Bruce, and Buck (1996) and Murphy and Oyer (2001) argue that executive compensation is strongly *positively* related to corporate performance. This is not to say that all academic thinking — even before the financial crisis — had supported executive packages. Several studies had argued that the greater the pay disparity in corporations, the weaker the financial performance, the poorer the internal collaboration, and the lower the product quality (e.g., Cowherd & Levine, 1992; Siegel & Hambrick, 2005). More cynical views are that stock options have been

"not so much an incentive device but a covert mechanism of self-dealing" which is the process they were supposed to eliminate (Yermack, 1995); and that

"top managers . . . appear to be an averagely ineffectual officer class who do, however, know how to look after themselves" (Froud, Johal, Leaver, and Williams, 2006).

Dodd and Johns (1999) and Bolton, Scheinkman, and Xiong (2006) confirm that executive remunerations have intensified management focus onto pleasing, and at times manipulating, financial markets, motivating them toward stock repurchases and an emphasis on short-term stock market valuation, with consequent reductions on attention to product and service markets and at the expense of long-term corporate value. See also McSweeney (2009) and, for example, Coles, Hertzel, and Kalpathy (2006), Ellsworth (1983, 2002), Fuller and Jensen (2002), Graham, Harvey, and Rajgopal (2005), Sanders and Carpenter (2003), and Stinchcombe (2000). Justin Fox (2009) concludes that options to executives in the bull market of the 1990s made a few superstar CEOs into billionaires and a lot of mediocrities into centi-millionaires (*The Myth of the Rational Market*, p. 279).

markets". It has taken the global financial crisis to bring the disparity between pay and performance into sharp relief.

The mantra of "efficient markets" as espoused by academics implies an effectiveness and efficiency of the system as steward and protector of common shareholder savings. Against such complacency, John Bogle is a rare outspoken critic.[7] He has repeatedly accused the funds management industry of emphasizing management bonuses driven by short-term per-formance and salesmanship with an attendant "churning" of client funds (the holding period for a stock is typically less than one year) — with the outcome that desired outcomes are misaligned with incentives (Bogle, 2005*a*, 2005*b*). Bogle concludes that citizens who have entrusted their savings to the care of mutual fund managers have not been well served by the industry. He receives support from Richard Ennis (2005) who considers that for the majority of fund managers, fees are "beyond the pale of plausibility" (p. 48).[8]

It has been left largely to non-academic writers to observe that gross pay and bonuses continue to be awarded to managers and executives even when their company does badly or an investment fund performs mediocrely. In his introduction to the reprint (2006) of Fred Schwed's (1940), *Where are the Customers' Yachts?*,[9] Jason Zweig of *Money Magazine*

---

[7]John Bogle is the founder of the Vanguard Group of Investment Companies — built on principles of low cost. Bogle insists that it is foolish to attempt to pick actively managed mutual funds and expect their performance to beat a low-cost index fund over a long period of time, after accounting for the fees that actively managed funds charge.

[8]Richard Ennis is a principal at investment advisory firm, Ennis, Knupp & Associates, Chicago.

[9]The book title refers to the story that a Wall Street broker was showing off his luxury yacht and indicating those of his fellow bankers and brokers to a friend, who asked rather naïvely, *Where are the customers' yachts?* As Jason Zweig recounts, the game remains the same. In the mid-1990s, a series of reports (the Cadbury, Greenbury, and Hampel reports, culminating in the Combined Code) had enquired into Britain's corporate governance system following sustained public outcry and the media voicing that executive remunerations were spiraling out of control. Such a case was in 1995, when protestors outside British Gas's annual meeting paraded against the 75% pay award to its chief executive officer (CEO), Cedric Brown. Packed inside the general meeting and outside, they were intent on overturning the pay increase. A sense of drama leading up to the general meeting had captured the newspaper front pages. However, a sense of anti-climax prevailed when the protestors were outvoted by the fund managers who constitutionally held the voting rights for the shares under their management — including the votes of those protesting in the street outside against the pay rise.

considers:

> "The names and faces and machinery of Wall Street have changed completely from Schwed's day, but the game remains the same. The individual investor is still situated at the very bottom of the food chain, a speck of plankton afloat in a sea of predators."

16.3.   Academic Finance: Responsible Enquiry or Stamp Collecting?

Keasey and Hudson (2007) consider that academic finance succeeds in having its papers published when they are upbeat and confirmatory of the system; in effect, adhering fundamentally to the paradigm of market efficiency. They point out that for finance academics, it is far safer, and more productive, in terms of the research game being played, to narrowly select data from the outside world and produce puzzles on the periphery of what is already established. This keeps the research community busy without seriously threatening the imposed belief system, be it banking or corporate behavior, executive pay, or fund management fees.

The idea that finance theory must learn to look beyond the limitations of its core precepts is stoutly resisted by the vast majority of academics (Whitley, 1984, 1986). In relation to asset pricing, the need to connect financial markets with economic cycles — each of which is capable of leading the other (up or down) — and thereby to connect with the imperatives in practice of institutional behavior in coherent explanations, has received scant academic attention. So, also, has the need to align market valuations with the needs of the accounting profession. In relation to corporate financial management, the notion that the subject matter might link to insights from management and organizational disciplines — of strategy and organizational behavior — is even more stoutly resisted.

Thus, the system continues to be held hostage to itself as the aspiring young finance person seeking a PhD and needing to produce a "job paper" to promote an academic career, is effectively obliged to follow the route of an econometrically sound contribution to empirical data mining, rather than the uncertainty associated with endeavoring to contribute to a meaningful understanding of the economic system. And so the self-protecting mechanism of academia continues with the vast majority of finance journals ranked primarily on the econometric closure of their contributions rather than the subjective insightfulness of their research.

Nevertheless, as an outcome of the global financial crisis, the mirror has been held up to academic finance as to how it wishes to see itself: either committed to meaningful and responsible enquiry, or content with an economic foundation that is at arm's length from reality and which is focused on achieving econometric closure within increasingly narrow domains of inquiry, without moral content, and which finds itself unable to accept the profession's excesses and inefficiencies.

At least, that is my opinion.

Adieu!

References

CHAPTER 1

Lintner, J. (1965), "The Valuation of Risk Assets and the Selection of Risky Investments in Stock Portfolios and Capital Budgets", *Review of Economics and Statistics*, 47, 13–37.

Markowitz, H. (1952), "Portfolio Selection", *Journal of Finance*, 7, 77–91.

Modigliani, F. and Miller, M. (1958), "The Cost of Capital, Corporation Finance and the Theory of Investment", *American Economic Review*, 48, 261–297.

Modigliani, F. and Miller, M. (1963), "Corporate Income Taxes and the Cost of Capital: A Correction", *American Economic Review*, 53, 433–443.

Mossin, J. (1966), "Equilibrium in a Capital Asset Market", *Econometrica*, 34, 768–783.

Sharpe, W.F. (1964), "Capital Asset Prices: A Theory of Market Equilibrium under Conditions of Risk", *Journal of Finance*, 19, 425–442.

Treynor, J.L. (1961), "Market Value, Time, and Risk", unpublished manuscript.

Treynor, J.L. (1962), "Toward a Theory of Market Value of Risky Assets", unpublished manuscript. A final version was published in 1999, in *Asset Pricing and Portfolio Performance: Models, Strategy and Performance Metrics* (15–22), Korajczyk, R. (ed.) (Risk Books, London).

CHAPTER 2

Black, F. (1973), "Capital Market Equilibrium with Restricted Borrowing", *Journal of Business*, 45, 444–455.

Black, F. (1993), "Beta and Return", *Journal of Portfolio Management*, 20, 8–18.

Black, F., Jensen, M. and Scholes, M. (1972), "The Capital Asset Pricing Model: Some Empirical Tests", in *Studies in the Theory of Capital Markets* (Praeger Publishers, New York).

Dempsey, M. (2013a), "The Capital Asset Pricing Model (CAPM): The History of a Failed Revolutionary Idea in Finance", *Abacus*, 49, 7–23.

Dempsey, M. (2013b), "The CAPM: A Case of Elegance is for Tailors?" *Abacus*, 49, 82–87.

Douglas, G. (1969), "Risk in the Equity Markets: An Empirical Appraisal of Market Efficiency", *Yale Economic Essays*, 9, 3–45.

Fama, F. (1976), *Foundations of Finance* (Basic Books, New York).

Fama, E. and McBeth, J. (1973), "Risk, Return and Equilibrium: Empirical Tests", *Journal of Political Economy*, 81, 607–636.

Fox, J. (2009), *The Myth of Rational Markets* (Harper Collins, New York).

Jensen, M.C. (1972), "The Foundations and Current State of Capital Market Theory", in *Studies in the Theory of Capital Markets* (Praeger Publishers, New York).

Jensen, M.C. (1978), "Some Anomalous Evidence Regarding Market Efficiency", *Journal of Financial Economics*, 6, 95–101.

Kuhn, T. (1962), *The Structure of Scientific Revolutions* (University of Chicago Press, Chicago).

Lo, A.W. and Mueller, M.T. (2010), "Warning: Physics Envy May be Hazardous to Your Health", *Journal of Investment Management*, 8, 13–63.

Mehrling, P. (2007), *Fisher Black and the Revolutionary Idea of Finance* (John Wiley & Sons, New Jersey).

Miller, M. and Scholes, M. (1972), "Rates of Return in Relation to Risk: A Re-examination of Some Recent Findings" in *Studies in the Theory of Capital Markets* (Praeger, New York).

Modigliani, F. and Miller, M. (1958), "The Cost of Capital, Corporation Finance and the Theory of Investment", *American Economic Review*, 48, 261–297.

Putnam, H. (1979), "The Corroboration of Theories", in *Philosophy As It Is* (353–380), Honderich, T. and Burnyeat, M. (eds) (Penguin Books, Middlesex).

Roll, R. (1977), "A Critique of Asset Pricing Theory's Tests", *Journal of Financial Economics*, 129–176.

Ross, S.A. (1978), "The Current Status of the Capital Asset Pricing Model", *Journal of Finance*, 33, 885–901.

Ryan, R.J. (1982), "Capital Market Theory — A Case Study in Methodological Conflict", *Journal of Business Finance and Accounting*, 9, 443–458.

CHAPTER 3

Black, F. (1993), "Beta and Return", *Journal of Portfolio Management*, 20, 8–18.

Black, F., Jensen, M. and Scholes, M. (1972), "The Capital Asset Pricing Model: Some Empirical Tests", in *Studies in the Theory of Capital Markets* (Praeger Publishers, New York).

Campbell, J., Hilscher, J. and Szilagyi, J. (2008), "In Search of Distress Risk", *Journal of Finance*, 63, 2899–2939.

Campbell, J. and Vuolteenaho, T. (2004), "Bad Beta, Good Beta", *American Economic Review*, 94, 1249–1275.

Daniel, K. and Titman, S. (1997), "Evidence on the Characteristics of Cross Sectional Variation in Stock Returns", *Journal of Finance*, 52, 1–33.

Dempsey, M. (2013), "The Capital Asset Pricing Model (CAPM): The History of a Failed Revolutionary Idea in Finance", *Abacus*, 49, 7–23.

Dichev, I. (1998), "Is the Risk of Bankruptcy a Systematic Risk?" *Journal of Finance*, 53, 1131–1147.

Fama, E. and French, K. (1992), "The Cross-Section of Expected Stock Returns", *Journal of Finance*, 47, 427–466.

Fama, E. and French, K. (1993), "Common Risk Factors in the Returns on Stocks and Bonds", *Journal of Financial Economics*, 33, 3–56.

Fama, E. and French, K. (1994), "Industry Costs of Equity", Working paper, Graduate School of Business, University of Chicago.

Fama, E. and French, K. (1995), "Size and Book-to-Market Factors in Earnings and Returns", *Journal of Finance*, 50, 131–155.

Fama, E. and French, K. (1996), "Multifactor Explanations of Asset Pricing Anomalies", *Journal of Finance*, 51, 55–84.

Griffin, J. and Lemmon, M. (2002), "Book-to-market Equity, Distress Risk, and Stock Returns", *Journal of Finance*, 57, 2317–2336.

Kuhn, T. (1962), *The Structure of Scientific Revolutions* (University of Chicago Press, Chicago).

Lakonishok, J., Shleifer, A. and Vishny, R.W. (1994), "Contrarian Investment, Extrapolation and Risk", *Journal of Finance*, 49, 1541–1578.

Lakonishok, J. and Shapiro, A.C. (1986), "Systematic Risk, Total Risk and Size as Determinants of Stock Market Returns", *Journal of Banking and Finance*, 10, 115–132.

Merton, R.C. (1973), "An Intertemporal Capital Asset Pricing Model", *Econometrica*, 41, 867–887.

Reinganum, M.R. (1981), "A New Empirical Perspective on the CAPM", *Journal of Financial and Quantitative Analysis*, 16, 439–462.

Ross, S.A. (1976), "The Arbitrage Theory of Capital Asset Pricing", *Journal of Economic Theory*, 13, 341–360.

CHAPTER 4

Amihud, Y. and Mendelson, H. (1986), "Asset Pricing and the Bid-ask Spread", *Journal of Financial Economics*, 17, 223–249.

Brennan, M., Wang, A. and Xia, Y. (2004), "Estimation and Test of a Simple Model of Intertemporal Capital Asset Pricing", *Journal of Finance*, 59, 1743–1775.

Campbell, J. and Vuolteenaho, T. (2004), "Bad Beta, Good Beta", *American Economic Review*, 94, 1249–1275.

Carhart, M.M. (1997), "On Persistence in Mutual Fund Performance", *Journal of Finance*, 52, 57–82.

Chopra, N., Lakonishok, J. and Ritter, J. (1992), "Measuring Abnormal Returns: Do Stocks Overreact?" *Journal of Financial Economics*, 31, 235–268.

Chordia, T., Huh, S. and Subrahmanyam, A. (2009), "Theory-based Illiquidity and Asset Pricing", *Review of Financial Studies*, 22, 3629–3668.

Chordia, T., Roll, R. and Subrahmanyam, A. (2002), "Order Imbalance, Liquidity and Market Returns", *Journal of Financial Economics*, 65, 111–130.

Chordia, T., Roll, R. and Subrahmanyam, A. (2008), "Liquidity and Market Efficiency", *Journal of Financial Economics*, 87, 249–268.

Chordia, T., Sarkar, A. and Subrahmanyam, A. (2005), "An Empirical Analysis of Stock and Bond Market Liquidity", *Review of Financial Studies*, 18, 85–129.

Chordia, T. and Shivakumar, L. (2002), "Momentum, Business Cycle, and Time-varying Expected Returns", *Journal of Finance*, 57, 985–1019.

Cochrane, J. (2005), *Asset Pricing* (Princeton University Press, Princeton and Oxford).

Cohen, L. and Frazzini, A. (2008), "Economic Links and Predictable Returns", *Journal of Finance*, 63, 1977–2011.

Conrad, J. and Kaul, G. (1993), "Long-term Market Overreaction or Biases in Computed Returns?" *Journal of Finance*, 48, 39–63.

Cooper, M., Gulen, H. and Schil, M. (2008), "Asset Growth and the Cross-section of Stock Returns", *Journal of Finance*, 63, 1609–1651.

Da, Z. (2009), "Cash Flow, Consumption Risk, and the Cross-section of Stock Returns", *Journal of Finance*, 64, 923–956.

DeBondt, W. and Thaler, R. (1985), "Does the Stock Market Overreact?" *Journal of Finance*, 40, 793–808.

DeBondt, W. and Thaler, R. (1987), "Further Evidence on Investor Overreaction and Stock Market Seasonality", *Journal of Finance*, 42, 557–581.

Dempsey, M. (2013), "The Capital Asset Pricing Model (CAPM): The History of a Failed Revolutionary Idea in Finance", *Abacus*, 49, 7–23.

Fama, E. and French, K. (1993), "Common Risk Factors in the Returns on Stocks and Bonds", *Journal of Financial Economics*, 33, 3–56.

Fama, E. and French, K. (2008), "Dissecting anomalies", *Journal of Finance*, 63, 1653–1678.

Griffin, J., Ji, S. and Martin, S. (2003), "Momentum Investing and Business Cycle Risk: Evidence from Pole to Pole", *Journal of Finance*, 58, 2515–2547.

Grinblatt, M. and Moskowitz, T. (2004), "Predicting Stock Price Movements from Past Returns: The Role of Consistency and Tax-loss Selling", *Journal of Financial Economics*, 71, 541–579.

Haugen, R. and Baker, N. (1996), "Commonality in the Determinants of Expected Stock Returns", *Journal of Financial Economics*, 41, 401–439.

Heston, S. and Sadka, R. (2008), "Seasonality in the Cross-section of Stock Returns", *Journal of Financial Economics*, 87, 418–445.

Hong, H., Lim, T. and Stein, J. (2000), "Bad News Travels Slowly: Size, Analyst Coverage, and the Profitability of Momentum Strategies", *Journal of Finance*, 55, 265–295.

Jagannathan, R. and Wang, Z. (1996), "The Conditional CAPM and the Cross-section of Expected Returns", *Journal of Finance*, 51, 3–53.

Jegadeesh, N. and Titman, S. (1993), "Returns to Buying Winners and Selling Losers: Implications for Stockmarket Efficiency", *Journal of Finance*, 48, 65–92.

Loughran, T. and Ritter, J. (1996), "Long-term Market Overreaction: The Effect of Low-priced Stocks", *Journal of Finance*, 51, 1959–1970.

Malkiel, B. (2004), "Can Predictable Patterns in Market Returns be Exploited Using Real Money? Not Likely", *Journal of Portfolio Management*, 30, 131–141.

Petkova, R. (2006), "Do the Fama–French Factors Proxy for Innovations in Predictive Variables?" *Journal of Finance*, 61, 581–612.

Rouwenhorst, K. (1998), "International Momentum Strategies", *Journal of Finance*, 53, 267–284.

Santos, T. and Veronesi, R. (2006), "Labor Income and Predictable Stock Returns", *Review of Financial Studies*, 19, 1–44.

Shiller R.J. (1981), "Do Stock Prices Move Too much to be Justified by Subsequent Changes in Dividends?" *American Economic Review*, 71, 421–436.

Subrahmanyam, A. (2010), "The Cross-Section of Expected Stock Returns: What Have We Learnt from the Past Twenty-Five Years of Research?" *European Financial Management*, 16, 27–42.

The Economist (2010), "Economics Focus: Data Birth." November 18th, p. 83.

CHAPTER 5

Baker, M. and Wurgler, J. (2004), "A Catering Theory of Dividends", *Journal of Finance*, 73, 271–288.

Ben-David, I., Graham, J. and Harvey, C. (2007), "Managerial Overconfidence and Corporate Policies", NBER Working Paper: No. w13711 (2007), SSRN, http://ssrn.com/abstract=1079308.

Brennan, M.J. (1995), "Corporate Finance over the Past 25 Years", *Financial Management*, 24, 9–22.

Daniel, K., Hirshleifer, D. and Subrahmanyam, A. (1998), "Investor Psychology and Security Market Under- and Overreactions", *Journal of Finance*, 53, 1839–1885.

Dempsey, M. (1996), "Corporate Financial Management: Time to Change the Cost of Capital Paradigm?" *Critical Perspectives on Accounting*, 7, 617–639.

Dempsey, M. (2003), "A Multidisciplinary Perspective on the Evolution of Corporate Investment Decision Making", *Accounting, Accountability and Performance*, 9, 1–33.

Dempsey, M. (2014), "The Modigliani and Miller (MM) Propositions: The History of a Failed Foundation for Corporate Finance?", *Abacus*, 50, 279–295.

Dewing, A. (1919), *The Financial Policy of Corporations* (Ronald Press, New York).

Doukas, J.A. and Petmezas, D. (2007), "Overconfident Managers and Self-Attribution Bias", *European Financial Management*, 13, 571–577.

Fama, F. (1976), *Foundations of Finance* (Basic Books, New York).

Ferris, S.P., Jayaraman, N. and Sabherwal, S. (2011), "CEO Overconfidence and International Merger and Acquisition Activity", *Journal of Financial and Quantitative Analysis*, 48, 137–164.

Fisher, I. (1930), *The Theory of Interest* (Macmillan Company, New York).

Gervais, S. and Odean, T. (2001), "Learning to be Overconfident", *Review of Financial Studies*, 14, 1–27.

Goel, A.M., and Thakor, A.V. (2008), "Overconfidence, CEO Selection, and Corporate Governance", *Journal of Finance*, 63, 2737–2784.

Griffin, D. and Tversky, A. (1992), "The Weighing of Evidence and the Determinants of Overconfidence", *Cognitive Psychology*, 24, 411–435.

Hackbarth, D. (2008), "Managerial Traits and Capital Structure Decisions", *Journal of Financial and Quantitative Studies*, 43, 843–881.

Heaton, J. (2002), "Managerial Optimism and Corporate Finance", *Financial Management*, 31, 33–45.

Hilary, G. and Hsu, C. (2011), "Endogenous Overconfidence in Managerial Forecasts", *Journal of Accounting and Economics*, 51, 300–313.

Hilary, G. and Menzly, L. (2006), "Does Past Success Lead Analysts to Become Overconfident?", *Management Science*, 52, 489–500.

Hudson, R., Keasey, K., Littler, K. and Dempsey, M. (1999), "Time Diversification: An Essay in the Need to Revisit Finance Theory", *Critical Perspectives on Accounting*, 10, 501–519.

Kahneman, D. and Lovallo, D. (1993), "Timid Choices and Bold Forecasts: A Cognitive Perspective on Risk Taking", *Management Science*, 39, 17–31.

Kahneman, D. and Tversky, A. (1979), "Prospect Theory: An Analysis of Decision under Risk", *Econometrica*, 47, 263–291.

Keasey, K. and Hudson, R. (2007), "Finance Theory: A House without Windows", *Critical Perspectives on Accounting*, 18, 932–951.

Keynes, J.M. (1936), *The General Theory of Employment, Interest and Money* (Macmillan and Company, London).

Lo, A.W. and Mueller, M.T. (2010), "Warning: Physics Envy May be Hazardous to Your Health", *Journal of Investment Management*, 8, 13–63.

Malmendier, U. and Tate, G. (2005a), "Does Overconfidence Affect Corporate Investment? CEO Overconfidence Measures Revisited", *European Financial Management*, 11, 649–659.

Malmendier, U. and Tate, G. (2005b), "CEO Overconfidence and Corporate Investment", *Journal of Finance*, 55, 2661–2700.

Malmendier, U. and Tate, G. (2008), "Who Makes Acquisitions? CEO Overconfidence and the Market's Reaction", *Journal of Financial Economics*, 89, 20–43.

McGoun, E.G. (1995), "The History of Risk Measurement", *Critical Perspectives on Accounting*, 6, 511–532.

Miller, M.H. (1977), "Debt and Taxes", *Journal of Finance*, 32, 261–275.

Miller, M.H. (1988), "The Modigliani–Miller Propositions after Thirty Years", *Journal of Economic Perspectives*, 2, 99–120.

Minsky, H. (1986), *Stabilizing an Unstable Economy* (McGraw-Hill, Columbus).

Modigliani, F. and Miller, M. (1958), "The Cost of Capital, Corporation Finance and the Theory of Investment", *American Economic Review*, 48, 261–297.

Modigliani, F. and Miller, M. (1963), "Corporate Income Taxes and the Cost of Capital: A Correction", *American Economic Review*, 53, 433–443.

Montier, J. (2002), *Behavioural Finance: Insights into Irrational Minds and Markets* (John Wiley & Sons, Chichester).

Putnam, H. (1979), "The Corroboration of Theories", in *Philosophy As It Is* (353–380), Honderich, T. and Burnyeat, M. (eds.) (Penguin Books, Middlesex).

Rabin, M. and Schrag, J. (1999), "First Impressions Matter: A Model of Confirmatory Bias", *Quarterly Journal of Economics*, 114, 37–82.

Ross, S.A. (1988), "Comment on the Modigliani–Miller Propositions", *Journal of Economic Perspectives*, 2, 127–133.

Shefrin, H. (2001), "Behavioral Corporate Finance", *Journal of Applied Corporate Finance*, 14, 113–124.

Shefrin, H. and Statman, M. (1984), "Explaining Investor Preference for Cash Dividends", *Journal of Financial Economics*, 13, 253–282.

Shiller, R.J. (2010), "How Should the Financial Crisis Change How We Teach Economics?", *Journal of Economic Education*, 41, 403–409.

Shiller, R.J. (1981), "Do Stock Prices Move Too much to be Justified by Subsequent Changes in Dividends?", *American Economic Review*, 71, 421–436.

Smith, C.W. (1990), *The Modern Theory of Corporate Finance* (2nd Edition, McGraw-Hill, New York).

Stiglitz, J.E (1988), "Why Financial Structure Matters", *Journal of Economic Perspectives*, 2, 121–126.

The Economist (2013), Free exchange: "Methods for all Moments", October 19th, p. 83.

Weston, J.F. (1989), "What MM Have Wrought", *Financial Management*, 18, 29–38.

CHAPTER 7

Dempsey, M. (2002), "The Nature of Market Growth, Risk and Return", *Financial Analysts Journal*, 58, 45–59.

Fama, F. (1976), *Foundations of Finance* (Basic Books, New York).

Jackwerth, C.P. and Rubinstein, M. (1996), "Recovering Probability Distributions from Contemporaneous Security Prices", *Journal of Finance*, 51, 1611–1631.

Malkiel, B.G. and Xu, Y. (1997), "Risk and Return Revisited", *Journal of Portfolio Management*, 23, 9–14.

Markowitz, H. (1952), "Portfolio Selection", *Journal of Finance*, 7, 77–91.

CHAPTER 8

Bernstein, P. (1998), *Against the Gods: The Remarkable Story of Risk* (John Wiley & Sons, New York).

Bierman Jr., H. (1998), "A Utility Approach to the Portfolio Allocation Decision and the Investment Horizon", *Journal of Portfolio Management*, 25, 81–87.

Black, F. (1993), "Beta and Return", *Journal of Portfolio Management*, 20, 8–18.

Brealey, R.A. and Myers, S.C. (1996), *Principles of Corporate Finance* (McGraw-Hill, New York).

Copeland, T.E. and Weston, J.F. (1988), *Financial Theory and Corporate Policy* (Addison Wesley, New York).

Dempsey, M. (2002), "The Nature of Market Growth, Risk and Return", *Financial Analysts Journal*, 58, 45–59.

Jorion, P. and Goetzmann, W.N. (1999), "Global Stock Markets in the Twentieth Century", *Journal of Finance*, 54, 953–980.

Kritzman, M. (1994), "What Practitioners Need to Know About Time Diversification", *Financial Analysts Journal*, 50, 14–18.

Kritzman, M. and Rich, D. (1998), "Beware of Dogma", *Journal of Portfolio Management*, 24, 66–77.

Lintner, J. (1965), "The Valuation of Risk Assets and the Selection of Risky Investments in Stock Portfolios and Capital Budgets", *Review of Economics and Statistics*, 47, 13–37.

Olsen, R.A. and Khaki, M. (1998), "Risk, Rationality and Time Diversification", *Financial Analysts Journal*, 54, 58–63.

Osborne, M. (1964), "Brownian Motion in the Stock Market", *Operations Research*, 7, 45–173.

Schwert, W.G. (1991), "Market Volatility: Review", *Journal of Portfolio Management*, 17, 74–78.

Van Eaton, R.D. and Conover, J.A. (1998), "Misconceptions about Optimal Equity Allocation and Investment Horizon", *Financial Analysts Journal*, 54, 52–59.

Von Neumann, J. and Morgenstern, O. (1947), *Theory of Games and Economic Behavior* (Princeton University Press, Princeton NJ).

CHAPTER 9

Merton, R.C. (1973), "An Intertemporal Capital Asset Pricing Model", *Econometrica*, 41, 867–887.

Merton, R.C. (1969), "Lifetime Portfolio Selection Under Uncertainty: The Continuous-Time Case", *The Review of Economics and Statistics*, 51, 247–257.

Roll, R. (1977), "A Critique of Asset Pricing Theory's Tests", *Journal of Financial Economics*, 129–176.

Sharpe, W. (2007), "Expected Utility Asset Allocation", *Financial Analysts Journal*, 63, 867–888.

CHAPTER 10

Arnott, R.D. (2005), "What Cost 'Noise?'", *Financial Analysts Journal*, 61, 10–13.

Arnott, R.D., Hsu, J. and Moore, P. (2005), "Fundamental Indexation", *Financial Analysts Journal*, 61, 83–99.

Asness, C. (2006), "The Value of Fundamental Indexing", *Institutional Investor*, 19, 67–71.

Avramov, D., Chordia, T. and Goyal, A. (2006), "Liquidity and Autocorrelations in Individual Stock Returns", *Journal of Finance*, 61, 2365–2394.

Black, F. (1986), "Noise", *Journal of Finance*, 41, 529–543.

Blitz, D. and Swinkels, L. (2008), "Fundamental Indexation: An Active Value Strategy in Disguise", *Journal of Asset Management*, 9, 264–269.

Bogle, J.C. and Malkiel, B.G. (2006), "Turn on a Paradigm?", *Wall Street Journal* (27 June).

DeBondt, W. and Thaler, R. (1985), "Does the Stock Market Overreact?", *Journal of Finance*, 40, 793–808.

DeBondt, W. and Thaler, R. (1987), "Further Evidence on Investor Overreaction and Stock Market Seasonality", *Journal of Finance*, 42, 557–581.

Dempsey, M. (2012), "The Controversy in Fundamental Indexation: Why both sides of the argument are (mostly) correct", *Journal of Investment Management*, 10, 4, 54–63.

Dempsey, M. (2014), "Mispricing and the Fama and French Three Factor Model", working paper.

Fama, E. and French, K. (1993), "Common Risk Factors in the Returns on Stocks and Bonds", *Journal of Financial Economics*, 33, 3–56.

Fama, E. and French, K. (1996), "Multifactor Explanations of Asset Pricing Anomalies", *Journal of Finance*, 51, 55–84.

Jegadeesh, N. (1990), "Evidence of Predictable Behavior of Security Returns", *Journal of Finance*, 45, 881–898.

Jegadeesh, N. and Titman, S. (1995), "Short-Horizon Return Reversals and the Bid-Ask Spread", *Journal of Financial Intermediation*, 4, 116–132.

Jun, D. and Malkiel, B. (2008), "New Paradigms in Stock market Indexing", *European Financial Management*, 14, 118–126.

Kaplan, P.D. (2008), "Why Fundamental Indexation Might — or Might Not — Work", *Financial Analysts Journal*, 64, 32–39.

Malkiel, B. and Jun, D. (2009), "Creating Indexed Portfolios: Weighing the Possibilities of Creating Portfolios through Fundamental Indexing", *Yale Economic Review*, 5, 45–49.

McQuarrie, E. (2008), "Fundamentally Indexed or Fundamentally Misconceived: Locating the Source of RAFI Outperformance", *Journal of Investing*, 17, 29–37.

Pastor, L. and Stambaugh, R. (2003), "Liquidity Risk and Expected Stock Returns", *Journal of Political Economy*, 111, 642–685.

Perold, A. (2007), "Fundamentally Flawed Indexing", *Financial Analysts Journal*, 63, 31–37.

Schiller, R. (1984), "Stock Prices and Social Dynamics", *Brooking Papers on Economic Activity*, 2, 457–498 (Brooking Institute Press).

Shi, T. (2013), *Fundamental Indexation: Essays on Stock Mispricing, Portfolio Diversification, and Rebalancing*, submitted as thesis for awarded Doctor of Philosophy, Monash University.

Shi, T., Dempsey, M. and Irlicht, L. (2015), "Fundamental Indexation and the Fama-French Three Factor Model: Risk Assimilation or Stock Mispricing?", *Journal of Investment Management*, forthcoming.

Smith, A. (1968), *The Money Game* (Random House, New York).

Subrahmayham, A. (2005), "Distinguishing Between Rationales for Short-Horizon Predictability of Stock Returns", *Financial Review*, 40, 11–35.

CHAPTER 11

Abel, A.B. (2002), "An Exploration of the Effects of Pessimism and Doubt on Asset Returns", *Journal of Economic Dynamics and Control*, 26, 1075–1092.

Alvarez, F., and Jermann, U.J. (2000), "Efficiency, Equilibrium, and Asset Pricing with Risk of Default", *Econometrica*, 68, 775–797.

Basak, S. and Cuoco, D. (1998), "An Equilibrium Model with Restricted Stock Market Participation", *Review of Financial Studies*, 11, 309–341.

Campbell, J.Y. and Cochrane, J.H. (1999), "By Force of Habit: A Consumption-Based Explanation of Aggregate Stock Market Behavior", *Journal of Political Economy*, 107, 205–251.

Campbell, J.Y. and Mankiw, N.G. (1990), "Permanent Income, Current Income, and Consumption", *Journal of Business and Economic Statistics*, 8, 265–278.

Canner, N., Mankiw, N.G. and Weil, D.N. (1997), "An Asset Allocation Puzzle", *American Economic Review*, 87, 181–191.

Cochrane, J. (2005), *Asset Pricing* (Princeton University Press, Princeton).

Constantinides, G.M. (1990), "Habit Formation: A Resolution of the Equity Premium Puzzle", *Journal of Political Economy*, 98, 519–543.

Constantinides, G.M., Donaldson, J.B. and Mehra, R. (2002), "Junior Can't Borrow: A New Perspective on the Equity Premium Puzzle", *Quarterly Journal of Economics*, 117, 269–296.

Constantinides, G.M. and Duffie, D. (1996), "Asset Pricing with Heterogeneous Consumers", *Journal of Political Economy*, 104, 219–240.

Epstein, L.G. and Zin, S.E. (1991), "Substitution, Risk Aversion and the Temporal Behavior of Consumption and Asset Returns: An Empirical Analysis", *Journal of Political Economy*, 99, 263–288.

Gordon, S. and St. Amour, P. (2004), "Asset Returns and State-Dependent Risk Preferences", *Journal of Business and Economic Statistics*, 22, 241–252.

Hudson, R., Keasey, K., Littler, K. and Dempsey, M. (1999), "Time Diversification: An Essay in the Need to Revisit Finance Theory", *Critical Perspectives on Accounting*, 10, 501–519.

Kocherlakota, N.R. and Pistaferri, L. (2009), "Asset Pricing Implications of Pareto Optimality with Private Information", *Journal of Political Economy*, 117, 555–590.

Mankiw, N.G. and Zeldes, S.P. (1991), "The Consumption of Stockholders and Non-Stockholders", *Journal of Financial Economics*, 29, 97–112.

Mehra, R. and Prescott, E.C. (1985), "The Equity Premium: A Puzzle", *Journal of Monetary Economics*, 15, 145–161.

Mehra, R. (2003), "The Equity Premium: Why is it a Puzzle?", *Financial Analysts Journal*, 59, 54–69.

Merton, R. and Samuelson, P. (1974), "Fallacy of the Log-normal Approximation to Portfolio Decision-making over Many Periods", *Journal of Financial Economics*, 1, 67–94.

Rietz, T.A. (1988), "The Equity Premium Puzzle: A Solution", *Journal of Monetary Economics*, 22, 117–131.

Samuelson, P. (1963), "Risk and Uncertainty: A Fallacy of Large Numbers", *Scientia* (6th series, 57th year), 108–113.

Samuelson, P. (1969), "Lifetime Portfolio Selection by Dynamic Stochastic Programming", *Review of Economics and Statistics*, 51, 239–246.

Samuelson, P. (1989), "The Judgement of Economic Science on Rational Portfolio Management: Indexing, Timing, and Long-Horizon Effects", *Journal of Portfolio Management*, 16, 4–12.

Samuelson, P. (1994), "The Long Term Case for Equities and How It Can Be Oversold", *Journal of Portfolio Management*, 21, 15–24.

Savov, A. (2011), "Asset Pricing with Garbage", *Journal of Finance*, 66, 177–201.

Siegel, J.J. (2005), "Perspectives on the Equity Risk Premium", *Financial Analysts Journal*, 61, 61–71.

Tversky, A. and Kahneman, D. (1992), "Advances in Prospect Theory: Cumulative Representation of Uncertainty", *Journal of Risk and Uncertainty*, 5, 297–323.

Weil, P. (1989), "The Equity Premium Puzzle and the Risk-Free Rate Puzzle", *Journal of Monetary Economics*, 24, 401–421.

CHAPTER 12

Black, F. and Scholes, M. (1973), "The Pricing of Options and Corporate Liabilities", *Journal of Political Economy*, 81, 637–654.

Merton, R.C. (1973), "Theory of Rational Option Pricing", *Bell Journal of Economics and Management Science*, 4, 141–183.

Merton, R.C. (1990), *Continuous-Time Finance* (Basil Blackwell, Oxford).

CHAPTER 13

Armitage, S., Hodgkinson. L. and Partington, G. (2006), "The Market Value of UK Dividends from Shares with Differing Entitlements", *Journal of Business Finance and Accounting*, 33, 220–244.

Auerbach, A.J. (1979), "Share Valuation and Corporate Equity Policy", *Journal of Public Economics*, 11, 291–305.

Boyd, J. and Jagannathan, R. (1994), "Ex-dividend Price Behavior of Common Stocks", *Review of Financial Studies*, 7, 711–741.

Cannavan, D., Finn, F. and Gray, S. (2004), "The Value of Dividend Imputation Tax Credits in Australia", *Journal of Financial Economics*, 73, 167–197.

Chu, H. and Partington, G. (2008), "The Market Valuation of Cash Dividends: The Case of the CRA Bonus Issue", *International Review of Finance*, 8, 1–20.

Clubb, C. and Doran, P. (1992), "On the Weighted Average Cost of Capital with Personal Taxes", *Accounting and Business Research*, 23, 44–48.

Cooper, I.A. and Nyborg, K.G. (2006), "The Value of Tax Shield Is Equal to the Present Value of Tax Shields", *Journal of Financial Economics*, 81, 215–225.

Cooper, I.A. and Nyborg, K.G. (2007), "Valuing the Debt Tax Shield", *Journal of Applied Corporate Finance*, 19, 50–59.

Dempsey, M. (1996), "The Cost of Equity Capital at the Corporate and Investor Levels Allowing A Rational Expectations Model with Personal Taxations", *Journal of Business Finance and Accounting*, 23, 1319–1331.

Dempsey, M. (1998), "The Impact of Personal Taxes on the Firm's Weighted Average Cost of Capital and Investment Behaviour: A Simplified Approach using the Dempsey Discounted Dividends Model", *Journal of Business Finance and Accounting*, 25, 747–763.

Dempsey, M. (1998), "Capital Gains Tax: Implications for the Firm's Cost of Capital, Share Valuation and Investment Decision-Making", *Accounting and Business Research*, 28, 91–96.

Dempsey, M. (2001a), "Valuation and Cost of Capital Formulae with Corporate and Personal Taxes: A Synthesis using the Dempsey Discounted Dividends Model", *Journal of Business Finance and Accounting*, 28, 357–378.

Dempsey, M. (2001), "Investor Tax Rationality and the Relationship between Dividend Yield and Equity Returns: An Explanatory Note", *Journal of Banking and Finance*, 25, 1681–1686.

Dempsey, M. (2008), "The Implications of Personal Taxes for Project Valuation", working paper.

Dempsey, M. and Partington, G. (2008), "The Cost of Capital Equations under the Australian Imputation Tax System", *Accounting and Finance*, 48, 439–460.

Dempsey, M., McKenzie, M. and Partington, G. (2010), "The Problem of Pre-Tax Valuations: A Note", *Journal of Applied Research in Accounting and Finance*, 5, 10–13.

Dempsey, M. (2013), "Consistent Cash Flow Valuation with Tax-Deductible Debt: A Clarification", *European Financial Management*, 19, 830–836.

Elton, E.J. and Gruber, M.J. (1970), "Marginal Stockholder Tax Rates and the Clientele Effect", *The Review of Economics and Statistics*, 52, 68–74.

Fama, E. and French, K. (1997), "Industry costs of equity", *Journal of Financial Economics*, 43, 153–193.

Fenech, J.P., Skully, M. and Xuguang, H. (2014), "Franking Credits and Market Reactions: Evidence from the Australian Convertible Security Market", *Journal of International Financial Markets, Institutions & Money*, 32, 1–19.

Fernandez, P. (2004), "The Value of Tax Shields is Not Equal to the Present Value of Tax Shields", *Journal of Financial Economics*, 73, 145–165.

Feuerherdt, C., Gray, S. and Hall, J. (2010), "The Value of Imputation Tax Credits on Australian Hybrid Securities", *International Review of Finance*, 10, 365–401.

Graham, J.R., Michaely, R. and Roberts, M. (2003), "Do Price Discreteness and Transactions Costs Affect Stock Returns? Comparing Ex-dividend Pricing before and after Decimalization", *Journal of Finance*, 58, 2611–2637.

Gray, S. and Hall, J. (2006), "Relationship between Franking Credits and the Market Risk Premium", *Accounting and Finance*, 46, 405–428.

Inselbag, I. and Kaauford, H. (1997), "Two DCF Approaches for Valuing Companies under Alternative Financing Strategies (and How to Choose Among Them)", *Journal of Applied Corporate Finance*, 10, 114–122.

Lally, M. (2004), "The Fama and French Model, Leverage, and the Modigliani-Miller Propositions", *Journal of Financial Research*, 27, 341–349.

Lally, M. and van Zijl, T. (2003), "Capital Gains Tax and the Capital Asset Pricing Model", *Accounting and Finance*, 43, 187–210.

Massari, M., Roncaglio, F. and Zanetti, L. (2008), "On the Equivalence between the APV and the WACC Approach in a Growing Leveraged Firm", *European Financial Management*, 14, 152–162.

Modigliani, F. and Miller, M. (1963), "Corporate Income Taxes and the Cost of Capital: A Correction", *American Economic Review*, 53, 433–443.

Oded, J. and Michel, A. (2007), "Reconciling DCF Valuation Methodologies", *Journal of Applied Finance*, 17, 21–32.

Ruback, R.S. (2002), "Capital Cash Flows: A Simple Approach to Valuing Risky Cash Flows", *Financial Management*, 31, 85–103.

Siau, K.-W., Sault, S. and Warren, G. (2013), "Are Imputation Credits Capitalised into Stock Prices?", *Accounting and Finance*, 55, 241–277.

Taggart, R.A. (1991), "Consistent Valuation and Cost of Capital Expressions with Corporate and Personal Taxes", *Financial Management*, 20, 8–20.

Truong, G. and Partington, G. (2008), "Relation between Franking Credits and the Market Risk Premium: A Comment", *Accounting and Finance*, 48, 153–158.

Walker, S. and Partington, G. (1999), "The Value of Dividends: Evidence from Cum-dividend Trading in the Ex-dividend Period", *Accounting and Finance*, 39, 275–296.

CHAPTER 14

Ackoff, R.L. (1970), *A Concept of Corporate Planning* (John Wiley & Sons, New York).

Astley, W.G. and Van de Ven, A.H. (1983), "Central Perspectives and Debates in Organization Theory", *Administrative Science Quarterly*, 28, 245–273.

Bower, J.L. (1972), *Managing the Resource Allocation Process* (Richard D. Irwin, Homewood, IL).

Bruner, R. (2004), *Applied Mergers and Acquisitions* (John Wiley & Sons, New York).

Bruner, R. (2005), *Deals from Hell: Lessons that Rise above the Ashes* (John Wiley & Sons, New York).

Butler, R., Davies, L., Pike, R. and Sharp, J. (1991), "Strategic investment decision-making: Complexities, politics and processes", *Journal of Management Studies*, 28, 395–415.

Carr, C., Tomkins, C. and Bayliss, B. (1994), *Strategic Investment Decisions: A Comparison of UK and German Practices in the Motor Components Industry* (Avebury Books, Avebury).

Chami, R. and Fullenkamp, C. (2002), "Trust and Efficiency", *Journal of Banking and Finance*, 26, 1785–1809.

Dempsey, M. (1996), "Corporate Financial Management: Time to Change the Cost of Capital Paradigm?", *Critical Perspectives on Accounting*, 7, 617–639.

Dempsey, M. (2003), "A Multidisciplinary Perspective on the Evolution of Corporate Investment Decision Making", *Accounting, Accountability and Performance*, 9, 1–33.

Dempsey, M. (2014), "The Modigliani and Miller (MM) Propositions: The History of a Failed Foundation for Corporate Finance?", *Abacus*, 50, 279–295.

Dent, J.F. (1990), "Strategy, Organization and Control: Some Possibilities for Accounting Research", *Accounting, Organizations and Society*, 15, 3–25.

Duhaime, I.M. and Thomas, H.W. (1983), "Financial Analysis and Strategic Management", *Journal of Economics and Business*, 35, 413–440.

Durand, D. (1989), "Afterthoughts on a Controversy with MM, Plus New Thoughts on Growth and the Cost of Capital", *Financial Management*, 18, 12–18.

Fama, E. and French, K. (1997), "Industry Costs of Equity", *Journal of Financial Economics*, 43, 153–193.

Hopwood, A. (1974), *Accounting and Human Behaviour* (Prentice Hall International, London).

Hopwood, A. (2009), "Exploring the Interface between Accounting and Finance", *Accounting, Organizations and Society*, 34, 549–550.

Keynes, J.M. (1936), *The General Theory of Employment, Interest and Money* (Macmillan and Company, London).

King, P. (1975), "Is the Emphasis on Capital Budgeting Misplaced?", *Journal of Business Finance and Accounting*, 2, 69–82.

Mason, R.D. and Mitroff, I.I. (1981), *Challenging Strategic Planning Assumptions* (John Wiley & Sons, New York).

Miller, D. and Friesen, P.H. (1980), "Momentum and Revolution in Organizational Adaptation", *Academy of Management Journal*, 23, 591–614.

Miller, D. and Friesen, P.H. (1984), *Organizations: A Quantum View* (Prentice Hall, Englewood Cliffs, NJ).

Mintzberg, H. (1978), "Patterns in Strategy Formulation", *Management Science*, 24, 934–948.

Mintzberg, H., Raisinghani, D. and Theoret, A. (1976), "The Structure of Unstructured Decision Processes", *Administrative Science Quarterly*, 21, 246–275.

Mitroff, I.I. and Emshoff, J.R. (1979), "On Strategic Assumption Making: A Dialectic Approach to Policy and Planning", *Academy of Management Review*, 4, 1–12.

Mukherjee, T.K. and Henderson, G.V. (1987), "The Capital Budgeting Process: Theory and Practice, Interfaces", 17, 78–90.

Mukherji, A. and Nagarajan, N. (1995), "Moral Hazard and Contractibility in Investment Decisions", *Journal of Economic Behaviour and Organization*, 26, 413–430.

Pettigrew, A. (1985), *The Awakening Giant, Continuity and Change in ICI* (Blackwell, Oxford).

Petty, J.W., Scott, D.F. and Bird, M.M. (1975), "The Capital Expenditure Decision-Making Process of Large Corporations", *Engineering Economist*, 20, 159–171.

Pfeffer, J. and Salancik, G.R. (1978), *The External Control of Organizations: A Resource Dependence Perspective* (Harper and Row, New York).

Ross, M. (1986), "Capital Budgeting Practices of Twelve Large Manufacturers", *Financial Management*, 15, 15–22.

Starbuck, W.H. and Hedberg, B.L.T. (1977), "Saving an Organization from a Stagnating Environment", in *Strategy + Structure = Performance* (249–258), Thorelli, H.B. (ed.) (Indiana University Press, Bloomington, IN).

Tinsley, C.H., O'Connor, K.M. and Sullivan, B.A. (2002), "Tough Guys Finish Last: The Perils of a Distributive Reputation", *Organizational Behaviour and Human Decision Processes*, 88, 621–645.

CHAPTER 15

Bowie, N.E. (1991), "Challenging the Egotistic Paradigm", *Business ethics Quarterly*, 1, 1–16.

Dempsey, M. (2000), "Ethical Profit: An Agenda for Consolidation or for Radical Change", *Critical Perspectives on Accounting*, 11, 531–548.

Denhardt, R.B. (1981), *In the Shadow of Organization* (Regents Press, Lawrence, KS).

Dobson, J. (1993), "The Role of ethics in Finance", *Financial Analysts Journal*, 49, 57–61.

Frank, R. (1988), *Passions Within Reason* (W.W. Norton & Co., New York).

Foucault, M. (1977), *Madness and Civilization: A History of Insanity in the Age of Reason* (Tavistock, London).

Lovell, A. (1995), "Moral Reasoning and Moral Atmosphere in the Domain of Accounting", *Accounting, Auditing and Accountability*, 8, 60–80.

Mitchell, A., Puxty, T. and Sikka, P. (1994), "Ethical Statements as Smokescreens for Sectional Interests: The Case of the UK Accountancy Profession", *Journal of Business Ethics*, 13, 39–51.

Neimark, M.K. (1995), "The Selling of Ethics: The Selling of Ethics Meets the Business of Ethics", *Accounting, Auditing and Accountability*, 8, 81–96.

Seedhouse, D. (1988), *Ethics: The Heart of Health Care* (John Wiley & Sons, New York).

CHAPTER 16

Ball, R. (2009), "The Global Financial Crisis and the Efficient Market Hypothesis: What Have We Learned?", *Journal of Applied Corporate Finance*, 21, 8–16.

Bogle, J.C. (2005a), "The Mutual Fund Industry 60 Years Later: For Better or for Worse?", *Financial Analysts Journal*, 61, 15–24.

Bogle, J.C. (2005b), "The Relentless Rules of Humble Arithmetic", *Financial Analysts Journal*, 61, 22–35.

Bolton, P., Scheinkman, J. and Xiong, W. (2006), "Executive Compensation and Short-Termist Behaviour in Speculative Markets", *Review of Economic Studies*, 73, 577–610.

Cai, C.X., Clacher, I. and Keasey, K. (2013), "Consequences of the Capital Asset Pricing Model (CAPM) — A Critical and Broad Perspective", *Abacus*, 49, 51–61.

Coles, J.L., Hertzel, M. and Kalpathy, S. (2006), "Earnings Management Around Employee Stock Options Reissues", *Journal of Accounting and Economics*, 41, 173–200.

Conyon, M.J. and Murphy, K.J. (2000), "The Prince and the Pauper? CEO pay in the United States and United Kingdom", *The Economic Journal*, 110, 640–671.

Cowherd, D.M. and Levine, D.I. (1992), "Product Quality and Pay Equity between Lower-Level Employees and Top Management: An investigation of Distributive Justice Theory", *Administrative Science Quarterly*, 37, 302–320.

Dempsey, M. and Jones, S. (2015), "Financial Measurement and Financial Markets", Ch. 17 in *Routledge Companion to Financial Accounting Theory*, Jones, S. (ed.) (Routledge, UK).

Dodd, J.L. and Johns, J. (1999), "EVA Reconsidered", *Business and Economic Review*, April–June, 13–18.

Ellsworth, R.R. (1983), "Capital Markets and Competitive Decline", *Harvard Business Review*, September–October, 171–183.

Ellsworth, R.R. (2002), *Leading with Purpose: The New Corporate Realities* (Stanford University Press, Stanford).

Ennis, R.M. (2005), "Are Active Management Fees Too High?", *Financial Analysts Journal*, 61, 44–51.

Fox, J. (2009), *The Myth of the Rational Market* (Harper Collins, New York).

Froud, J., Johal, S., Leaver, A. and Williams, K. (2006), *Financialization and Strategy: Narrative and Numbers* (Routledge, London).

Fuller, J. and Jensen, M.C. (2002), "Just Say No to Wall Street: Putting a Stop to the Earnings Game: Courageous CEOs are Putting a Stop to the Earnings Game and We Will All be Better Off for It", *Journal of Applied Corporate Finance*, 14, 41–46.

Graham, J.R., Harvey, C.R. and Rajgopal, S. (2005), "The Economic Implications of Corporate Financial Reporting", *Journal of Accounting and Economics*, 40, 3–73.

Jensen, M.C. and Murphy, K.J. (1990), "Performance Pay and Top-Management Incentives", *Journal of Political Economy*, 98, 225–264.

Jensen M.C. and Zimmerman, J.L. (1985), "Management Compensation and the Managerial Labor Market", *Journal of Accounting and Economics*, 7, 3–9.

Keasey, K. and Hudson, R. (2007), "Finance Theory: A House without Windows", *Critical Perspectives on Accounting*, 18, 932–951.

MacKenzie, D. and Millo, Y. (2003), "Constructing a Market, Performing Theory: The Historical Sociology of a Financial Derivatives Exchange", *American Journal of Sociology*, 109, 107–145.

Main, B.G.M., Bruce, A. and Buck, T. (1996), "Total Board Remuneration and Company performance", *The Economic Journal*, 106, 1627–1644.

McSweeney, B. (2009), "The Roles of Financial Asset Market Failure Denial and the Economic Crisis: Reflections on Accounting and Financial Theories and Practices", *Accounting, Organizations and Society*, 34, 834–848.

Moosa, I.A. (2013), "The Capital Asset Pricing Model (CAPM): The History of a Failed Revolutionary Idea in Finance? Comments and Extensions", *Abacus*, 49, 62–68.

Murphy, K.J. (1985), "Corporate Performance and Managerial Remuneration: An Empirical Analysis", *Journal of Accounting and Economics*, 7, 11–42.

Murphy, K.J. and Oyer, P. (2001), "Discretion in Executive Incentive Contracts: Theory and Evidence", Available at SSRN 294829, papers.ssrn.com.

Sanders, W.G. and Carpenter, M.A. (2003), "Strategic Satisficing? A Behavioral-Agency Theory Perspective on Stock Repurchase Program Announcements", *Academy of Management Journal*, 46, 160–178.

Siegel, P.A. and Hambrick, D.C. (2005), "Pay Disparities within Top Management Groups: Evidence of Harmful Effects on Performance in High-Technology Firms", *Organization Science*, 16, 259–274.

Stinchcombe, A.L. (2000), "Social Structure and Organizations: A Comment", in *Economics Meets Sociology in Strategic Management: Advances in Strategic Management*, Baum, J. and Dobbin, F. (eds) (JAI Press, Greenwich, CT).

Whitley, R.D. (1984), *The Intellectual and Social Organisation of the Sciences*, (Clarendon Press, Oxford).

Whitley, R.D. (1986), "The Transformation of Business Finance into Financial Economics: The Roles of Academic Expansion and Changes in US Capital Markets", *Accounting, Organisations and Society*, 11, 171–192.

Yermack, D. (1995), "Do Corporations Award CEO Stock Options Effectively?" *Journal of Financial Economics*, 39, 237–269.

Zweig, J. (2005) in Introduction to *Where are the Customers' Yachts?*, Schwed, F. (1940, 2005 edition) (John Wiley & Sons, New York).

Index